Dick Dougherty

DOUGHERTY REVISITED

*A Random Selection of Columns
by Dick Dougherty, veteran Gannett-Rochester Newsman*

Compiled by Pat Dougherty

Dougherty Editions, Rochester, New York

Pat - "midas"

Inquiries should be addressed to
Dougherty Editions
276 Dale Road
Rochester, New York 14625

First printing (Fall 2004)

Cataloguing-in-Publication Data

Dougherty, Dick
Dougherty Revisited

ISBN 0-9759333-0-2
LC 2004095981

Reprinted with permission of the Gannett Rochester Newspapers
(Democrat and Chronicle/Times-Union)

Compiled by Pat Dougherty
Cover photograph by Lauren Long
Cover design by Julie Findley, Esse Design, Aspen, Colorado

Printed in the United States of America by Empire State Weeklies, Webster, New York 14580

This book is dedicated to Dick himself, and to his legions of readers who together have shared a unique and mutually enriching relationship for more than 25 years.

Acknowledgments

This book was not Dick's idea — in fact, quite the opposite.

He resisted from the beginning, viewing it as "self-serving and self-promotional," two things utterly foreign to his nature.

But his family persevered, sensing that at age 84 and after 58 years on the job, he was facing imminent retirement despite his insistence that one day, after fully recovering from serious heart surgery, he would return to his desk at the Democrat and Chronicle. Thus the motivation for this collection was simply our own satisfaction, and, hopefully, that of his many readers.

We are deeply grateful to the Gannett Company for granting permission to reprint these columns, gleaned from Dick's turnout over the last decades. The cover photograph of Midas and his master, now framed and on our coffee table, was taken by Lauren Long.

This book would not have been possible had not his oldest son, Dick, picked off his computer every one of his Dad's columns every day since 1990 and preserved them on discs which he then reprinted in pamphlet form to present to his parents as a yearly Christmas present.

Nor could it have been done without the work of our daughter, Carolyn, who arranged for the book's design, printing and assembly from her home in Colorado, all while holding down two jobs and caring for her family, including two young daughters.

Helping me choose the columns from a mountain of more than 3,000 choices has been Dick's younger son, Steve, a freelance writer in Manhattan.

Heartfelt thanks are due to the many friends who have lent support during stressful periods and to those who have guided me through the maze of self-publishing — especially Donna Kittrell of Wegmans, Jeff Adams, Emerson Klees, longtime friends Larry and Barbara Howe, and Lynn Tabak and David Young of Empire State Weeklies.

My chief role has been to worry day and night whether this collection as chosen and presented is worthy of the writer and meets the expectations of his many readers through the years.

It's hard to tell if I have succeeded. I can only hope so.

Pat Dougherty

Contents

Preface

"Kansas," Dick Dougherty wrote in one of his earliest columns, "was like a blind date, expected to be plain or perhaps even ugly, who turned out to be warm and beautiful. It was a brief encounter, a romance that never had time to blossom."

It was phrases like that, filed while Dick and an artist/photographer colleague were on a 4,100 mile bike-trip across America, that convinced his editors that he should be writing full-time. When he returned home three months later (his arm in a cast after his bike hit a pothole in Salem, Oregon), he was a confirmed columnist.

That was in 1975; Dick was 55 years old. By then, he already had been a Gannett newsman for nearly three decades. Over the years, there were different responsibilities and desks, different deadlines and hours (a night copy editor on a morning newspaper, for instance, starts his work day at 4 p.m.) He started out typing on manual Underwood typewriters, later making the switch to computers. But the setting always has been the same —a Gannett newsroom, as much home to Dick as his family home in suburban Rochester.

All this started back in 1948 when he graduated from Syracuse University's journalism school, which he attended on the GI Bill after World War II. His four years with the Army included combat in the European theater as a forward observer with the 36th Infantry Division.

Dick's first job with Gannett was as "chief" of a one-man bureau in Oneonta, New York. He moved on to Endicott and nearby Binghamton, and in 1950, to Rochester, where he and I both worked as reporters for *The Democrat & Chronicle*. We married in 1956.

Over the years, Dick has played just about every role on the journalistic stage — first as a "lightweight" (his word) features and general assignment reporter, then copy editor, wire editor, city editor and Sunday magazine editor.

Sometime in the mid-seventies, the idea arose to send a reporter and photographer across the country by bicycle as part of the newspaper's coverage of the U.S. bicentennial. Dick and Herm Auch, an artist and photographer as well as a friend, were the natural choices, as they both rode their bikes to work at the paper every day. The two mapped out their route along the Bike-Centennial Trail, packed their panniers full of reporter's notebooks and took off from Williamsburg, Virginia in the spring of 1975.

In the days before laptops and digital cameras, they mailed in their stories and film or dictated from pages of notes while standing in phone booths beside the road. Increasing numbers of Gannett newspapers began carrying the pieces, and as they did, the bikers raised their living standards from campsites to bed and breakfasts and finally to motels. After three months of cycling — Dick wrote, "Quite simply, the world is uphill all the way" — the two returned home, Dick with his arm in a cast as a result of an accident when his bike hit a pothole in Salem, Oregon.

For the nearly three decades that followed he has written a five-day-a-week column, (an assignment he calls "on-the-job retirement"), first for the *Times-Union* and then for the *Democrat and Chronicle.* This continued up until the very morning he underwent emergency heart surgery in July 2003.

While thousands of readers have been delighted for many years by his unique style combining wit and wisdom, no one has enjoyed his tenure at the newspaper as much as the writer himself: "One of the perks at the paragraph factory," he notes, "is that I do not have to submit to close supervision. The fact is, no one is exactly sure what I am supposed to be doing around here, so I am not often told how to do it."

Collecting some of Dick's columns (chosen from about 4,000 just since 1990) has been a backward glance over wonderfully happy years on and off the job. As the song says, "Who could ask for anything more!"

Pat Dougherty

Chapter One

Across America

A Little Fife and Drum
Amber Waves of Grain
Wild Headlong Mountain Rivers
The Pacific

A Little Fife and Drum
Goes a Long Way

Williamsburg, Va. (18.0 miles into the trip) — To come right out and say it: I haven't often felt the stirring in the breast that everyone says should accompany the sight of the flag going by.

But the other day on Market Square when that kid fife and drum corps played "The Harriott," "White Cockade" and the authentic version of "Yankee Doodle," there were moments when I would have re-enlisted to fight any old imperialistic war anywhere.

Even the boy rifleman wearing sunglasses failed to break the spell.

Herm Auch, my riding partner on this trip, looked ready to charge up San Juan Hill on his 10-speed.

As they marched off the parade ground, we chased them to get a head-on picture of the massed flags of the state regiments, but they quickly dissolved back into gum-chewing sub-teenagers and headed off in all directions, shucking their uniforms as if a foreign army had just entered the outskirts of town.

The guidebook poses that familiar old cliché: If the 18th Century resident could return today and see Williamsburg as it is now, would he be amazed at how little it had changed?

Sure he would, says the guidebook predictably. Then it adds, surprisingly:

He would wonder what happened to the "streets and paths mired in mud or deep in dust, an the clouds of flies and mosquitoes in summer… The life of this bygone century was crude by modern standards, even for white Virginians. The death rate for children was appalling. The average man had little education. Women had few legal rights."

Today Williamsburg is a tonic for the disillusion and cynicism that encrusts us all. At Jamestown you get the aching feeling of pity and wonderment at the fact that the first colonists survived at all in such terrible surroundings. Here you are reassured that they did survive. They did work things out and start building a country.

Tomorrow we head down the James River toward Richmond, Charlottesville, Pueblo, Cheyenne and Oregon, confident that we will find the Northwest Passage. A little fife and drum goes a long way.

Amber waves of grain,
purple mountain majesties

C anon City, Colorado (2,162.1 miles into the trip) — It's too bad we squandered all those adjectives on the Flint Hills of Kansas and amber waves of grain, because now that we're into purple-mountained majesty, our superlatives have run dry.

We talked about things dissolving into infinity in Kansas, but we didn't know how infinite infinity could be until we climbed up out of the desert terrain of Canon City — pronounced "canyon" city here — into the crystal clear, Kodachrome, multi-dimensional world of South Park.

"We've talked about things dissolving into infinity but, we didn't know how infinite infinity could be until we climbed up out of the desert terrain..."

This is a high-altitude grassland plateau surrounded by mountains. It looks like an air conditioned, elevated (8,000-10,000 feet) Flint Hills with a purer blue sky, an atmosphere completely free of heat distortion, and an impossibly spectacular backdrop of snow-capped peaks on all sides.

The road is nearly deserted, the wind is blowing strongly to our backs, the air is cool, the sun is bright, the odometer is clicking happily, and again we look out across those perplexing vistas. Are those ducks? No, they're not ducks, they're cattle 20 miles away. No, there's a water tower, it must be a town.

We are heading north now, going in back of the Front Range of the Rockies, across this vast South Park bowl, into Fairplay, then over Hoosier Pass, crossing the Continental Divide at 11,541 feet, to Dillon and on through the Arapaho National Forest to Kremmling, then over Muddy Pass (8,772 feet) to Walden and into Wyoming.

The air is thin up here. It takes a lot of panting to keep that leaden feeling from creeping up the legs to the brain. But the human body is indeed an amazingly sophisticated machine. Ours have received this new information about the oxygen content of our environment and have made mysterious adjustments that make the machine able to function.

Pikes Peak is a beautiful Lorelei of a mountain from out here. Seen from a plane, it looks like a cloud that doesn't move. But now we've circled it slowly and its shape has changed with every mile and shift in the sun's angle.

We will have to put this down as the most spectacular leg of our trip so far — perhaps because of the contrast with the dusty, dry plains from Eads through Pueblo to Canon City, or perhaps because the images of the smoky hills of Kentucky have faded.

Wild, headlong mountain rivers

Kooskia, Idaho (3,298.6 miles into the trip) — Really, when you think about it, travel is all rivers and passes.

The animals traveled the same riverside route we're taking now. So did the Indians who followed them, then the settlers, then the road and railroad builders.

These past few days our rivers have been the Bitterroot, Lochsa and Middle Fork of the Salmon — fantastic wild rivers with personalities that imprint the memory.

The Lochsa, which runs from the Bitterroot Mountains down through the Selway-Clearwater wilderness area, is our nomination for the handsomest river of the trip so far.

The Ohio and Mississippi are wider, but muddier and domesticated. They are just damp interstate superhighways and sometimes sewers.

The Bitterroot is sparkling, wild and headlong.

It has a deep, throaty constant voice and it creates its own wind as it hurls itself down the gorge below Chief Joseph Pass to Missoula, Montana. But it loses in our ratings because some of its fire is dissipated as it levels off down the valley.

But the Lochsa — ah, the Lochsa! It moves through the huge, forested Bitterroots with sustained power, gliding swiftly and silently for short periods just to heighten the dramatic contrast, then building to crescendo after crescendo.

We sat watching it flow through a towering mountain gorge in a forest of lodgepole pine the other night. The sun was backlighting the whitecaps downstream, and just in front of us we could feel its power as it ground away at a huge boulder just offshore.

It seemed impossible that this massive, living thing was simply the sum of thousands of those small springs and vertical creeks we had seen on the way down from Lolo Pass, feeding it with melted snows.

Along its entire hundred-mile length it moved in huge arching curves — alluring, irresistible curves that pull the traveler forward with anticipation to the next bend.

The idea that it carved his gorge out of the rock doesn't seem an academic geological concept at all — it seems an obvious, visible fact. You can feel it happening as you watch.

All day long, from early morning to late afternoon, we raced the river around those bends. We could outrun it by a slight margin on the level, but it passed us on the hills and gained miles on us at rest stops. While we sleep, the waters we raced this morning may be turning turbines in the state of Washington, more than a hundred miles away.

The Sailish Indians named the Lochsa. It means "Rough Water." The Selway means "Smooth Water." Good descriptive names, if your vocabulary doesn't have a word that sums up "wild, relentless and beautiful."

The Pacific, at last:
"one of us made it the honest way"

Lincoln City, Oregon (4,026.8 miles into the trip) — The guy with the broken arm got to the Pacific first. (The arm broke when his bike hit a pothole in Salem, Oregon, just a few miles from the coast.)

The other half of the expedition did it the honest way.

Route 18 climbs a final hill by the Safeway store just outside Lincoln City, and suddenly there it is — the Pacific Ocean — a couple of acres of it visible around the corner.

But then, as you turn down Logan Road toward the "Road's End" cottage community, the panorama opens.

"It doesn't seem possible that we've really gone all this way on those ridiculous machines."

The last leg of this trip is supposed to come two days from now when we pull into Astoria at the mouth of the Columbia. But this was to have been the dramatic moment — seeing the "other" ocean. Somehow it didn't come off.

There's nothing wrong with the Pacific Ocean. It is magnificent. On this afternoon, the breakers were starting far out and making satisfactory deep pounding noises as they crashed on the beach.

There are large volcanic reefs offshore that look like mountaintops, and the shoreline has high bluffs — not just beaches, dunes and tidewater marshes like the Atlantic shore.

No, the trouble was our vision.

We sat there on the porch of a lovely beach house, walked down along the sand, and stared at the sea as everyone does. But the vision wouldn't come.

Here we have crossed this whole country — Appalachians, Rockies, Cascades, plains and deserts, snowy passes, fields of lava, magnificent forests — you would think that we could sit here and look out over these waves and get some of those scenes to flash back at us.

Nope.

It doesn't work that way.

It doesn't seem possible that we've really gone all this way on those ridiculous machines.

Yesterday, we headed north along the coast, one of us in the borrowed car. This week, we'll be flying back east, taking about six hours to cover almost the same ground we've been laboring over since May 4.

Maybe then the perspective will come into focus.

Chapter Two

Canine Chronicles
(starring Midas)

Genetics yield the ultimate dog

Y ou made the Top Dog list!" I told Feeney.
°°The *what* list?°°
"The American Kennel Club's list of the 10 most popular dog breeds in America," I told him. "The black Labrador retriever was No. 1, German shepherd No. 4, Golden retriever No. 6. You're all of those and many, many more."

°°This means you're going to do one of those silly columns with the little thought-transfer circles, right?°°

Naturally, I said.

°°Well, make it up without me. I've got a nap going here.°°

As I've explained before, Feeney is a multi-purebred triumph of the famous "catch-me-if-you-can, big boy" school of genetic selection. His genes are mingled with those of the large breeds that have inhabited or visited his native Peaks Island, Maine, since the beginning of time.

His mother was a mostly-Shepherd-golden retriever named Dubba whose last romantic partner was mostly Newfoundland. He would be Feeney's father, probably a Summah Dog from Away. ("Away," in local talk, means "not Peaks Island.")

It is my theory, validated by Dubba's owner Kenny Brown, that Dubba met all the ferries to inspect disembarking dogs for breeding partners. Then whenever she felt ovulation coming on, she'd go down the list.

After years of this, Dubba finally got it right and out popped Feeney, the Ultimate Dog. Then two tragic things happened.

First, Feeney was adopted by some kindly but stupid Summah People named Dougherty. They named him after the island market, then took him home to and had him "altered".

A vet told them it would spare him the ordeal of lying in the snow all night staking out bimbo dogs in heat.

Secondly, Mrs. Brown, sick of having new pups underfoot, shipped Dubba off to relatives who had her spayed, bringing to an end one of the most promising breeding programs in the annals of dogdom.

Evidence of its promise can be seen today on Peaks where most dogs, except for newcomers, resemble Feeney, one way or another.

Meanwhile, the meddling AKC keeps trying to tell dogs to socialize only with their "own kind."

Feeney told me once: °°I could have done something about that if that vet hadn't sneaked up on me.°°

He's right. A few hundred generations and all dogs would have been exact replicas of Feeney.

Feeney slips away
By Pat Dougherty

This is a column my husband could not write. It is not easy for me either, but I feel we should let Dick's readers know that we had to put our beloved Feeney to sleep last Friday morning.

Feeney was often mentioned in this space and had been part of our family for 14 years (98 in people years, if the old formula is to be trusted).

For the last month he had experienced increasing difficulty in breathing and decreased mobility, due less to his arthritis than to inoperable tumors at the back of his throat which were cutting off his oxygen supply.

Dr. Mike (Foley) came out to our car in front of the Brighton Animal Hospital, and patted his old patient who had previously been tranquilized and was lying on the back seat. While Dick and I sat on a nearby hillside, he performed his final service to the Feen. Our friend went painlessly and with dignity.

No dog's life could have been better. From the autumn day he acquired us as servants and foster parents on Peaks Island, Maine - a tiny ball of fur who fell asleep on my foot in front of Feeney's Market - he has had a good home, better perhaps than could have been provided by his original owner who had given him up for adoption.

Each summer Feeney revisited his native Peaks for reunions with his biological family. He accompanied us on camping trips and slept in tents and motels, chased uncountable cats and seagulls, had loyal friends in Loki (who preceded him in death just recently), Mike and Ming, all neighborhood cronies.

He outwitted one electric fence and charmed two dog wardens, but most important, he received loved and gave love in equal measure.

Now all that remains is to fill in the cool, dusty hole under the hedge, reseed the brown spots in the yard and shampoo the carpet. At last we'll have a respectable lawn and a relatively clean house, two things that, by comparison, we couldn't care less about.

Finally, we must start getting used to the awful emptiness and not hearing the thumping tail when we get up in the night.

But I can hear the Feen now, in his circle-enclosed °°thought transference°° quotes:

°°Hey, you two, get real. It's been great from start to finish. No, I never fathered any puppies. You took care of that, remember? Too bad. You could have had a duplicate replacement all ready.

°°And look, I went off peacefully, thanks to Dr. Mike. I hope you two can slip away as quietly when your time comes.

°°Don't mourn. Just remember the good times. Another dog will find you sooner than you think.°°

Mob scene at the Rainbow Bridge reunion

Someone sent us a sentimental sob-inducing tale about the "Rainbow Bridge" to eternity where deceased pets, cured of all their ills, romp and wait to be reunited with their loved ones.

We've been sending copies along with our thank-you notes to the 200-plus readers who wrote to console us.

Almost all the writers told their own version of a Rainbow Bridge (not the one at Niagara Falls, the other one, to Heaven) and told how they still mourn their devoted, long-dead animal friends.

Well, the tear-sharing worked.

We realized we were just about sobbed out when I felt a guilty giggle coming on at the prospect of actually being mobbed simultaneously by Feeney and the other nine: Rocky I and II, Simba, Copper, Partly, Mostly, Nicky, Beagle and Bonnie.

In the previous listing, I forgot Red and Rex from my youth and Pat's added these seven Fallon family dogs, Girly, Boy, Jackie, Patsy, Terry, Bing and Bozo.

So make that 19 dogs and at least four cats descending upon us at the newcomer's cocktail party tent at the bridge and wreaking havoc with their furious tail-wagging and yelping.

The chances of surviving this mob scene seem pretty remote, even though, according to the legend, we'll have been totally reconditioned physically. (Even our natural bridge-work will be restored, I've been assured by Jack Pitlick, DDS, the workman who built most of mine.)

"The phrase 'drenched in drool,' comes to mind," I told Pat.

"Remind me to wear a nametag," she said.

"Right. Last time Rocky the First saw us I had hair. He'd say who're these old ducks?"

"But if they restored our youth, Feeney wouldn't recognize us!"

"You're forgetting dogs believe their noses, not their eyes. 'Sniff-sniff. Hold everything! It's THEM! I smell their DNA!' "

We're both agnostics when it comes to mythology like this. We're pretty sure it's not true, but why rule it out prematurely?

"Before we leave the subject, I wonder if the human ancestors' receiving line is on the near side of the bridge," I asked.

"I hope it's the far side. That's bound to be a tedious affair," she said.

Mine were an inhibited, undemonstrative bunch, No tails, for one thing, at least after the first few million years. A lot of beards and celluloid collars. A few hairy grunters in animal skins.

The point of telling you all this is that we seem to be healing.

Now if we can just survive this lonely week on Peaks Island without blubbering, we may be on our way to becoming whole again and ready for the Feen's replacement to find us.

Midas Finds the Doughertys

To all the dog fanciers out there who have been feeling sorry for us, we have news. Mourn no more. We are healed!

A new dog found us last weekend in a saloon in the Wyoming County village of Arcade.

He is a golden retriever-Irish setter pup, six weeks old. We named him Midas.

(No, not the muffler, although he could use one; after the Greek king whose touch could turn anything, even opportunities, to gold).

Take this remarkable opportunity, for example:

We were in Gray's Pub having lunch while waiting for the Arcade & Attica leaf-watchers' express to Curriers. For mysterious reasons, the subject of dogs came up in conversation with the proprietor, former Rochesterian Doug Gray.

He told us that villager Laura Bigelow had been in the pub giving away a litter of non-pedigree retriever pups. He volunteered to call her while we were taking our train ride and see if any were left.

On the train we played it cool.

"Let's not make a commitment right off," my wife warned

"Right, we'll stall her until we think it over carefully. We have other options, and we'd be foolish to get into all that puppy training. Let's not let the dog make the decision for us this time."

"Good. I thought you might go off half-cocked again on this."

When we got back from the excursion, Doug handed us a phone number. We called, and soon Laura appeared with Midas who turned our day to gold.

We took our time thinking it over — about one millisecond.

"We'll take him, right?" I said to Pat.

"Of course," she said, and suddenly we were parents of an infant once again.

Midas can't yet talk in comic strip bubbles like our late beloved Feeney, of course, but I swear I heard him murmur as he fell asleep in Pat's arms: °°See you, Laurie baby. Say good-bye to Mom.°°

Now here we are, the second of many sleepless nights behind us and boring all our friends (including you) to death.

One regret: Until Midas came along we were agonizing over whether or not to buy Chauncey, a big, gentle, gorgeous, friendly Bernese Mountain Dog from Marion in Wayne County. His only flaw was his distinguished pedigree. He had papers!

Feeney's ghost would haunt us if we bought any dog instead of letting one find us. He would be furious at the idea of being replaced by a dog with only one breed in his lineage. Chauncey was a beauty. Sorry, fella.

Television as Dog Trainer

Those dog obedience videos are amazing. All you have to do is invite your dog up on your lap, press "play" on your VCR and the dog absorbs the training lesson by lesson.

He intently watches his peers go through their paces, learning to heel, sit, stay, come, as well as to stop jumping on people, gnawing on the furniture, pulling down the drapes, shredding mom's lingerie in the front yard - the whole syllabus.

As each segment ends, you say "See?" and the dog understands.

°°You want me to do that? Why didn't you say so? No problem.°°

That's all there is to it.

If it hadn't been so cold out the other night, and the three of us hadn't been so sleepy, I'd have taken him out and run through the routines, just to make sure he had them down pat.

Midas weighs about 75 pounds now. When you've had a dog that heavy on your lap for over an hour, your circulation is impaired and you're lucky if you can hobble off to bed.

When the TV golden retriever, a Midas look-alike, was jumping up on the instructor, Midas' ears went up and he raised his head.

> *"When you have a 75-pound dog on your lap for over an hour, your circulation is impaired."*

The TV dog kept whirling and jumping, but the instructor kept walking along, seemingly oblivious. Finally the dog gave up and fell into step in a perfect "heel" position.

"See?" I said.

°°The dumb mutt had him going but he lost it,°° Midas was thinking.

(I've talked about the uncanny phenomenon of dog thought-transference before. I denote it with those little °°bubble°° quotes. Now back to our story.)

°°He fell for the old Ignoring Ploy. If there's anything I've learned, it's that you have to be patient and firm with them. Keep jumping up on them until they get the idea and know you mean business. Never give up.°°

This wasn't quite the reaction I'd been expecting, but Midas teaches us something new every day and we're always careful to express our gratitude. We wouldn't want to hurt his feelings by suggesting he's a dog. He's so sensitive.

The off-leash heeling lesson went a little better. Midas looked at me astonished.

°°That dog is amazing. He's got that man following him like a shadow. All he has to do is fake that look of adoration and he's got the poor stiff eating out of his hand.°°

"Just shows what concentrated training will do; I can't wait!" I said.

°°Down, boy. Easy, fellah,°° said Midas.

Man domesticates dogs (Hah!)

"**D**NA dates dogs' domestication to 100,000 years ago," read a recent headline that caught my eye.

Something didn't ring true. My wife agreed. "Who domesticated whom, that is the question," she said.

°°You can say that again,°° said Midas, the golden retriever asleep on her lap.

The story quoted a scientist explaining that he analyzed the "mutations in the mitrochondrial DNA of 140 dogs representing 67 breeds and in the DNA of wolves from 14 countries."

Don't ask me what that means. Let's just take his word that it somehow establishes that dogs diverged from wolves and joined human households 100,000 instead of 14,000 years ago, as archaeologists claim.

However, lifelong behavior studies conducted by dog servants suggest that the premise itself is cockeyed: It was the dogs who domesticated humans and bent them to their will.

As I imagine that first encounter, an early human was ambling along, minding his own primitive business, when a wolf looked up and thought: °°I think I'll follow that guy and wag my tail at him. Maybe it will lead to something.°°

The rest is history:

Wolf hypnotizes man, says °°Call me doggie.°° Man says "Nice doggie." Wolf says °°Let's go to your place and share that mastodon shank you've got there.°°

Man arrives at cave: "Honey I'm home. I've got a doggie!."

Spouse says""Don't let him up on the furniture!" Dog smiles at her, wags tail and climbs up on sofa for nap before dinner.

"Oh well. We'll domesticate him later," says the woman.

°°Sure you will, honey,°° muses the dog. °°Wake me when dinner's ready. Afterwards we'll start training you to respond to my body language and barking.°°

Anyone who "owns" a dog will immediately confirm that this is the most plausible scenario. Whether it happened 100,000 years ago or last Tuesday is immaterial.

The point is that we humans have learned our role as domesticated humans is to respond promptly to all barked or otherwise signaled commands.

"That about cover it, Midas?" I asked.

°°Good boy! Bend over and let me lick you.°°

Midas talks politics

"This 2000 election is driving me crazy," the man was saying. "It never ends. We're always waiting for something. Anything I write about is sure to be outdated by events by the time the paper comes out. If I want to get home by suppertime tonight, I'll have to write about you again."

°°So what's the problem? You've written about me or some other talking dog hundreds of times, beginning back with Partly, Mostly, Nicky, Uncle Beagle, Feeney and all the others °°

"But it's such a cop-out. The country is having a constitutional crisis and what do I do? I interview a golden retriever named Midas."

°°You could do worse. It happens that we dogs know a lot more than you think about transfers of power, which is what this silly election business of yours is really all about. °°

"I don't follow you."

°°Well, HEEL then.°°

"Very funny."

°°I thought so. Just trying to lighten the mood. But as I was about to explain, an election is essentially a transfer of power. We dogs do it all the time. We're what is known as a pack society. It's run by an alpha, or dominant, dog. What he or she says goes. Like a chief executive officer, you might say. °°

> °°*Our dog elections are nothing as barbaric as yours. We just let two contenders duke it out and the winner becomes leader...*°°

"Do you have specified term limits like we do?"

°°Not really. I guess you could say the alpha dog serves at the pleasure of the pack; but usually we don't have a lot of turnover. Sometimes a challenger will come along and may or may not be successful. °°

"So you mean dogs really do have elections?"

°°Nothing as barbaric as yours. We just let the two contenders duke it out and the winner becomes leader and the loser steps aside. °°

"With no hard feelings?"

°°I wouldn't go that far. There is the traditional licking of the wounds, as in your society, but with us it's more than just a figure of speech. °°

"So who is your alpha dog right now?"

°°It's you, silly. You wanted to dominate and I let you. What the heck. I'm easy. As long as you feed me on time and don't make a lot of stupid, unreasonable demands, I let you play boss. I'll even 'heel' and 'come' if I happen to be going your way. It's no big deal. °°

"So it's not all that different from our system after all."

°°Except for the recounts, of course. When a guy is nursing a shredded ear or a lacerated tail, he isn't anxious to prolong the 'process,' as you call it. °°

Back when dogs roamed the neighborhood

For years the high point in the lives of Dougherty dogs was the departure and return of the school bus.

It was their duty to see the kids safely off, wagging their tails and looking forlorn as the bus pulled away and jumping and whirling with glee when it returned.

In between, they were free to go about their business, inspecting the boundaries of their territories for unauthorized smells and performing other important duties.

There was an animal control ordinance in effect but it was enforced only in response to complaints. All dogs in our neighborhood dogs were deemed to be "under control."

"Sorry, kid. Times have changed. Its a 'no pets' and 'keep off' world out there now."

There was an unwritten no-fault rule on out-of-yard waste accumulations. ("If it's in your yard, it's yours to keep.") Everyone had a dog and all specimens were anonymous.

Obviously this system was too relaxed and uncivilized to endure.

The last Dougherty dogs who had neighborhood permission to roam were Nicky and his young sidekick Beagle, both strays who picked us up downtown during blizzards in the 1970s. It's hard to explain to a footloose stray that his world ends at your property line, so we didn't try.

Beagle used to roam all over town. When he got tired, he'd knock on the nearest door and ask °°Can I use your phone?°° Then we'd come and get him.

Then one day a neighbor down in Corbett's Glen found him asleep on his couch.

"You won't believe this," his host told me after repeated visits, "but I'm the regional Alpo salesman. How did he know that?"

"Obviously he's been reading your mail," I said.

Subsequent dogs had to be tied up or leashed and weren't allowed to do school bus duty. I don't know who suffered most, dogs or kids.

Our present resident dog, Midas, lives inside a compound defined by a buried wire that causes his collar to beep when he approaches too close and zaps him if he crosses the boundary. It does the trick, but he has to bark at passing kids until they come inside his yard to visit.

°°Tell me again about Beagle,°° he asks me. °°What do I have to do to get out of this yard?°°

"You could learn to heel without dragging me, for one thing. Once this knee loosens up we'll be hitting the road again."

°°But no school buses? No off-leash explorations?°°

"Sorry, kid. Times have changed. It's a `No Pets' and `Keep Off!' world out there now."

Wild pup turns angelic

The time has come to rehabilitate the reputation of Midas, the former golden retriever demolition puppy.

We would like to have you think that our rigorous training regimen did the trick, but I think he just got bored with gnawing furniture and shredding clothing.

Still exuberant when revved up, he has intervals of sanity that are getting longer and longer day by day.

His most spectacular behavioral advance is one he thought up himself. When he wrestles with his German shepherd friend Heidi he often gets muddy and we'd manhandle him into the shower.

He'd wriggle frantically, slipping and sliding, running in place on the tile floor, grabbing the toilet bowl and hanging on. But just recently, Pat went next door to pick him up.

"Watch this," she said. "You won't believe it."

When she let him in the back door, he ran into the bathroom and stood in the tub, waiting expectantly. As she lathered him up and rinsed him with the hand spray, he stood immobile.

"How did you ever train him to do that? It's amazing."

"Are you kidding? He just decided he liked it and trained me to do what he wanted."

As she toweled him off he stretched luxuriously.

°°A little more on the belly — ah, that's the spot,°° he said. Then she fluffed him up using the hair dryer.

I should add that he has never had to be housebroken from the day he joined the family at five weeks of age and he still remembers his Denali Farms heeling and staying lessons. He'll actually perform them if he's in the mood.

Off the leash, he'll come when called if he feels like it, but when you ignore him and walk the other way, he'll turn up at your heel in an instant.

This is the same dog his mistress once threatened to have a taxidermist make into a floor lamp. Now when she reads on the recliner, he insinuates his 70 pounds alongside, his head draped over the armrest, paws dangling.

When we're eating, he'll crouch at the edge of the dining room, alert and drooling, but won't beg.

He knows from his mistress' costume whether she's headed somewhere he's eligible to go. If she's in a tennis outfit, he'll sigh and go back to sleep. But when I invite him into my car, he tries to take the wheel because he knows it means "park!"

I hesitated to write this progress report, fearful that he might see it and decide to teach me not to jump to conclusions. But the threat of a libel suit made me go public with this apology.

Watching the Westminster dog show

Midas and I were watching the Westminster Kennel Club show finale Tuesday night.

His reactions were so predictable I had no problem reading the thoughts in the imaginary comic strip balloons connected to his head by tiny bubbles.

°°What's wrong with that poodle?°° he snorted. °°If you did that to me, I'd take your arm off at the elbow!°°

"If you did, you'd be disqualified," I told him.

The handler was simply adjusting the dog's hindquarters with one hand and raising his head with the other, but I had to admit that it was demeaning to the point of being a little obscene.

°°It's bad enough to make her prance around in that stupid fur costume. Look what they've done to her tail! The way she's waving that pompon on the end, she's just asking for it. She must be in heat. Check out the look that Rhodesian ridgeback hound is giving her!°°

I explained that the hound was wasting his time.

"His owner would never let romance blossom. It would lead to a litter of hyphenated-breed pups," I said, forgetting for a moment that Midas, a golden retriever look-alike, had a philandering Irish setter father.

°°Of course you saw to it that I grew up celibate. I can imitate some of the instinctive moves I've seen my buddies perform, but it's just for show,°° he explained.

> °°**What's wrong with that poodle? If you did that to me, I'd take your arm off at the elbow...**°°

I've always regretted that I fell for that "fixing" myth. Now if I wanted to exactly duplicate him I'd have to go the cloning route. If I'd thought it through, I could have had a near-replica standing by as a replacement and a dad to show him the ropes.

But, on the other hand, then I'd never have known the wide variety of wonderful mutts who've adopted us every 14 years or so.

Impurebred Midas and I are in agreement about the Westminster. It's an elitist exercise in arranged one-night stands — a big sex-for-hire audition, you might say.

"We're both for 'natural selection,' aren't we, Mighty, old buddy?" I said.

°°Right. It worked for you and Mom, and it would have worked for me and that poodle, if it hadn't been for that vet.

°°If she'd let her hair grow out uncombed and rolled in a ripe Irondequoit Creek fish carcass, we'd have had a bright future together.°°

18

Buddy, Clinton's dog, seeks sex advice

"**D**ear Dr. Sex:
Socks the cat told me what it means to be 'fixed.' When I told her I didn't even know I was broken she laughed hysterically, then gleefully explained. (Cats are so mean!)

Naturally I feel betrayed by my best friend. What can you tell me about this terrifying procedure? They say it is for my health!

Everyone in this town is going crazy about sex. I wanted to try some and see what makes it such a big deal. Now I'll never know."

"Dear Buddy,

You have a right to feel betrayed, but look at it this way: You will gain lifelong immunity from sexual harassment charges. In today's climate of testosterone hysteria, that is a plus.

You will be able to ogle any dog that strikes your fancy. If she threatens to sue, you can get her for libel because you will have an absolutely foolproof alibi, one your friend You-Know-Who might consider.

(I have withheld his name out of left-wing sympathies, respect for his high office and to prevent Kenneth Starr from getting bizarre ideas.)

I don't know if you have encountered a female dog in "heat" as yet, but believe me, it is no picnic. Consider yourself lucky.

Dogs we know used to stake out the homes of females in this condition, lying in the snow for hours and getting in fights with other single-minded suitors. They welcomed their new-found freedom from the rigorous demands of lust.

Veterinarians have told us that "neutering" (which has no connection to the Speaker of the House Newt Gingrich) helps curb aggression and encourages docility, but don't worry.

Like our friend Midas, you floppy-eared hounds are born without the troublesome aggression gene. Docility means tranquillity. It is mostly a function of maturity, not hormones.

Don't worry, you will still be able to demolish furniture at will, shred clothing and mark your territory indoors and out.

Some say it is a shame to rob you of the ability to procreate, but believe me, this is highly overrated.

Leave that to the snooty purebreds who are condemned to stand immobile while judges poke at their bodies. Then they have to make their handlers lumber around show rings on leashes.

One day, when you have run out of longevity, your friend will be overcome with remorse and wish he had left you intact so he could duplicate you.

That's his problem. Let the him grieve a little. It won't hurt him.

Animals: Got a sex problem? Write to Dr. Sex care of this newspaper."

Publicity hound jumps from speeding car

Midas, the golden retriever publicity hound, gets depressed when weeks go by without seeing his name in print, so last weekend he was forced to take strong measures.

°°Watch this!°° he barked as he wriggled through the back window of his car as it sped up Route 590 toward Sea Breeze last Sunday.

"BACK! BACK, stupid!" his mistress shouted. "Midas! NO!" I cried. Too late.

Somehow, by turning sideways, he had managed to get head, front feet and chest through the six-inch opening. From there, it took only a simple twist to allow the weight of his front end to drag the rest of him through.

As I jammed on the brakes and pulled to the side, I could see him in the side mirror tumbling end over end in front of a red car. Its alert driver somehow was able to hit the brakes and swerve to avoid him. (Nice driving, whoever you are. You drove off before we could thank you.)

> "As *I* jammed on the brakes and pulled to the side, I could see him... tumbling end over end in front of a red car."

I opened the door, screaming his name, and Midas came galloping back as traffic sped by in the passing lane. He was unhurt but momentarily subdued as he scrambled into the back.

"Didn't turn out quite the way you planned, did it, you poor silly baby?" his mistress said, her voice close to hysteria. Then we three hugged, silently waiting for our coronary episodes to subside.

We had been on our way to revisit Durand Eastman Beach for swimming and stick retrieval practice.

A few days earlier Midas had been nearly strangled by his German shepherd wrestling companion. Her protruding canine teeth became caught in his chain collar. Then Midas rolled over twice and tightened it into a noose. He was wide-eyed and making terrible gurgling noises.

After some hysterical screaming and calls to 911, a siding contractor working nearby appeared with a boltcutters just as we were about to give up on Midas.

The episode was sobering for both dogs. They were subdued for at least 30 seconds. The human participants were limp.

Little did we know at the time that this was just a warmup. "I hope you've learned your lessons," Midas' mistress scolded him yesterday.

°°Now for my next trick ... °° he replied.

Golden gathering unites man and beast

We accompanied Midas to his third semiannual "gathering" of golden retrievers near the Seneca Park trout pond Saturday.

Don't ask why. It's sort of hard to explain.

The Golden Gatherings were Cheddy Harvey's idea. She picks the date and notifies everyone by postcard or e-mail, and the participants just show up.

The event has been going on for several years, we were told, but we've been to only three because we had been associated only with "multi-purebreds." (To have a true "gathering" you have to have an identifiable homogenous assembly. That's the rule.)

Cheddy said she just thought it would be interesting to get a whole bunch of nearly identical hyperactive blondes together for no real reason except to see what happened.

What happened this time was that the dogs went berserk porpoising through the deep snow, playing dominance games, sniffing private parts, wrestling and growling and sometimes knocking down geezers like me, silly enough to bring treats.

We so-called "handlers" just stood around watching, flailing arms and stamping feet while flirting with hypothermia and discussing behavior problems and our sanity. When everyone was suitably frozen we posed for a group picture (dogs and people), then trooped home exhausted and took naps.

Last Saturday, when the wind chill was well below zero, the whole thing lasted about an hour, not including the naps.

In the summer we gather at a private beach on Lake Ontario for stick throwing and chasing, which is much more interesting for dogs and spectators. Until you've seen 15 dogs tearing into the lake and swimming after one stick, you haven't lived. Sometimes you'll see three growling dogs swimming to shore with a length of the same long stick in their mouths.

At the winter gathering in Seneca Park, the dogs have to be satisfied to simply chase each other and think up their own roughhouse games.

As we were driving home afterward, I asked my wife why we enjoyed these outings so much.

"The dogs are all just manic. But what do "we see in such a pointless activity?" I wanted to know.

"The pointlessness is the whole point," she said.

Midas, half asleep in the back seat, agreed. He raised his head and floated one of his comic-strip balloons aloft, the text set off in °°double bubble°° quote marks.

°°It's a metaphor for a dog's life, stupid,°° it said.

Man's best friend a good nurse, too

Midas the golden retriever was confused when I got up from the table after lunch and sat down at the computer in the den.
°°What's this? It's our nap time.°°

He was already up on the bed pawing at the bedspread, making his nest, when he discovered I wasn't right behind him.

"I know I've upset your routine," I said, "but I'm warming up for my possible return to the office. They don't let us nap on the job down there, at least not openly, even if you're an old coot like me, prone to nodding off while digesting food."

°°In our world we'd call that an unfair labor practice.°°

"Our management calls it unprofessional."

°°That's the trouble with management, even the pitiful version you try to inflict on me. I find it laughable. Especially the short leash stuff. I mean, who's managing who?

> *"I thought I had a lifetime nursing career ahead of me, but the old coot seems to have come back to life."*

"Whom. It's managing whom."

°°See what I mean? Picky picky.°°

When I sat down at the computer I didn't intend to start off my comeback career with another dog interview, but Midas looked so bewildered by my behavior, I had to discuss it with him, even if I had to translate his imaginary but eloquent °°thought transference°° responses.

The poor guy had seen me off to the doctor, then to the hospital a few weeks earlier with what he we both thought was a routine case of kennel cough.

Instead the doctors performed open heart surgery and installed a cow's heart valve.

When I finally got home and tottered into bed, he put two and two together and was extremely solicitous, staying at his post at the foot of the bed, eyes shut, pretending to be fast asleep but ready in an instant to jump up and escort me to the bathroom.

Now everything has changed.

°°I thought I had a lifetime nursing career ahead of me, but the old coot seems to have come back to life,°° I heard him mutter this morning.

°°Ah well, might as well turn in for the nap without him.°°

(This column was written following Dougherty's heart surgery in July, 2003)

Chapter Three

House & Spouse

Thinking of moving? No way!
State of our union just fine, thanks
Assertiveness training at home
Camping OUR way
Move, Midas! Mom's coming home
Telecommuting: What really happens
Guests impressed — no dust balls!
Bermuda revisited — again
Grandparents' rights date from Adam and Eve
Farewell to our four-wheel friend
Reading a newspaper from a ladder
Sounds of passing trains hypnotic
Personal barber owed for 4,144 haircuts
Give a hug, shed a tear

Leaf & Lawn

Lawn care experts just dreaming
Burning the ceremonial nostalgia leaf
Grass is yellow all over
Need Dr. Ruth's advice on sexy trees
Leaf harvesting delayed
Neighborhood lovely under snow
Farming out future snow jobs
Dark harbingers of spring

Thinking of moving? No way!

My years of grumbling about the burdens of home ownership were almost over. We had decided to move to a carefree townhouse in Fairport. Goodbye lawn. Goodbye leaking pipes and drafty windows. Somehow the idea of giving up the place we'd lived in since we got married, where we brought up three kids and nine dogs, didn't seem to faze us.

"Look, no water stains on the ceiling!" one of us remarked during a tour of our new home.

"And a dining room that's not in the kitchen! Look at this tub!"

Everything was moving along briskly when two real estate agent friends stopped by to suggest things we might do to make our place sell.

"Of course, you'd be painting this hallway," Norman said.

"Oh, of course," we said, snorting at the laughable suggestion we had given it a thought.

"Ceilings pure white. Walls off-white. Makes the place seem brighter, cleaner. In fact, do the entire interior. Exterior too, in the bad spots."

"Naturally," my wife said, giving me a look. "Right, dear?"

"Oh, absolutely. No big deal."

Downstairs in the cellar we thought spotless, we were told:""It helps to get rid of the junk. All of it. Throw it out."

But then suddenly we were outdoors on our deck overlooking the glen and one of them said:

"Oh, well now! You'll have no trouble selling. People will look at this and just fall in love with it."

That did it.

I looked at Pat. She looked at me, beaming a shared thought: "Fall in love with OUR house? WE'RE in love with OUR house. We were here first!"

As the briefing went on, we were relieved to find that there were insoluble financial problems that would kill the move. The real estate market is comatose in winter when we'd be selling. We could never come close to our tentative offer. How long could we handle the two stories?

"Tell you what . . ," I started to say. She was way ahead of me.

"Take the money and fix up THIS house!" she shouted.

What a woman! What a genius! I had to hug her. The dog did too.

"Let's get a drink and go sit on the deck," she said.

State of our union just fine, thanks

The state of our union is excellent.

We'd like to report to the two houses of Congress meeting in joint session tonight, and to the American people watching on TV, that another year has gone by with no extramarital affairs or other nuptial contract violations.

That makes 43 in a row.

We're not counting repeated failures to "obey" that were rashly promised in the original marriage contract. We just said "I do" back then because we didn't want to make a fuss.

Of course neither of us expected obedience because we couldn't decide who was in charge of the union in the first place. I'm sure if I'd asked about her obeying my orders, she'd have said, "Don't be silly" or "Are you kidding?" but we wanted to get on to the "cleave" part.

If it's any of your business, we cleaved (clove?) exclusively to each other as promised and still do.

We don't expect you to leap to your feet and applaud each and every one of these triumphs as the audience will do tonight, but we have no objection.

Consider it optional. Just keep it brief so we don't have to stand there with those dumb smiles on our faces.

There will be some similarities between the two reports on the states of the two unions.

Not only will both of us outline plans for spending more money, but in both cases it will be OUR money.

We'll want increases for household maintenance and improvements and debt service. His will be for what he calls "programs." He'll propose spending more money on health care, and so will we.

Clinton will propose tax breaks, and so do we. His will be for the working poor. We say sure, give them some too, but don't go overboard.

He favors safeguarding Social Security. So do we. We're already drawing it, so safeguarding it would be nice.

The president will talk about continuing the present prosperity and the unprecedented economic expansion. We're for that too.

Likewise safeguarding the world's peace and the nation's security, raising the educational levels or our children (as long as it includes grandchildren), reducing crime, enacting a patients' bill of rights.

They say Clinton's programs will increase spending by $30.4 billion. Ours are more modest because we don't have huge surpluses lying around.

But those are minor differences. The important thing is that we preserve our unions.

To preserve ours, I'll try to see to it that my spouse doesn't move out and run for the U.S. Senate.

Assertiveness training at home

Y ou don't hear too much about assertiveness training these days. It seems only yesterday it was all the rage.

I'm guessing that this is because women have succeeded in becoming totally assertive and no longer need to learn the fundamentals. Guys, of course, have always had assertiveness to burn.

Years ago (would you believe 22?) I did the definitive treatise on this subject to accompany a special section for bridegrooms.

Unlike normal males, they are pathologically assertiveness-challenged because romance has altered their hormone balances.

Here are some exercises from that important handbook:

Situation No. 1: The lawn needs mowing. How do you interrupt your bride, who is doing the dishes, and tell her to mow it?

A: "The grass is getting pretty high out there, honey." (Non-assertive. Namby-pamby but sensible.)

B: "As soon as you're through with the dishes, I want you to get out there and mow the lawn." (Assertive. Direct. Foolhardy.)

C: "Hurry up with those dishes. The grass is getting higher even as we speak."(Pack a suitcase and leave it by the door before using this one.)

Situation No. 2: Your bride says: "Where have you been? Why didn't you call?"

A: "It was kind of you to be concerned about me. How lucky I am to have someone who cares so deeply." (Non-assertive. Ingenious. Transparent. Dubious.)

B: "Traffic was terrible." (Non-assertive. Effective response. Works whether true or false.)

C: "Stopped for a drink with (person of same sex)." (Assertive. Honest. Perishable. Good for one-time use only.)

Situation No. 3: The dog is scratching at the door.

A: "YOUR dog is scratching at the door. I think he wants to go out." (Flawed attempt at non-assertiveness. Won't work.)

B: "Did you hear something?" (Non-assertive. Transparently sneaky. Lacks finality.)

C: "Can't you hear the dog scratching? Get up and let him out. Do I have to do everything around here?" (That's her line!)

I could go on but I can sense I am losing my audience. Perhaps I have had too much experience.

Oh, all right. One more.

Situation No. 4: "I've been meaning to tell you, honey, I'm having an affair. I wanted you to be the first to know."

A,B,C: "That's nice, dear." (Non-assertive.)

Camping OUR way

The First Family allegedly went camping in the Wyoming Tetons and the president pronounced it a "wonderful" experience.

Personally, I doubt he was talking about real camping.

The Clinton camping experience included horseback rides, hikes, a chuckwagon steak dinner, singing around the campfire and, finally, sleeping "under the stars."

That's not what I call real camping.

Real camping, which we did last week in Stony Brook Park outside Dansville, is erecting a tiny mountain tent and forgetting to bring the adapter for the air mattress pump.

Then it's having a friend who lives down the road blow up the mattress with a compressor, cramming it into the back seat, then having a hell of a time getting it out again at the campsite as other campers grin and point.

That's real camping.

Real camping is when you are sleeping on the queen size air mattress and your partner gets up to go into the bushes and all the air shifts to the vacant side causing your side to drop abruptly to the ground onto a pointed rock that bruises your lower spine and makes you emit a loud oath that causes other nearby campers to yell "Quiet over there!"

That's real camping,

Real camping is when the person getting up to go into the bushes cannot find the flashlight and says the hell with it and stumbles around in the dark in bare feet and steps on something sharp and it turns out to be the missing pump adapter.

That's real camping.

Real camping is a guy with bongo drums (BONGO DRUMS!) banging away until 10 p.m. What do you bet nobody in the Clinton party remembered to bring the bongo drums? And these people call themselves campers!

Real camping is when you finish "dinner" and head into town for supplemental nourishment at the drive-through window of a well-known fast food chain that provides emergency rations for real campers.

Real camping is lying back and marveling at the dazzling canopy of stars and trying to decide whether you absolutely must get up immediately or can wait until your bridgework floats away.

That's real camping.

What Bill, Hillary, Chelsea and all the Secret Service guys did was something entirely different.

Actually, we didn't do the entire real camping experience this last time either, but it wasn't our fault.

The weather wasn't right for real camping

It didn't rain.

Move, Midas! Mom's coming home

"I t's O.K.," I told the dog, "get up on the bed. She's not here."
°°Are you kidding? She knows everything.°°

He's right about that. I can see her now: She's sitting up there in Maine, gazing out to sea and chatting with her sister and her friends when suddenly she falls silent. "Uh-oh!" she says. "I knew it, he's let the dog up on the bed."

It's not simply a guess based on past performance. She's psychic. Tonight when I phone for my daily instructions, she'll say: "Did you let the dog up on the bed again?"

When I ask how she could think such a thing, she'll say:

"You asked him and he refused. He was afraid I'd walk in, right?"

"Right," I'll sigh.

Sometimes she uses deduction instead of her psychic powers.

She knows, for example, the dishes are piled in the sink and the dishwasher is full. She knows this because she knows I do not wash dishes until there are no clean dishes left in the cabinet. What's the point?

She knows the place needs vacuuming and the bed isn't made. That's because I don't believe in vacuuming until there's plenty of dirt underfoot. I like to see major, not minor, transformations. I don't make beds that are going to be slept in the same day.

She knows I haven't eaten a vegetable all week but have had plenty of cream ale and potato chips because the TV football season got under way Sunday.

Mostly she knows these things because she knows it isn't Friday yet. Friday is when she gets home.

> *"She knows that married men are basically slobs when left alone without supervision."*

She also knows that married men are basically slobs when left alone without supervision. When their wives are around, a well-trained husband will pitch in eagerly, make beds, do dishes, vacuum and help heat up food.

But when the wife is absent, forget it. He will clear a path through the accumulating debris but that's it.

He will wait until she gets home and says: "I can't go on living like this."

I have been told that bachelors are not like this, but I can't remember that far back. I've been under the care and supervision of a wife or a sergeant since my youth.

And you know something? I secretly like it that way. So does the dog. We like being housebroken. If the truth were known, we're really getting anxious for Friday to come. It's lonesome here and the place is a mess.

I can't wait to hear her walk in and exclaim: "Wow! The place looks spotless!"

Telecommuting: what really happens

People say: "You've got a computer; why not write at home and send your stuff to the office by phone line?

I've been keeping this log as I write today's piece. Perhaps it will shed some light on the matter:

2:30: Great time to work. Nobody here except me and the dog. Sitting at computer, staring at wall, notice wallpaper flap hanging loose. No problem. Fix in a jiffy with paste. Down to cellar. Burrow into workbench debris. Find paste solid as rock, useless.

2:53: Drive to hardware store. Buy paste. On way back, pass park. Dog goes wild. Barking, jumping back seat to front. Turn back to park. He dives out of window, chases German shepherd friend, Uno. They wrestle. Run though creek. Roll in mud.

3:35: Back home, Midas, runs into bathroom, stands in tub awaiting shower. Bathe, towel him off, blow dry with wife's hair dryer, clean up muddy tub, make sandwich, fill bird feeder.

3:47: Back to handy den/office computer station. Resume staring at wall. Notice wallpaper. Uh-oh. Forgot! Back to car. Retrieve wallpaper paste. Mix in bowl. Back to cellar for wallpaper brush. Find it dried out and useless. Grab sponge. Back to den. Ah! Finished! Admire handiwork.

> *"I've been keeping this log...*
>
> *Perhaps it will shed some light on the matter."*

4:08: Resume staring at wall waiting for download from muse. Spouse appears. Tell her about wallpaper. "That little flap took all this time?" Explain about paste, store, park, dog. "But you started at 2:30! Seriously, great job! But not a column."

4:22: Resume "writing." Hear vacuum running. Guilt feelings. Yell into living room: "Want me to do that?" No response. Repeat. "WAIT TILL I TURN OFF THIS VACUUM." "WANT ME TO DO THAT?" "You don't have to shout. Nice timing. I'm done."

4:35: Thinking: Crowded newsroom would be full of smart-aleck colleagues regaling each other with fascinating stories instead of putting them in the paper. Quiet here. No distractions. But no inspiration either. Resume musings.

4:51: Informed by spouse that work station closes in 15 minutes. Decide to upload these raw notes, call it a day.

5:00: "Quittin' time!" she announces. I reply: "I say when it's quittin' time 'round here. QUITTIN' TIME!" (Old family joke.)

5:30: Getting dressed to go out for dinner, I casually say: "Didn't get around to the yard cleanup. Too busy writing."

Guests impressed: no dust balls!

"**L**ook honey, no dust balls in the corners!"
"And no cobwebs on the ceiling! Check the bathroom, I'll bet there's no ring around the tub. These people are real pros."
"You said it. Great job, you guys!"

Funny how the people we call "company" never have the courtesy to say those things. You work all day to get the house in shape to receive them and they don't even notice. What ingratitude. It makes you wonder why we bother.

"You get no extra credit for neatness. It's compulsory."

We were talking about this the other night. The least "company" could do in exchange for all that food, drink and brilliant conversation is acknowledge our efforts, we agreed.

"Hey! Great vacuuming job, Big Guy! And no streaks on the windows! Fantastic! Way to go, babe." Something like that. Praise where praise is due.

But no. They just hand you their coats and head for the kitchen to pour themselves a drink. They figure that the absence of dirt is simply the way things are supposed to be.

You get no extra credit for neatness. It's compulsory. No matter how much labor you put in, you still get just a C. There are no A's, B's, C-pluses, gold stars or little smile faces.

I realize now that I've been guilty of this myself in the past and I'm ashamed. Next time we go out I'm going to behave differently and give credit where credit is due.

"Boy!" I'll say, "I love the way you cleaned up that lawn. It must have been a chore collecting all that dog stuff. How many bags did it take, if I may ask? Really? Wow! Good show, old boy! Now let's have a look at the master bedroom. Hey, great hospital corners! How did the cellar look, honey?"

"All shipshape. Debris neatly stacked, toolroom spotless. Winter clothes put away, screens ready to go up as soon as the storm windows come down. Garage all swept. These kids can really housekeep. Well done, folks! We can see you've been working like fastidious little beavers."

"Gee, thanks," they'll say. "Coming from you guys, that's special. In all the years we've been coming to your place, we never spotted a smudge on a molding or a wallpaper wrinkle."

"Well, we try," I'll say, "I'm glad you noticed. Some people think a clean house just happens."

The amazing thing about all this is that we do it all with volunteer labor. She volunteers hers and I volunteer mine.

And, you may not believe this, but there are no illegal aliens involved.

Bermuda revisited — again

We're revisiting the scene of that historic personal assignation again.

That's another way of saying it's our 46th wedding anniversary this Sunday so we're flying to Bermuda tomorrow for a long weekend.

An assignation, according to *Webster's New World Dictionary (Third College Edition)*, is defined as "an appointment to meet, especially one made secretly by lovers; a tryst; a rendezvous."

That's surely more romantic and accurate than the silly term "honeymoon," a weird compound word that inexplicably combines insect secretions with astronomy.

The""secret tryst" element jibes nicely with the way the original opening scene played out: As our plane descended over St. George we were peering out the window and my bride said the immortal words: "Well, by golly, we got away with it!"

The concept that we were putting something over on the fates stuck with us and on this, our sixth visit, one of us is bound by tradition to resurrect some variation of that expression of wonder and delight.

"Thirty years elapsed before we returned in 1986. Then we went back four more times."

"Outwitted them again!" has been used at least once by one conspirator or the other.

The May 5, 1956, trip was financed by several months of our *Democrat and Chronicle* reporters' paychecks.

Thirty years elapsed before we returned in 1986, then we went back four more times, all on our son's airline passes.

Needless to say, we're very high on Bermuda, for several reasons, most importantly, the friendly welcoming people.

We'll be riding on a crowded bus and the black teenager sitting next to us will ask "How do you like Bermuda?" Then others will chime in: Have you seen this? Have you seen that?

There is little, if any, poverty, so there is little of the guilt we felt in Caribbean cruise destinations.

So what if we're paying higher income taxes because big corporate tax cheaters are using Bermuda as a haven to escape the U.S. Internal Revenue Service?

They've got their ways of getting away with something, we've got ours.

The only difference is that we can live with ourselves, as the record shows.

Their honeymoon is bound to be over one day. Ours has passed the long-term durability test.

Grandparents' rights date from Adam and Eve

The Supreme Court is mulling over the question of grand-parents' rights. Can the right to visit grandchildren be denied?

I don't think so.

It's my highly educated guess that the justices will rule in favor of us grandparents, since they're geezers themselves and, if not grandparents, desperately wish they were.

This ruling is a no-brainer.

The right of grandparents to spoil their grandchildren rotten must never be abridged. The feelings of the parents are immaterial.

Similarly, the rights of grandparents to criticize their own children and interfere in all aspects of their lives are sacrosanct.

> *"When Adam protested that he and Eve would bring up the kids their way, God blew up."*

These rights have been woven into the fabric of civilization ever since God told Adam and Eve that His grandchild Cain was (and I quote Him exactly here) "a rotten kid and it's your fault. I should never have left him in your care."

When Adam protested that he and Eve would bring up the kids their way, God blew up.

"Look Buster or whatever your name is, I made you two and I can unmake you. I can turn you back into primordial ooze with a simple finger snap and bolt of lightning!" He thundered.

Naturally the "First Family" was "sore afraid," as the Bible used to say before the revisionists started tinkering with it. So I don't see how the Supreme Court thinks it could possibly reverse this practice at this late date.

Here is the case before the court:

A couple had two children out of wedlock — both girls. The father committed suicide. A court ruled that his parents could continue to see his daughters regularly. Then the mother married. Her husband adopted the children. They both refused to let the grandparents visit because it would remind the children of their genetic father.

Complicated? Sure. But the principle is crystal clear:

Parents have no constitutional right to interfere with the right of grandparents to meddle in all aspects of their offsprings' lives.

That includes diet, dress, hair length, manners, choice of friends, money management, career choices and especially the conception, rearing and educating of children. Parents should be grateful we care enough to interfere. Footnote: See God v. Adam and Eve, Celestial Law Review, Case No. 1.

Farewell to four-wheel friend

I felt a twinge when they led away the 10-year-old Honda wagon. She looked back at me with those big accusing tail lights. I couldn't meet her gaze. "How could you, after all we've been through?" she seemed to be saying.

How could I indeed?

Simple.

For money, that's how.

I know some of you read how I'd planned to put the old girl out to pasture in our front yard on Peaks Island, Maine, and let her rust away gazing out over the Atlantic Ocean at Halfway Rock lighthouse. They say the real Atlantic salt spray is so painless you're oxidized in half the time and don't even know it's happening to you.

But when Bob the salesman said he'd take another thousand bucks or so off the price of her sleek new successor, I realized I was being excessively sentimental.

I also learned that my insurance company wouldn't extend my liability policy to cover an unregistered "island car." Apparently it's too risky, despite the fact that an islander's lucky if he can get his junker up anywhere near the 20 mph speed limit before he runs out of island.

"In these affluent times, people look down on you if you're driving a wrinkled old car with a limp."

But the truth is that I lusted after the new Honda Civic DX 4-door with sun roof and CD player. It was just like a Bill and Monica thing when we saw each other. She was all silver to match my hairdo.

When I took her out for a spin we were like Fred and Ginger together. It was magic. When we came back and I pulled in alongside the old girl, it was no contest. I took one look at that scaly psoriasis-ridden complexion and thought, "she's revolting enough now; think what she'll be like when she's 20 and I'm 90."

Sure, we had good times together, we two. (Actually we four, counting wife and dog.) Nights camping at Stony Brook Park, the trips to Maine. I remembered how she'd come out of the car wash feeling so proud and frisky. It's too bad she let herself go like that.

In these affluent times, people look down on you if you're driving a wrinkled old car with a limp.

So what's the big deal? I don't have to apologize for getting a new car, do I? Come on, DO I? Of course not.

Cars don't have feelings, do they? Come on, DO they? Of course not.

They're just metal, plastic and rubber after all, aren't they?

Aren't they?

Sure they are.

Reading a newspaper from a ladder

If you are one of those wrongheaded critics who say there is nothing of compelling interest in the newspaper, try this little test:
1. Decide to paint a bedroom.
2. Assemble essentials: can of paint, brush or roller, masking tape, screwdriver, stepladder, stirring implement.
3. Open can with screwdriver. Stir paint with implement. Apply masking tape as needed. Grasp brush and can. Mount stepladder. Place paint can on ladder shelf. Dip brush in paint.
4. Mumble:
"Uh-oh. Forgot to spread newspapers."
5. Go to garage get old newspapers. Spread on floor.

After remounting the ladder, you will look down and see a startling headline and feel compelled to descend and read it.

If you are honest with yourself, you will think: "I have often said there is nothing in the newspaper, but obviously I was wrong."

In a recent example I observed first hand, the headline was: "Seven asteroids could cause Earthly havoc."

> *"After mounting the ladder, you will look down and see a startling headline and feel compelled to read it."*

How could I have missed that?" the reader muses. "Must remember to read the rest of the paper, not just my own column. Otherwise an asteroid could easily sneak up on me."

Presumably the rest of you saw the story in time to take cover. It went on to say that NASA had detected seven objects larger than half a mile across that could smash into the Earth causing worldwide devastation.

Then it added the comforting news that NASA was confident none of the asteroids would hit the Earth in the next 200 years.

But then it cautioned that only 10 percent of the sky had been surveyed for asteroids so "most of the potentially hazardous objects remained unknown."

It took several minutes for the reader to decide whether it made sense to go on painting the bedroom. Then he noticed that the story was a month old.

Suddenly the man's supervisor appeared.

"There was a planetary emergency, but it's O.K. now," he said, showing her the paper and remounting the ladder once again.

I rest my case. There are important stories in the paper. Ignore them at your peril.

Just to be safe, try to read all them the day they appear rather than waiting until you stumble upon a riveting one that throws off your whole day.

You might splatter paint on your obituary, making the whole painting exercise unnecessary.

Sound of passing trains is hypnotic

About 30 years ago a real estate agent was showing our house to a prospective buyer when the little girl who lived with us chirped: "Wait till you hear a train go by - they shake the whole house!"

What could we say? It was the truth. So we just stood there grinning and looking sheepish. "We hardly notice them any more," my wife lied.

The buyer and his wife, suddenly non-prospective, smiled too. They left soon after.

The little girl sensed that we were not pleased. She looked at her mom questioningly.

"It's O.K., sweetheart. Some people just don't like trains as much as we do."

We gave up the idea of moving and remodeled instead. Our little girl saved us from making an expensive mistake.

We've been living with the trains for 42 years now. Today we enjoy 50 freights and six (soon to be eight) passenger trains a day.

At night we can lie in bed and hear them blow (two longs a short and a long) for the Fairport grade crossing. From the "doppler effect" (rising tone of the whistle) we can tell whether it's a fast Amtrak turbo or a slower Conrail (soon to be CSX) freight. The Amtraks are said to speed by at 79 mph, but I'd swear some go much faster on the downhill grade past our house. (Soon they'll be hitting 120.)

> *"It's o.k., sweetheart. Some people don't enjoy trains as much as we do."*

On hot summer nights in the old days, we'd be entertained for hours by switch engines banging cars back and forth outside our window as they shunted them into the East Rochester car shop yards.

Since the old 39-foot bolted-together rails were replaced by the quarter-mile lengths, welded together into mile after mile of continuous steel, the old "clickety-clack, echoing back" (Blues in the Night) sound has been eliminated. Now we get a smooth seamless hum that's actually soothing.

If the little girl had found her audience more responsive that day, she no doubt would have exclaimed that "we can see the trains on our TV set!"

It's true. Shadowy outlines of passing boxcars were visible on our tube because the railroad embankment rises between our house and the Pinnacle Hill transmitters. Now, with cable, we've lost that dramatic special effect.

Admittedly, all this is what you could call an "acquired taste." Less romantic folk would probably call it noise pollution. We think of it as a reasonable substitute for the foghorns and bell buoys of Maine.

Personal barber owed for 4,144 haircuts

My wife figures she saved the family something like $10,000 over the years by cutting my hair with her trusty Sears haircutting kit. That's 44 years of barbering, every other week, at a cost of perhaps $9.95 for the kit, purchased years ago.

Before 1956 I used to get my hair cut by Tony in the barbershop at the old Central YMCA at a cost of maybe $1.50 including tip.

Now I'm told that guys pay $15 and up.

I tried to do the math, roughly figuring 44 years times 26 weeks equals 1,144 haircuts at prices ranging from $1.50 to $15, including 15 percent tip. Her figure of $10,000 sounded accurate enough, considering that some weeks she let me go shaggy.

> *"She is armed with clippers and I'm a sitting, non-tipping duck. (There's nothing more pitiful than a bald duck.)"*

If I'd kept on with Tony he'd probably have talked me into shampoos and "razor cuts" when all the barbers became "hairstylists."

But when my spouse took over, she scorned those vanities. She just slides a rake-like guide over the clippers and starts mowing away with abandon, often humming to herself.

Occasionally she will mutter an "Oops" or a "Sorry," followed by a "Don't worry; it will grow out." But usually the operation goes forward without serious blood loss.

Like Tony, she insists on working without mirrors. Otherwise I might distract her with instructions such as "Careful with the sideburns, and watch the bald spot."

But I rarely complain. After all, she is armed with clippers and I'm a sitting, non-tipping, duck. (There's nothing more pitiful than a bald duck.)

Seriously, she's become a skilled barber over the years, if not a stylist. There's no waiting, and once in motion she's very, very fast.

She also monitors me continuously for scruffiness.

"You're getting that Charley Winniger look," she'll tell me. (Charley was the feathery silver-haired Capt. Andy Hawkes in the 1936 movie Show Boat.)

Sometimes I'll check the mirror afterwards and be reminded of the young face I saw in the mirror of the barracks latrine at Fort Sill, Okla., years ago.

But most of the time I'll think, "Not bad, considering what she had to work with."

When you're paying $9.95 instead of $10,000 for 1,144 haircuts in 44 years, you don't get picky about quality control.

Give a hug, shed a tear

*(The following column was written on the eve of Dick's daughter's graduation
from Bowdoin College in Brunswick, Maine)*

A close friend of the family, who is also the newest member of it, is graduating from college this weekend and we've been wondering what to give her, aside from good wishes, as a graduation present.

We've thought of giving her optimism, since we seem to have alot of it on hand, but nobody seems to want it anymore. We've thought of giving her self-discipline, but she's already got more of that than anyone else in the family.

She's got kindness. She's got good looks. She's got brains, concern, humility, character. What do you give somebody who has everything?

Her mother would like to give her a haircut. Her father says no. She wouldn't like that.

How about wisdom? But we had to say no to that, too, because we don't have any to spare. Maturity? We've got lots of maturity but what did it ever do for us except make us geriatric supplement junkies?

"We've been getting calls from companies that mistakenly assume we have a lawn under circulation."

Sometimes we think she is short on realism. She finds it difficult to think of reasons why things can't be done. She tends to go ahead, unrealistically, and somehow they wind up done.

Let's give her some luck! Look what luck has done for us. If it hadn't been for luck her mother and father might never have met.

But where are we going to get any luck these days? Whoever gives it out is certain to tell us that we've already had our share. (That's just being realistic.)

Luck can be dangerous. It can corrode the character. You might get to rely on it and you overdraw the account and your luck bounces.

Wonder? She's got wonder. Reverence, too. Got that the first time we took her outdoors and she saw a bird. Strength? Her mother gave her that. Courage? Let's hope she already has it. Besides, we don't have any extra ourselves.

It would be nice to give her something like world peace and a guarantee of freedom, but the people who could help give her those seem to have carelessly misplaced them and don't seem to care.

No, they're saying "power" is what matters. Forget it. She doesn't need or want power. Thank God for that!

Tell you what.

Let's give her a hug.

And maybe a tear.

She'd like that.

Lawn care "experts" just dreaming

I t begins to look as though the dreaded outdoor improvement season is almost upon us, at least according to the calendar and the lawn care solicitors.

Ever since New Years we've been getting calls from companies that mistakenly assume we have a lawn under cultivation.

Despite past experience, they persist in expressing confidence they can make it all nice and green like in the magazines.

What dreamers!

They want to drop by and give us a no-obligation consultation. We've told them to call back when the lawn turns from white to brown again. In the past when we've consented to give it "one more try," they've signed us up for a "program" of pest control spraying and fertilizing.

In midsummer, when nothing has come up except dandelions and crabgrass, we consult again and they tell us we'll never have a lawn until we get rid of all those trees and the dog.

Maybe next year, we say.

Now here it is next year again. Should we go through the same drill again?

It has always been my feeling that, since we don't plan on living forever, we should leave lawn improvement to the new owners and heirs. I've been saying that since we moved in in 1956, but now I'm no longer joking.

One of the offending trees, with a sunblock rating of 1,000, is a mongrel spruce. Just after we moved in, I was walking the dog and encountered the late Mr. Beers and was admiring his infant spruce forest on his Glen Road property.

"We've been getting calls from companies that mistakenly assume we have a lawn under cultivation."

"Here," he said, yanking a two-foot seedling out of the ground, "take it home and stick it in the ground. It'll grow."

Today it towers menacingly 60 feet over the house. It must know it's getting old because it showers us constantly with cones, desperately trying to give birth to little spruces.

The other large tree is a silver maple. It too is over-sexed. It masturbates those whirling "helicopter" seedlings all over the driveway. We suspect the other big maple is a brazen female hussy getting him all excited.

There is another conifer, a crab apple, a Japanese maple and a fat bush. Too much horticulture? We think not.

Is one golden retriever one too many? Don't be silly. Midas the most decorative living thing on the property, except for the mistress of the house.

If the grass doesn't like our yard, the hell with it, I say.

Burning the ceremonial nostalgia leaf

We burned a single leaf in the fireplace last weekend just to get the nostalgia juices flowing.

It did the trick, taking us back to autumn days long ago when leaf smoke was considered a fragrance, not a noxious carcinogenic pollutant and ozone layer perforator.

Try it. You'll not only enjoy the aroma, you'll also know the thrill of breaking the law, knowing that any moment an environmental SWAT team of municipal leaf smoke-cops could break down the door.

"I don't see why the environmental ordinances can't be suspended just one weekend a year, just so our kids can get a sniff of real autumn," I told my wife. "If one of those town board candidates had campaigned on that issue, I'll bet she'd have won in a landslide."

"Couldn't do it. Politically impossible. Too radical. Undermine values. Introduce kids to substance abuse," she said.

"They could say they didn't inhale. Like our president."

"Or maybe legalize it for medical treatment purposes only?"

We'd been raking leaves until our back, shoulder and buttocks muscles were throbbing and our hands proudly blistered. The ceremonial burning, toasted with a glass of sacramental liquid relaxant on the rocks, was our reward.

Later we sat on the front steps and viewed our handiwork.

"Nice crop this year," I said.

"By cracky," my wife replied.

"What?"

"By cracky. That's the way we rubes talk down on the farm."

She was actually born in Manhattan but grew up in the Wayne County outback of Clyde, so she can fake the talk.

It was a fine crop indeed, by cracky or otherwise.

The leaf mound filled the gutter and spilled into the road. With our neighbors, we had done our part to make our suburban street a meandering one-lane country road.

Soon, perhaps today, the town trucks and front loader will be along to scoop up the harvest and haul it to "market" outside the DPW garage near the salt pile.

Our town has a compassionate leaf redistribution program. It takes from us, the leaf-rich, and gives to the leaf-poor composters.

"It sure gives you a feeling of satisfaction, bringing in a bumper crop like this, knowing that we're helping out those less fortunate, doesn't it?" I said.

"Yup," she replied.

"By cracky?"

"Of course."

Grass is yellow all over

The lawn looks gorgeous these days. It has lovely yellow flowers growing all over it.

Of course it isn't as beautiful as it was in February when it was all a glistening white, but it's better than when it was infested with unsightly patches of green sprouts.

I remarked to my spouse that it reminded me of the time I was out "wandering lonely as a cloud o'er vales and hills when all at once I saw a host of golden dandelions."

"That's funny," she said, "William Wordsworth had the same reaction when he came upon a host of golden daffodils."

"Daffodils, dandelions, whatever," I muttered.

All up and down the street last weekend our neighbors were attacking the little yellow flowers with deadly weed poppers and mowers and throttling them barehanded. Some were even waging chemical warfare.

You'd think they'd know by now that the dandelion is our friend and should be welcomed and protected from its natural enemy, grass.

According to the encyclopedia, dandelions have been used since the 10th century to treat piles, liver and kidney ailments, gallstones, jaundice and dropsy.

The blooms are high in potassium, lecithin (the memory enhancer) and calcium. They make excellent diuretics and can be made into tea and wine.

> *"...the dandelion is our friend and should be protected from its natural enemy — grass."*

With this kind of pedigree, you'd think folks would feel more kindly toward them.

But the only true celebration of the dandelion that I know of is the University of Rochester song "Dandelion Yellow," music by the late Charley Cole, class of '25 and veteran *Democrat and Chronicle* newsman:

> *O, Azariah Boody's cows were sleek and noble kine*
> *They wandered o'er verdant fields where grew the dandelion.*
> *And when they drove the cows away*
> *To build a home for knowledge*
> *They took the color from the flow'r*
> *And gave it to the college.*

The chorus ends with these stirring lines:

> *O, let Harvard have her crimson*
> *And old Eli's sons the blue*
> *To the dandelion yellow we will e'er be true.*

I wonder if UR grads mouth those words as they whack away at the hosts of golden dandelions spreading o'er their verdant lawns.

Leaf harvesting delayed

L eaf harvesting season looms again, and this time I was going to pull a fast one.

I had planned to compose a simple anonymous but official-sounding note and stuff photocopies into the mailboxes on our street:

Notice: Leaves may be allowed to lie where they fall until all are safely on the ground. Bureau of Foliage Management.

But then I came to my senses. The neighborhood isn't ready.

The counterfeits would be traced to me and an ugly crowd would gather out front.

"The leaf rules cannot be changed without years of tireless consultation," they'd shout, brandishing their rakes and leaf blowers.

Then I'd have to convince them I was only kidding.

"It was just a trial balloon," I'd say. Finally they'd quiet down and begin to drift off.

"Return to your homes," the police chief would shout through his bull-horn. "It's all over, folks."

Luckily, I stopped myself in time and none of this happened.

The situation cries out for reform, but I'm not the courageous leader the neighborhood needs.

It started as I stood in the yard last weekend, looked up at the trees and lost my grip on reality.

I shook my fist: "Come down out of there!" I shouted, but they just rustled at me, as if to say: "We'll come down when we're ready, one day at a time all month long, and you'd better be ready!"

As I've complained in autumns past, the rule on our street has always been that a leaf must not be allowed to lie unmolested for more than 24 hours Monday through Friday. On weekends it is customary to keep one's lawn leaf-free at all times.

When a leave falls on Saturday, it is to be promptly raked into a central pile. This pile must be deposited at the curb by nightfall. On Sunday the procedure must be repeated. Violators risk being clucked at by inspectors from the leaf surveillance committee.

I don't mean to suggest that enforcement is unreasonable.

If there is a death or serious illness in the family, applications for brief extensions may be filed.

But it is the law throughout the realm that leaves are essentially litter. They are in the same category as gum wrappers and cigarette butts and are to be treated as such.

Whenever I have questioned this, people say: "You're one of those liberals, aren't you? We don't need your kind around here."

I hate that. Let someone else be a hero this time.

Need Dr. Ruth's advice on sexy trees

I was so upset that I composed a letter in my head to Dr. Ruth, the sex lady, as I angrily raked up under the tree.

"Dear Dr. Ruth: We've got one of those shamelessly sexually- active silver maple trees in our front yard. Its behavior is a neighborhood scandal. Every year about this time, in broad daylight, it showers its seed on the lawn. We are so embarrassed! Please help. Easily Shocked, Rochester, N.Y."

"Dear Easily: I am so sick of you prudish suburbanites complaining about the sexual behavior of trees when there are so many serious problems facing suburbia, such as garage debris overload and junk mail pollution. Your tree is doing what comes naturally. It is trying to fill your yard with little silver maples. Leave it alone or it will become sexually repressed. Send for my free pamphlet, Sex and Your Tree, in care of this newspaper."

I knew Dr. Ruth would give me a snippy brushoff, so I didn't actually write. I just kept raking and fuming.

Dr. Ruth has always been too liberal about sex, if you ask me. She comes from the Cole Porter Let's Fall in Love School of Sex Education whose anthem is: "Birds do it, bees do it, even educated fleas do it, let's do it, etc."

I don't have a violent argument with that, but in broad daylight, and in the presence of another maple tree apparently of the opposite sex? My goodness!

> *"I was right. The show-off tree was a male. Wouldn't you know!"*

The other maple does not spew helicopter seeds all over the lawn. It sits there demurely with its branches folded in its lap, blushing and trying not to notice.

The next day I went to the science division of the main library where they keep the dirty books about tree sex. I was right, the show-off tree was a male. Wouldn't you know!

I don't want to repeat all the explicit details about stamens, pistils and, ugh, pollen, but I was surprised to learn that there are bisexual (both male and female) trees, unisexual (one sex) trees and, get this, trees that are both bisexual and uni-sexual!

Talk about sexual orientations!

Male maple trees indulge in a practice called "wind pollination." (Don't ask.)

And talk about naive! I had no idea. And right in front of my eyes, with the neighbors laughing at me behind the curtains!

I was right to decide not to discuss this with Dr. Ruth. She'd just tell me all the tree was trying to do was make a forest. "Get a life," she'd say. I hate it when they tell me that.

No, I should have gone to Cal Thomas right off the bat.

Neighborhood lovely under snow

The neighborhood has rarely looked better. Everything is all white and clean. Even *our* yard is spotless.

If the neighborhood lawn contest were held today, we'd be a cinch for an honorable mention.

At last we've got the dandelions and crabgrass under control, and there are no unsightly leaves lying around or hanging aloft. Nor is there any evidence we have a housebroken dog on the premises. It's as though he has his own secret septic system.

Many times in the past we've thought how nice it would be to have a carefree asphalt lawn, but this is even better. The nicest part is that everyone else has one, too.

Ed, the perennial lawn champion up the street whom we all hate with a passion, now is one of us — or, rather, we're all up there on the podium with him at last.

> **"Many times I have thought how nice it would be to have a carefree asphalt lawn, but this is even better."**

During the off-season, when the town is covered with unsightly crew-cut stubble, some of us stop by Ed and Lorraine's and admire his handiwork. We'll ask Ed what he's putting on his crop that makes it look like a vast pool table.

Not that we listen intently to the answer, you understand. We're just trying to make him feel good.

I wish I could preserve my lawn in its present all-white state throughout the year. In the fantasy that I often indulge in, Ed comes by and pumps me for lawn care tips.

"How do you make it so smooth and clean like that, with that interesting pattern of dog, bird and rabbit tracks on it?" he'd ask me.

"Nothing much to it," I'd tell him and the gathering crowd of neighbors.'"You just let the yard lie there fallow and unmolested until enough of this white stuff accumulates, then you refrigerate the whole thing."

"Everything?" they'd exclaim.

"Absolutely," I'd say. "Especially the trees and shrubs. Otherwise you'll have leaves falling all over the place. Keep it down in the single digits for the best results."

I was standing in the yard yesterday, enjoying this fantasy while waiting for the NFL playoff game to begin, when I heard a familiar voice.

"What are you doing standing out there with that stupid smile on your face? You'll catch your death" the voice said.

It was my spouse. I recognized the tone right off.

"Nothing," I said.""Just checking the estate and hoping this weekend cold heralds the beginning of the new ice age."

Farming out future snow jobs

F orget about this snow. You've seen the last of it.

You guessed it; in a fit of sanity, accompanied by lower back spasms, I signed up for snow removal. Here's how it happened:

Midas, the dominant pup who heads our household, and I were out in the driveway playing with my Canadian snow scoop. I was shoving it back and forth while Midas barked at it hysterically.

(A Canadian snow scoop is, as you might expect, sort of a scoop. As you shove it along, it scoops up the snow, instead of just shoving it aside into furrows.

(When the scoop is full, you veer off to the side and dump it with a quick push-pull. There is no lifting. Now back to our story.)

While we were barking and giggling together, a sobering sanity, accompanied by fatigue, came over me unexpectedly. I could feel my playfulness leaking away.

Uh-oh, I thought, I can see it now: Local Man Suffers Heart Attack While Scooping Snow to Entertain Puppy.

Then my back spasm hit. The driveway was unfinished.

That's when I remembered that my neighbors, most of them younger than I, all have driveways beautifully manicured by a man named Jim.

And that's when Jim, through mental telepathy, happened to pull into my driveway in his pickup. Minutes later we had a deal.

As I was writing the check, my wife said:

"You realize, don't you, that this means there will be no more snow this winter. You told all your readers it would be a bad winter and they all went out and signed contracts or bought blowers."

"Am I my brother's keeper? If the readers want to take the half-baked advice of a superstitious whacko, they deserve whatever they get."

"Ah, the great liberal speaks," she said.

When I went back outside with the check, Jim had finished the driveway. It looked beautiful.

"Sorry, pup," I told Midas. "No more playtimes. Pop is pooped."

He looked at me, disgusted, but I was unmoved. No dog is going to shove me around, I thought. I'm the alpha dog in this pack, you little runt.

So he went into his behavior modification routine, the plaintive whine and heartbreaking woebegone victim impersonation.

Naturally it worked. I haven't been the star pupil at obedience school for nothing.

Soon we were barking and giggling together again.

Too bad the snow is all over for the season. I'd have him riding in that scoop in no time.

Dark harbingers of spring

People ask me if spring is going to come this year. I try to be optimistic and say "I sure hope not."

But I know better.

There's no holding it back. Even biting cold snaps like the one we had over the weekend can't keep it at bay forever.

There is snow on the roof that has to melt and when it does, it has to go somewhere. As in previous years, it will flow down the roof until it reaches the ice dam that has formed in the gutters. Then it will back up under the shingles and drip through the living room ceiling.

The overflow will seep through the foundation walls and into the basement.

When you have lived in the arctic for as long as we have, you know these things. We call them "harbingers" of spring.

Spring is when the front yard turns from a glistening white to a dirty brown, covered with bones and dog toys and what we call "droppings."

Spring is also when dogs shed their fur underwear all over the carpeting and furniture. We collect it in our nasal passages and vacuum cleaner bags. Recently it has been blonde, as befits a golden retriever named Midas.

> *"Spring is when the lawn turns from a glistening white to a dirty brown."*

Not long ago it was black, the color of his predecessor, Feeney.

There are insects stirring everywhere and measures must be taken to prevent them from taking over.

Since we signed our snow removal contract, winters have been carefree and restful, with pleasant interludes watching electronic images of football players.

Now that's all over. Beginning in a few weeks, it will be porch and deck furniture moving time, screen repair time, window washing time and garage and basement reorganizing time.

But most of the weekends will be spent performing what I call ornamental agriculture chores — where we strive to make various non-edible crops grow using fertilizer.

At the same time we must prevent others from growing by feeding them toxic powders and sprays.

There are larvae lurking in the soil, preparing to become insects and grubs are stirring.

We must be ready for them!

Believe it or not, there was a time when I was a young man and had a "fancy" that turned lightly to thoughts of dalliance and baseball.

Now that's all just a memory.

Chapter Four

Presidents & Politics

Founding Fathers needed Founding Mothers

My wife attributes the recent constitutional unpleasantness to the failure of the Founding Mothers to assert themselves.

"You see all these references to the Founding Fathers. What about their spouses?" she wanted to know.

"Where were they when their husbands were hanging out in the Philadelphia pubs, supposedly founding a country?"

"Good question," I mumbled, a little miffed that I hadn't thought of it as a column.

But now that I have, I have to admit I do find it curious that so little has been made of the role of motherhood in all of this.

Even with my rudimentary knowledge of sex, it seems clear that if you're giving birth, to a country or a nation, you need a woman to do the hard part. Sure, the male role is fun, but fleeting. They plant the seed and then they're out of there.

> *"If you're giving birth to a country or a nation, you need a woman to do the hard part."*

I can hear Mrs. Madison telling Jim: "This is the third day in a row you've been late for dinner. I'm in my eighth month now. It's not easy, you know, being with country like this; being with child is bad enough."

"I'm sorry, dear, Ben and I and the guys were down at the City Tavern, talking about the electoral college, and lost track..."

"Sure you were. I'll bet you were playing darts. Let me smell your breath. I thought so! Your nose is as red as a beet."

"You're wrong, my dear. But next time I'll call."

"How are you going to call? Yell out the window?"

"Right. I forgot. No telephones. I'll send a messenger."

"So how's the world-shaking document coming?"

"Not bad, but we're hung up on the preamble. We don't know how to start it off."

"Simple. You start off with 'We, the people,' and explain you're trying to form a more perfect union and all that."

"You're a genius, my dear!"

"And don't forget about 'insuring justice and domestic tranquillity.' That's a must."

"Yes, dear. Hey! I guess this means you're having labor pains at last!"

"Just a twinge. Now let's talk about that electoral college thing. Mark my words, it will lead to trouble down the road."

"You mustn't bother your pretty little head about these pesky details, sweetheart. Daddy will take care of the electoral college. We're going to have a Supreme Court, you know."

"That's what I'm afraid of!"

Why do Presidents always have to build something?

Every time she hears our president talking about joining him in "building a bridge to the 21st Century," my irreverent spouse has to suppress a giggle. "Imagine him asking YOU!" she says. "That's hilarious."

Exactly. Hilarious and a little terrifying.

Why do presidents keep asking every Tom, Dick and Harry to help them build something?

Woodrow Wilson had his New Freedom project, Roosevelt his New Deal, Kennedy his New Frontier, Johnson his Great Society. But these were more concepts than structures.

Jimmy Carter had his New Foundation and Clinton has his crazy bridge in the sky. These are major engineering projects that could easily fall down and hurt somebody, especially if you ask Tom and Harry to help out. I won't even mention Dick.

As I pointed out to Jimmy Carter 20 years ago, his New Foundation would be no piece of cake, even for my neighbor Frank Boehm, the contractor who can build anything.

> *"There are major engineering projects that could easily fall down and hurt somebody."*

First, Frank would explain, you have to lift everything off the foundation and cover it with a tarp. Then you have some guy come in with a backhoe and dig out the old cement blocks. Then you lay the new foundation, maybe put in a new furnace, heat runs, sump pump and plumbing. Then you have to put the whole damn house, building or whatever back on top and connect up the wiring.

I imagined Frank licking his stub pencil, figuring on the back of a White House envelope, and saying "Vow, Chimmy, this is going to cost you a pretty pfennig."

(Frank was a German POW who was interned in Denver, liked the U.S., went back to Austria for his wife and moved to our neighborhood. If we'd met during the war, we'd have been expected to shoot each other. Now back to our story.)

As I imagined it, Frank would be telling Jimmy:

"Look, you've got four foundations here. You got your `foundation for the future,' you got your `foundation for the government that works for the people,' your `foundation for confidence in our economic system.' Then there's that `foundation for a peaceful and prosperous world' you mentioned. This is no easy chob. I may have to subcontract a lot of this stuff."

I'm sure his advice to Clinton would be to forget the bridge idea. Once everyone's across, nobody can get back, so it's useless anyway.

Miss Woolcott breaks up Clinton-Gingrich fight

They're saying the budget crisis has been settled but I'm not so sure. My old elementary school principal, Miss Woolcott, wouldn't call it settled. The conspicuous missing elements here are that Newtie and Billy did not have to endure the silent and withering Miss Woolcott Stare, nor were there admissions of guilt, apologies or promises of future good behavior.

When Miss Woolcott wrapped things up, there was finality, like this:

"Now, Billy Clinton, you march right over there and tell Newtie you're sorry you made him and Bobby use the back door of Air Force One," Miss Woolcott would have said, grabbing Billy by his ear and hauling him to his feet and leading him across the room to face Newtie.

"And make him say he's sorry for not talking to me and Bobby about the budget for 25 hours!" Newtie would have protested.

"Stand up and be quiet! I'm handling this," Miss Woolcott would have replied, grabbing Newtie by the ear with her other hand and yanking him to his feet to face Billy.

"Ouch!" Newtie would have replied convincingly.

"All right, Billy. We're waiting."

"Ouch! I . . .I . . . I'm sorry, Newtie. Ouch!"

"Look him in the eye, not at the floor!"

"Ouch! I'm sorry, Newtie."

"Once again, and this time with feeling and without the ouch."

"I'm sorry, Newtie."

"And I won't do it again!"

"And I won't do again!"

"And now you, Newtie."

"Ouch!"

"Tell Billy the next time you get angry you won't goad him into shutting down the government."

"Ouch! I promise."

"You promise what? Without the ouch this time."

"Lose my temper and make him shut down the government."

"Ever again."

"Ever again."

"Now both of you go stand in that corner facing the wall. When the bell rings, I want both of you to call your mothers from this phone and tell them about this."

(In unison) "Ouch! Yes, Miss Woolcott."

Now THAT'S a settlement.

All that remains is for the mothers to say, "We'll talk about this when your father comes home" and for Newtie to say "I'll get you for this" and Billy to reply: "You and what army!"

That evening, when the fathers say "This will hurt me more than it's going to hurt you," the entire episode would be considered over, perhaps even permanently.

Moving day at the White House

Eavesdropping on Laura and W:

Can't you DO something? Here it is almost inauguration time and I haven't seen the inside our new house since your parents left and those awful people moved in eight years ago.

Look, I'm doing the best I can, honey, but the other guy is dragging his feet.

My lord! I guess your best isn't good enough. You're the new president of the United States, for goodness sake. You said so yourself. But I don't even know if we can bring our own furniture.

Put it in storage. But remember, most of this stuff belongs to the state of Texas. Don't get it mixed up with our stuff.

Put it in storage! Put it in storage! You seem to forget that most of our own stuff is already in storage.

Meanwhile, in Washington, the Other Guy's wife is giving her spouse a similar piece of her mind.

Can't you do something? Here it is almost inauguration time and I haven't even met with the movers!

Look, I'm doing the best I can, honey, but the other guy is dragging his feet.

The best you can! The best you can! And you still call yourself President of the United States for goodness sakes, and you can't even tell me when we're going to move out? You're still the chief executive. Let's make an executive decision here!

And you're the first lady! LADY! LADY! Try to remember that.

Oh, listen to him. Hail to the chief! Ruffles and flourishes! Well answer this, Mr. Chief Executive, what are we going to do with the dogs and cats?

Take them with us. I'm in politics, remember? I'll need them for photo ops. The dogs, anyway.

Aha! An executive decision! If you'd stop suing everybody and his brother, you'd have time for your own family.

Try to cool it. Remember, we're not moving to the moon. It's still only Washington, D.C.

Meanwhile, back at the governor's mansion, the usually amiable lady of the house is getting testy.

Do you remember what color the drapes are? No, of course you don't. Men never know the important things.

The place comes furnished, you know. And it's a national monument. It's not like you can redecorate the Lincoln Bedroom in ranch bunkhouse decor.

You're no help at all. I should have known. I guess I'll have to go crawling to Hillary.

Funny she should say that, because back in Washington the Other Guy's wife has just turned on her heel and snapped:

Forget it! I'm calling Laura. Honestely! Men!!

Controlling guns (and militias)

"A well-regulated militia, being necessary to the security of a free state, the right of the people to keep and bear arms shall not be infringed."

So reads the Second Amendment to the U.S. Constitution so often cited by the National Rifle Association as the basis for its opposition to gun control legislation.

This leads to my plan for resolving the hostility between the pro and anti-gun control folks:

Just this: Draft all gun enthusiasts into militias. Not just any old militia, well-regulated militias.

Here's a fantasy that will illustrate my vision. A platoon of militia recruits is reporting for its first day of basic regulation.

"All right, you men, stop playing with them guns and give me your attention. You in the back there, yes you, did you hear what I just said?"

"Yes, sir."

"Don't call me sir, you idiot. I'm a non-commissioned officer."

"Yes, er, sarge."

"Sergeant! Never call me Sarge. Sarge is a term of affection. I don't want any of you to regard me with affection. Fear, yes, affection, no. Is that clear? I said is that CLEAR? That's better."

"Now listen up. You civilians are here to become well-regulated. You've heard of regularity. No, not that kind of regularity! I'm talking blind obedience. Standing at attention, eyes focused on the horizon, shoulders back, hands at your sides, thumbs along the seams of your trousers, heels together."

"I'm talking making your bunks, shining your shoes, scrubbing the barracks, standing inspection, watching venereal disease films, learning to salute, memorizing your serial numbers..."

As the scene unfolds, we see your kid from Brooklyn, your hayseed from Iowa, your sissy, your coward, your rich kid, your various racials, ethnics and females and of course your tough black drill sergeant (played by Lou Gossett Jr. of "An Officer and a Gentleman").

The kid from Brooklyn pipes up: "Hey Sarge, I mean Sergeant, We joined this outfit to shoot at stuff. When do we get our bullets?"

"Go read your Constitution again, city boy. It says we can't infringe on your right to keep and bear arms. It doesn't say anything about bullets. This militia is going to be well-regulated. You'll bear arms when I say you bear arms. In the meantime your arms will stay locked up in the supply room where they can't hurt anybody.

"Now when I say MARCH, you step off with your left foot. Forr-warrrd MARCH! Platoon HALT!

"City boy, show me your left foot. NO, NO! The other one! Let's get regulated here, troops."

"Forr-warrrd . . ."

Two good ol' farmboys chat it up

I have to admit I'm feeling better about the Mideast crisis. Early last week, I was depressed. The Arabs hated us and threatened to shut off our oil.

But then Saudi Prince Abdullah came to President Bush's Crawford, Texas, ranch to talk things over.

About time, I thought.

"This is the kind of initiative the whole world has been waiting for," I exclaimed.

Well, now we know. It was a resounding success!

The report I read said "the two men reaffirmed the abiding friendship between their two nations and agreed to work together to bring peace to the Mideast."

I attribute this remarkable diplomatic breakthrough to three developments mentioned just briefly in the dispatches:

Development No. 1: First Lady Laura Bush fed the prince, her husband and their combined entourages a sumptuous lunch of "pecan encrusted smoked beef." No Texas-style SOS (Something on a Shingle) for his royal highness.

For dessert, she gave them vanilla ice cream, an exotic treat for a poor hayseed used to frozen fermented camel milk with fig sauce.

Development No. 2: Afterwards the two piled into a pickup truck for a tour of the Bush spread.

"He's a man who's got a farm and he understands the land," Bush told reporters.

"We saw a wild turkey, which was good," said the president, doing his famous Ernest Hemingway imitation.

What a heartening scene: Two good ol' hardscrabble farm boys out for a spin, one in cowboy jeans, the other in a sheet and head towel. How could they NOT hit it off and come up with a formula for world peace?

Development No. 3: All the president's words were dutifully taken down by the alert journalists at the end of the day.

(Who says the media is not seeking out the story-behind-the-story and demanding answers from our leaders?)

I was reminded of the 1959 visit of Soviet premier Nikita Khrushchev's to Roswell (Bob) Garth's hog farm outside Coon Rapids, Iowa, during the Cold War.

The visit was a howling diplomatic success, concluding with a near riot as Garth and his guest pelted the press corps with corn cobs and handfuls of ensilage.

Again, like last week, just two plain farmers solving the problems of the world.

Did it work? You tell me.

The Cold War ended a mere 26 years later, didn't it?

Marriage tax credit? Make it retroactive

The Bush administration wants to spend $300 million to promote marriage. I don't know the details, but naturally I'm in favor of it. Who wouldn't be?

I assume there will be cash incentives to get married and I further assume that those of us who have already committed marriage will get some too.

If marriage, as they say, is a "great institution," it seems only fair that we who are already institutionalized should be first in line for the handouts.

I spoke to my cellmate in our institution and asked her what she thought we should do with our share of the $300 million when it comes.

"Let's go to Bermuda," she said without hesitation. That's where we were when we first started serving our life sentences together without parole.

(That doesn't sound quite right. Remind me to rewrite that paragraph before I hand this in.)

If I know the government, I suspect it will squander most of the $300 million on unwed mothers-to-be.

Meanwhile, we experienced marriage enthusiasts, who know how to handle money and not blow it all on essentials, will be lucky if we get a dime.

It's surprising that Republicans who historically disparage government interference should want to get involved that intimately in our private lives.

That turf is supposed to belong to us knee-jerk liberal Democrats and other mushhead Rush Limbaugh targets.

> *"Hey, when $300 million is being given away, ideology must not get in the way of sensible advice."*

But hey, when $300 million is being given away, ideology must not get in the way of sensible avarice, I say.

However, if you will pardon me a moment of uncharacteristic seriousness, I have to say that I have always thought that there are very practical incentives for a consorting couple to get married — especially for the woman.

The marriage contract is more than a romantic expression of endearment.

Among other things, it facilitates divvying up property and responsibilities if the union breaks up, leaving helpless little third parties in its wake.

Perhaps what we really need here is a pre-non-nuptial agreement for co-habitating couples who are not contemplating nuptials.

For starters, it might specify that sex is optional but pregnancy is a no-no without renegotiating the contract after the troth is securely plighted.

Did we miss SEC deadline?

"**D**id you meet the deadline for certifying your financial reports?" I asked the family CEO/CFO last night. "They were due at 5 p.m., you know."

"What are you talking about?" she snapped.

"Securities and Exchange Commission Chairman Harvey Pitt ordered it after all the corporate accounting scandals. Don't you read the papers? You're the chief executive and financial officer of this firm, you know. You were supposed to sign off, under oath, on the accuracy of your financial reports."

> *"We're not a corporation, we don't make anything."*
> *"We're not? We make ends meet, don't we?"*

I've long suspected that the lady might be cooking the books. I've had several modest raises that I've never seen reflected in my allowance. When I ask for an accounting, I get the brush-off.

"How much does it take to park a car and buy lunch and coffee?" she'll scoff. "If you'd take a sandwich and a thermos, you'd have a surplus."

I know the money is coming in. I see the pay stubs. But where it goes from there, who knows?

No wonder Harvey Pitt is cracking the whip.

"Don't get defensive," I said. "I just wondered if you'd met the SEC deadline."

Obviously, I'd overstepped my authority. I just thought that as the so-called "breadwinner," I had a right to a little more detailed disclosure.

"Let me explain something to you," she said in that patronizing tone she uses when she's talking to me or Midas, the dog, her only other employee.

"We are not a corporation. We don't make anything"

"We're not? We make ends meet, don't we?"

"We have no investors because we do not issue stock. Harvey Pitt does not have anyone to protect from us."

I could tell by her tone that she was heading into her martyrdom mode.

"Look," she hissed. "When you were CEO/CFO, you used to toss the bills in a shoebox and at the end of month you'd pull them out and decide which to pay. It was ridiculous. You were ousted fair and square."

She's right, although actually I stepped aside for the good of the firm. She had the head for figures and was ruthless enough to bring order out of chaos.

If we'd been a corporation, there'd have been a lot of ugly annual meetings, believe me.

And now I'd be facing a perjury rap for certifying my own accounting.

"Chuckles" Greenspan and his cute phrases

Some of these quaint economic terms being bandied about mystify some of us non-economists.

I call these terms Greenspanisms, after Chairman of the Federal Reserve Board Alan ("Chuckles") Greenspan.

Take the term "durable goods," which is in the news today because their sales fell 6 percent in January, an ominous sign of the looming of something or other.

Much to my hilarity, cars are considered examples of "durable goods." I don't know about you, but I have never owned a durable car. My experience suggests that cars are "perishable goods," only slightly more durable than unrefrigerated fish.

Sure, I once had a secondhand $75 Model A Ford roadster that served me for five years, including two cross-country round trips. It came close to durability but wound up spontaneously catching fire while in motion outside Spokane, Wash., in 1937.

Right now, an estimated 20-or-so cars later, I have a '95 Geo Prizm whose durability is fast expiring. Soon, I hope, it will be "pre-owned" once again and I'll trade it for another fleetingly durable machine.

> *"Much to my hilarity, cars are considered examples of 'durable goods'."*

I'll buy it with what economists laughingly call "disposable income." (Isn't all income disposable? Sure it is. Have you ever been in possession of a dime that wasn't disposable?)

The other kind of income I've heard about is "discretionary." Maybe I'll use some of that to buy a new, temporarily durable and ultimately disposable car.

I wonder where one gets "discretionary income." I suppose that's income that isn't ear-marked for something, like rent, food or taxes, and never used to finance long-term indiscretions.

Unsurprisingly, NOT listed under "durable goods" were new homes, sales of which were reported this week to have fallen 10.9 percent in January.

I've always known houses were non-durable items. Ask any homeowner if his house is durable, and he'll laugh in your face. The term "durable house" is an oxymoron, a figure of speech that contains a contradiction, such as "a thunderous silence." (One of my favorites is "military intelligence.")

Come to think of it, the term "homeOWNER" is an oxymoron, almost as silly as "dog-OWNER." One does not own houses or dogs. One is owned BY them.

It might be helpful if I could analyze these various terms, and explain how they "impact" upon the "leading indicators" that tell us whether a recession is looming or not.

I'd do it if I had the credentials, but my findings would be neither good nor durable.

Pity the Pontiff for being so politically naive

Good thing the Pope isn't running for public office. He wouldn't have a prayer.

The Pontiff made some appalling political boo-boos in his speeches in Newark, N.J., the other day. His words sounded dissonant in the political climate of today.

For example: How about the one praising America's "spirit of creative generosity" in "meeting the needs of the poor and disadvantaged!"

That sounds like a line out of the distant past, when "liberals" stalked the land and even George Bush dared speak of a "kinder, gentler nation" and "safety nets" for the poor.

Talk about out of touch! You'd think he lived on another continent. The pontiff even dared suggest the rich "share their blessings," unaware that this kind of proposal today smacks of subversion.

Talk like that will just make it all that much harder to dismantle welfare and poverty programs to give tax breaks to the rich.

If he hadn't been wearing those robes, he'd have been hooted off the podium. But wait. That wasn't all. The Pope also praised the United Nations as a valuable "instrument of dialogue and peace"!

This is the same United Nations that we have stiffed for $1.3 billion in back dues.

He went on to say that the "powerful and mighty (nations) ought to show meekness in their dealings with the weak"!

He seemed unaware that in today's world, power is in. Meekness is for wimps. To advocate meekness is political suicide.

As if that were not enough, the Pope appeared to actually praise our nation's past history of encouraging immigration.

He totally ignored the fact that the mood of the country today seems to be to slam the golden door to outsiders now that all of us good folks are safely inside.

Can you imagine any of the candidates now running for president coming out for immigration and praising our "rich ethnic and racial diversity"?

Plainly, the Pope hasn't read the fine print in the "Contract on America". Or perhaps he has no interest in public office. For all I know, he may even be ineligible to vote, being a Polish alien here on a temporary visa — without even a green card.

Which party is pure and innocent?

I f you want to hear some refreshingly cynical laughter, try saying this out loud sometime: "Aren't you glad Republicans never do any of those awful things the Clinton administration is accused of?"

I tried it in the YMCA steam room recently. The guffaws were deafening.

Admittedly, the loudest came from those of Democratic persuasion. The Republicans just sat there, rolled their eyes and grinned sheepishly.

I became thoroughly cooked and had to leave, but I like to think the conversation continued more or less along these lines:

"Boy, I'll say! If I thought for a minute that Jesse Helms' political action committee was accepting campaign donations from North Carolina tobacco companies, I'd be appalled. We don't have to worry about THAT."

> *"It's a blessing for me... to know which party is guilty of everything and which is totally innocent."*

"Absolutely not. And we know that when Bob Dole said cigarettes were not addictive, he was speaking from conviction. If he had discovered that any of his campaign funds came from the industry, he'd have hit the roof."

"And don't forget our Al D'Amato. He comes from Long Island, known far and wide for its squeaky clean Republican politics. If he were president, you can bet there'd be no politics of any kind allowed in the White House."

I'm reminded of the scene in the movie classic "Casablanca" when the police chief Renault (Claude Raines), under pressure from the Nazis, tells Rick (Humphrey Bogart) he is "shocked, SHOCKED" that gambling is taking place on the premises.

The words are no sooner out of his mouth than a croupier sidles up and says, "Your winnings, monsieur."

As a descendant of a federal judge in the Harding administration who ruled for the Sinclair Oil Co. in the Teapot Dome oil lease scandal, I knew Harding Republicans were straight arrows.

To say otherwise would be like saying my grandfather, a printer, got his no-show job as a court attendant because he was Irish and a Tammany Hall ward heeler who could deliver his all-Irish Manhattan district to the Democrats.

We in the family knew better. It was obvious he was appointed on merit alone.

It's a blessing for me, as a pure-as-the-driven-snow columnist, to know which party is guilty of everything and which is totally innocent. It simplifies everything.

School prayer: "Please God, don't let her call on me"

The Supreme Court just ruled that it's constitutional for a state to pass a law requiring a daily minute of silence in the schools.

A kid can even pray if he or she wants to, as in "Dear God, don't let her call on me."

The court didn't say whether it was OK to move your lips if you kept your hand in front of your face.

I've always been against making kids recite specific prayers in school, but much as I agree with just about everything the Civil Liberties Union stands for, I can't see why they fought the minute of silence.

I mean, one lousy minute? Come on!

Let's talk about multiple minutes of silence, all strung together, starting whenever the teacher gives the signal. Now you're talking real educational reform.

"The court didn't say whether it was OK to move your lips if you kept your hand in front of your face."

And I don't mean just a teacher option to restore order in the classroom. I'm talking pupil protection, too.

Many is the time, from kindergarten through my senior year in college, when I'd have given anything to be able to say: "I'd like to help you out with the answer to that one, Teach, but why don't you call on someone else while I observe another of my moments of silence, as required by law?"

According to the story I read, the court did not comment in turning down the appeal from opponents of the Virginia law. The critics had argued that the law was an unconstitutional encouragement of classroom prayer.

The justices obviously cherish silence themselves. They didn't even say "no comment."

The attorneys for the school system argued that the children could simply meditate or stare out the window for 60 seconds if they preferred, so long as they were quiet.

Personally, I'm a great believer in quiet reflection. I wish I did more of it and was more efficient at it.

Sometimes I do a little pondering. Sometimes some heavy-duty musing. But most of the time I sit here staring at this computer screen waiting for my fingers to move.

Then I just silently read what appears.

Only after the fingers stop moving do I break my silence.

"By golly, Dougherty, you've done it again," I say.

Then I sign off, turn out the light and go home.

Politics needs a gender-neutral pronoun

I n the upper left corner of the voting machine today, you'll find a proposal to make the New York State Constitution "gender neutral."

Because the constitution was written in 1777, when officeholders were all men, there are 170 references that will have to be changed if the voters approve the resolution.

"Assemblyman" would become "member of the Assembly." The governor, in the second reference, would not be "he," but would be "the governor."

The same with the chief judge of the Court of Appeals, who happens to be Judith Kaye, a "she."

I plan to vote "yes" on this matter, but I'd really like to see a permanent solution to the problem. What we really need is an all-purpose, gender-neutral singular pronoun.

> *"My first trial pronoun was 'sheesh', a logical contraction of 'he' and 'she'."*

I've given this matter the three seconds of thought it deserves but have not come up with the ideal word. I hope you readers can come up with the solution.

My first trial pronoun was "sheesh," a logical contraction of "he" and "she."

However, it sounds too much like a mispronunciation of the word "jeez," which is borderline blasphemy.

It also places the "she" first, which we male chauvinists regard as subtle gender favoritism. Feminists would feel the same about the contraction "heesh."

I tried to come up with a similar treatment of "him" and "her," but the word "herm" has a definite "guy" ring to it.

Those of us who pretend to have mastered the language have always felt burdened by the need to be perfectly accurate and write "he or she, as the case may be."

We have the same problem with the word "everyone." In the second reference it should be "he or she" or "his or her." However, some nonpurists simply jump into the gender-neutral plural and say "they" or "their."

I wish Miss Woolcott, my old English teacher, were available to help me work on this problem. She always made things perfectly clear.

I still remember asking, "Can I go to the bathroom," and being told, "You may go to the bathroom. Whether you can or not is entirely up to you."

If she knew I made a living writing in English, she'd say, "Sheesh, what's the world coming to?"

How government got its start

The worst thing about the Clinton health-care system seems to be the fact that the government is involved.

This means that it is dangerously close to "socialized medicine," and we all know how awful that is. It's what almost every modern industrial country in the world has, that's how awful. The only thing worse is socialized fire protection or a socialized army.

The only way to save a program, once it becomes socialized, is to sell it or give it away to a private company. Then the private company can provide the service at a higher price and make a profit. This saves money by eliminating waste and fraud.

Some people, like Bill Clinton and other subversives, just don't get this. They think that government should be allowed to do things for its citizens. Franklin Roosevelt was like that too. My uncle used to call him a communist.

How, you ask, did this crazy idea get started? I'll tell you how:

Some primitive tribesmen were sitting around talking and one of them said: "Wouldn't it be nice if someone could pick up all this garbage and take it somewhere else and bury it? This place is a mess."

Then someone said: "It sure would, but nobody is in the garbage collection business. It hasn't been invented yet."

"Well, why don't we all chip in and hire some guys and buy a wagon?"

"Are you kidding? That would be socialized garbage collection, you dummy."

"Oh."

(Long pause)

"Wait, I've got it! You all chip in and give ME the money and I'LL hire some guys and buy a wagon and I'll keep some of it for myself!"

"Great idea! You'll make a profit, we eliminate waste and fraud and keep the government off our backs at the same time! Everybody wins!"

It's this kind of thinking that undermines the fabric of our nation. People get the idea that the government can do things for them. They don't realize that this makes us soft.

It's all right for the government to give away money, provided they give it only to certain people, such as savings and loan companies. People like Clinton and his meddling wife can't get that through their heads.

Another thing: People say the president's plan relies heavily on "sin taxes." They say this is unfair. Sin should be tax-free, like municipal bonds, they say.

As lifelong sinners, you and I might welcome a little tax relief. Why not soak the virtuous instead? You ask.

I'll tell you why not: There aren't enough of them, silly. But nice try.

Just check "other" on census form

A federal task force has decided against adding a "multiracial" classification to the 2000 Census.

Instead it recommends allowing mixed-race Americans to check off more than one racial category.

That seems reasonable to me, so long as the categories accurately reflect our actual complexions in all their seasonal variations.

This is a complicated exercise and we'd certainly need more classifications.

For example, to be totally accurate, a multi-racial person like myself would want to check off the following boxes:

- White (chalky, pasty, pallid) in winter.
- Brown and white (mottled) in summer.
- Red and white (red neck and hands, other parts dirty white and peeling).
- Gray (when ill or hung-over).
- Pink (when embarrassed).
- Purple (when angry).
- Yellow (when jaundiced).
- Green (when envious).
- Olive (when envious and sunburned).
- Black-red (charred, well-done, first degree sunburn).
- Chocolate Royale.
- French Vanilla.

Admittedly this is a controversial proposal, especially since I have overlooked many important categories, possibly including yours.

It also would defeat the purpose of categorizing people, which is the whole idea of a census in the first place. It is the scientific principle behind gerrymandering, redrawing election districts to disenfranchise various groups hostile to the majority party.

The task force also recommended that a separate census question be asked about a person's ethnicity.

Apparently "American" is not considered enough, although it has always been considered sufficient by most folks.

Under the new rules, I would have to check off Irish-African-American, since my ancestors (and yours) all came from Africa millions of years ago.

You may be Hispanic-African-American or Chinese-African-American, but if you want to be accurate, don't forget the African part.

I agree that the current four census categories - black, white, American Indian/Alaskan Native, and Asian/Pacific Islander are too confining.

They were drafted in 1977 to help agencies enforce civil-rights laws.

I understand that.

But I would prefer that everyone be designated "other" or "don't know" and let it go at that.

The great thing is that neither requires a hyphen.

Working on GWB's walk

The operatives in charge of George W. Bush's image are said to be trying to get him to relax.

Make that appear to be relaxed. The president has never been charged with workaholism.

Never mind that I read about this in a column by *New York Times* acid-pen columnist Maureen Dowd, who is not exactly W's most enthusiastic booster, but then neither am I.

I think I know what the problem is. The man has been working out too vigorously on the White House gym's upper-torso weight machines.

Just look at the way he carries himself when he's reviewing an honor guard.

Sure, he's trying to look military — head erect, back straight, alert but solemn, marching smartly in cadence.

That's admirable, of course. If you're commander in chief of the greatest armed force in the world, you don't want to slouch in front of the troops.

> *"The man has been working out too vigorously on the White House gym's upper-torso weight machine."*

But the president goes too far. He looks muscle-bound. Look carefully at the way he holds his arms out from his body, like he's ready to pop somebody in the snoot. The chest is thrust out a little too far, and he's walking on the balls of his feet.

He even looks like this when he is appearing in the Rose Garden before an audience of languid civilians.

It is the look of a man who has been diligently working the weight machines and is too conscious of his biceps, triceps, quads, lats and delts.

How do I know this?

Because — you won't believe this — I still work out in the gym at the paragraph factory and sneak glimpses of myself in the mirror when no one is looking.

Usually I pedal more or less furiously on the stationary bicycle, but before I leave I work the weight machines and do some belly crunches. As I leave, I grab a look at the results in the full-length mirror. I may even strike one of those body-builder poses, if I am sure I am unobserved.

If I'm not careful, I may find myself walking like George W. Bush, unable to let my arms dangle relaxed at my side.

Perhaps George is cultivating the Ronald Reagan Look, a copy of the John Wayne Swagger.

This is not an impeachable offense, but perhaps it's time for the president to take some time off from the weights and cultivate a modest, dignified paunch.

Me, I suppose I'll continue my fruitless quest for the "not bad for an old geezer" look.

Tax praise for Congress and family CFO

The CFO (chief financial officer) does the taxes in our household. At a recent meeting, I stood up and made a little speech that came right from the heart.

"I'd just like to say, on behalf of the entire household consisting of the dog and myself, that, as always, you did a bang-up job this year. We are deeply grateful. Look for a little something extra in your paycheck."

Hmpff!

I read somewhere that Americans spend 6.1 billion hours a year filling out IRS forms.

It took me that long just to fill out the accountant's questionnaire.

I don't know about you, but I'm proud that once again we helped put the government's fund drive over the top. As a people, we raised a total of $1.8 trillion. That's more than twice the amount raised in 1987 when the Cold War was raging. No other country in the world can top that! You must be very proud.

Hmpff!

We should also be proud of our senators and congressmen. They are the ones, after all, who found such novel ways of spending such a vast fortune. Who would have thought of spending billions to try to impeach the president, for example? They rose to the challenge.

Hmpff!

Actually, come to think of it, they failed to spend it all. They had some left over. But, hey, they gave it a good try and I'm confident they'll find a way to get rid of that pesky surplus.

Hmpff!

But getting back to you, you can't imagine the guilt I felt when I came out to the kitchen night after night to get another beer and saw you hunched over the kitchen table, rummaging through those piles of papers and punching your calculator. I'd try to say something to convey my profound gratitude but all you'd say was ...

Hmpff!

Exactly! Such a self-effacing response, considering the lateness of the hour and your obvious exhaustion. I'll bet when we exchanged those marriage vows years and years ago you never dreamed you would wind up as CFO of this vast money-making and money-consuming enterprise, with responsibility for keeping the accounts for both the family and the nation.

Hmpff!

There it is again! What an eloquent word, hmpff. It conveys volumes. Volumes! Not many women would sit there and listen to such a heartfelt tribute without blushing. Most women would ... PUT THAT DOWN!

Would George Washington make it as a candidate today?

Y ou have to wonder what the voting public would make of George Washington if he were trotted out as a presidential candidate in this TV age. The first president's diaries went online the other day at the Library of Congress' Web site (www.loc.gov), so I went browsing for clues to the answer.

It turns out that the father of our country was a not an eager daddy.

"I feel not unlike a culprit who is going to the place of his execution, so unwilling am I in the evening of a life nearly consumed in public cares, to quit a peaceful abode for an ocean of difficulties," he told a friend.

(The TV folks would risk an oral hernia if they tried to make a sound bite out of that.) An April 16, 1789, diary entry elaborated:

"About ten o'clock I bade adieu to Mount Vernon, to private life, and to domestic felicity, and with a mind oppressed with more anxious and painful sensations than I have words to express, set out for New York ... with the best dispositions to render service to my country in obedience to its call, but with less hope of answering its expectations."

Of course GW didn't have to "run" for public office and wouldn't have understood the concept, but he allowed himself to be "drafted" by the electors.

When told of their decision by an emissary (who addressed him as "your excellency"), he is supposed to have said:

> *"It turned out the father of our country was not an eager daddy."*

"Sir, I have been long accustomed to entertain so great a respect for the opinion of my fellow citizens, that the knowledge of their unanimous suffrage having been given in my favor, scarcely leaves me the alternative for an option."

Translation: "I accept."

So the great man journeyed to "Elizabeth Town" (now Elizabeth, N.J.), where he crossed the Hudson in a barge built and rowed by 13 harbor pilots dressed in white uniforms.

"No language can point the beautiful display made on his excellency's approach to the city," a witness wrote.

"The shores were crowded with a vast concourse of citizens, waiting with exulting anxiety his arrival."

He was given two 13-gun salutes.

In my fantasy version, that's when GW turns to me, his old wartime sidekick, and mutters: "Well, that's it. No turning back now, eh, Dicky?"

Analyzing Barbie's presidential campaign

If Barbie is serious about running for president, will she balance the ticket by picking Ken for her running mate?

That's just one of the questions political analysts like me are pondering in the wake of the recent announcement that the former airline pilot, pro basketball player, race car driver, aerobics instructor, nurse and surgeon has tossed her astronaut's helmet in the ring.

Call me cynical, but I have a suspicion she's just in the race for the publicity. The fact that the announcement was made by press release at the headquarters of her employer, Mattel Inc., and not at a televised rally staged by a major political party, suggests that she could be just trying to help her boss market dolls.

But just for the sake of argument, let's assume she's on the level. After all, she has all the credentials.

She's served in the military. I forget which war and don't know if she's seen combat or been wounded, but I'm sure members of my profession are looking into her service record even as we speak.

You have to take a woman like that seriously. She's obviously more than a clothes horse, although she does seem obsessively neat. I understand her bust to height measurements are grotesque but we men could live with that. (Women may be another story.)

But the question remains: Is the country ready for a female president, especially one with no last name and no apparent party affiliation and stands only about 12 inches in her stocking feet?

"Is the country ready for a female president... who stands only about 12 inches in her stocking feet?"

But the running mate issue is the big problem. Her boyfriend Ken unfortunately does not seem to be presidential timber. He always seemed to me to be, let's face it, nerd-like. Handsome, yes, but somehow lacking in depth. Besides, who knows what went on between those two? (You know what I mean.)

Would we want Ken to be just a heartbeat from the presidency?

Preside over the Senate? Sure, but commander-in-chief? Forget it.

Somehow I doubt the country would go for two women at the top of the ticket, except possibly a Margaret Thatcher and a Susan B. Anthony look-alike.

Yes, I know we've had only men at the helm ever since 1789 and there've been some real losers, but old prejudices die hard.

If I were Barbie, I'd hang back a year and let the men screw things up one more time before making my move.

Back in those good old days
didn't we all love government?

They say the country is in an angry mood and furious at government. They say this is news. It never used to be like that. Or was it?

I was wracking my brain, trying to remember what it was like in the good old days when everybody just loved the government to death and couldn't wait to pay their taxes.

I asked my spouse: "Remember 60 years ago, around 1935, when we couldn't heap enough praise on the government?"

"Not really. You mean when nearly 30 percent of the people were out of work and everyone was sore at government for not doing anything about it?"

"Hmmm. Must have been some other year," I said.

"Today they want government to get out of the way and let the country fix itself. After 60 years of government meddling, things just kept getting worse, they say."

"Except that during those 60 years unemployment went down 24 percentage points," she said. "It's only around 7 today."

I can remember my father coming home depressed night after night having had to fire another friend. Then that meddler Roosevelt started the government job programs and things slowly began to pick up.

"Maybe those were the good old days." I said.

"But the country was riding on the government's back," she pointed out.

The war years couldn't have been the good old days, but it was sort of reassuring to know the government had not shut down.

The postwar years could not have been so good because government was meddling with my education, sending me to college, even paying me an allowance. I was on the "government dole!"

The Korea and Vietnam vets were lucky they didn't have to go through that humiliation.

We got a government guaranteed loan so we could buy our own home. Sixty years ago less than half of American families owned homes. Two thirds do now.

Back in the good old days the feds didn't knock down your door and invade your house. Not much! Sixty years ago Irish cops routinely rapped folks on the head for being Italian.

As I ponder these historical developments, it occurs to me that loving one's government is not in man's nature. Ranting at it is nothing new. We used to rant while begging its help.

Today everyone's angry and frustrated. It doesn't make sense.

Maybe after it has been dismantled and no longer does anything for us, we'll realize that it wasn't so bad after all.

Chapter Five

Health & Wealth

Colors fly for one physical, droop for another
Doughertys choose tax shelter: Bermuda
Getting fit without pesky 'fun'
Baldness in a jar
HMO inspects his aging chassis
Bears, bulls and irrationality
Will tomorrow's computers practice safe sex?
Inventors take adversity in racetrack stride
One arthritis victim consoles another
Remembering the 25-cent minimum wage
Social Security takes stock of Wall Street
Discussing TV ads with your doctor
Be patriotic and lay yourself off
A correction means an improvement?
Silver lining behind falling stock market
Sitting in on a modern sex education class
Wall Street gambling dens open all night
Flexibility can lead to unemployment
Did we evolve for the better?
Betting your Social Security on the Super Bowl
Erasing wrinkles with Botox
Memory software takes a brief vacation
Heart valve recipient thanks his bovine benefactor

Colors fly for one physical, droop for another

The president and I have just had our carcasses into the shop for inspection.

His emerged with "flying colors," the papers said.

My colors were a little limp by comparison. They were far from flying or snapping smartly in the breeze, but considering the miles I've got on me, I can't complain.

When you're talking physical exams, it's hard not to fall into the automotive metaphor trap because the ailments are so much the same.

Like the car, my chassis shows signs of wear and could use some replacement bearings (cartilage) wherever two moving parts meet, as in the knee joints, elbows, shoulders, engine mounts, valve lifters, springs and connecting rods.

The doc told me he heard some grating noises in one of the pump valves but nothing that would seriously affect my trade-in value. He said the same thing two years ago when I took the carcass in for the 80-year, 2,000,000-mile check.

The entire suspension system should be replaced or at least overhauled. You hear some ominous grinding noises when you get it up out of bed in the morning, but once it gets warmed up they subside.

Everyone talks about the fragility of the human body, but this one has outlasted 22 cars, only three of which are believed to be still in service somewhere.

Even the old 1950 Studebaker and the gutsy 1955 Nash Rambler American that caught fire and burned on a ski trip to Swain live on only in memory.

Meanwhile, the carcass keeps rolling along, taking me wherever I want to go. And back again, too!

Sure, sometimes it takes forever, but I'm not in a hurry to get anywhere these days. I don't care if some hotshots beat me away from the stoplight. Let 'em have their fun.

President Bush, on the other hand, works hard on carcass maintenance — lifting weights, jogging, playing golf and doing sit-ups. From the news photos, he appears to be in superb shape.

But lately I'm beginning to wonder if he hasn't overdone it.

I fear he may have let his testosterone levels get out of control to the point where he feels the need to lead us to war to prove his masculinity.

There is such a thing as becoming too fit and frisky for your country's own good, if you ask me.

Doughertys choose tax shelter: Bermuda

I nspired by that public-spirited company, Global Crossing Ltd., my wife and I have been planning to move our vast operations to Bermuda.
The idea came to her while she was gathering notes, receipts and other materials to hand over to Al, the long suffering genius who does our income tax returns.

This tax prep process gets them both strung out enough to be open to ideas like emigration as a tax avoidance strategy.

You see, *Bermuda doesn't HAVE an income tax!*

For some curious reason, moving a corporation's headquarters to a tiny offshore reef in the Atlantic Ocean to evade taxes is not considered tax evasion.

I assume this scam would apply to us. We're only two adults and a dog, but why should that matter? We must ask Al.

One company said it saved $30 million. I imagine our beloved Global Crossing saved a little something too, despite filing for bankruptcy and being accused of inflating its sales figures.

Just because its stock dropped from $60 a share to around 6 cents doesn't mean it doesn't have some taxes worth evading.

My wife is really excited about the move. We went there on our honeymoon in 1956, but couldn't afford to go back for about 30 years. Since then we've been back about 10 times on our son's airline passes.

According to a corporate consultant who favors the Bermuda strategy, "patriotism is a troubling issue, but profits trump patriotism."

I agree with that analysis. Move out. Let those who stay behind pay for the war on terrorism, national defense and all that other stuff.

"After all," I can hear them saying,""we're all Bermudians now; let those Americans take care of themselves."

But if we're smart, I think we should keep a little aside in escrow for campaign contributions to congressmen and presidential candidates who might try to end our little scam.

"The move to Bermuda is simple," said my wife, the chief financial officer (CFO).

"You just rent a P.O. box and pay an incorporation fee. We could keep our headquarters here in town and you could keep on with your columnist dodge at the paragraph factory."

What a woman!

You can see why I pay her my entire salary (less a small allowance) to keep the books.

She makes Arthur Andersen, the auditor/consultant firm, look like a real piker.

Getting fit without pesky "fun"

Y ou wouldn't believe the way we're squandering our energy resources these days.

Why, just in one big room at the Metro Y called the Cardio (should be "cardiac") Theater, you can witness giga-calories of energy being sucked up by the ventilation system and dispelled into the atmosphere without producing a single product or milling a single kernel of grain.

You'll see row on row of folks of all shapes and sizes running on treadmills, pumping vertical handlebars and spinning sprockets, all of them going nowhere, expelling used air and dripping perspiration just to burn off their own suet.

Right there in the front row you might see a geezer pedaling away on a stationary bicycle. He's wearing a headset that's connected to the bank of overhead TV sets in the front of the room.

That's me.

Sometimes I can't imagine that this is the same guy who once used exactly the same motions to propel himself 4,100 miles across the country on a noncaptive untethered bike.

Now there he is, pedaling and puffing away to no avail whatsoever except to get his pulse rate up to 130 beats per minute because a chart told him that's going to burn fat and get him "in shape."

(By "in shape," he means "into another shape," but never mind. Technical point.)

Every now and then (approximately every 10 minutes or less) he wonders why he and his fellow (and female) toilers do this to themselves.

"If we were in a union and someone ordered us to do this, we'd be picketing the place and screaming 'SCAB' at fitness nuts like us who went inside." He often mutters to himself.

The words of Neil Armstrong come to mind. He's the moon-walking astronaut who said he figured man had "an optimum number of heartbeats" coming to him in a lifetime and he wasn't going to squander his on exercise.

The words come to mind, all right, but they are flushed right out with the sweat.

The truth is we're becoming mentally ill by trying to get or stay "physically fit." In our younger days, we achieved fitness in sensible ways, like chasing a rubber ball around a small room and flailing at it ferociously with gloved hands or a racket.

That was called "having fun." Now, we've discovered how to get the same effect by avoiding fun and inflicting pain on ourselves using expensive machines instead.

Isn't technology something!

Baldness-in-a-Jar

The news about the new facial hair-remover has some of us worried: What if it got on the TOPS of our heads instead of the front?

That's all we need: Instant baldness in a jar — Easy-Off, the instant scalp and oven cleaner.

Right now only women need worry, but tests indicate it works for men too.

It's called Vaniqua and was developed by Bristol-Myers Squibb and, of all people, Gillette, a worldwide leader in the manufacture of hand-held facial hair harvesters.

The company said it will consider making the prescription drug available to men after first proving its effectiveness to women.

"On a clear day, from a step-ladder, you can see your face in my glistening bald spot."

While reading about the new product, I had a weird nostalgia reverie. Phil ("Holy Cow!") Rizzuto, the New York Yankee shortstop turned broadcaster, was commanding his listeners to "look sharp, be sharp and be on the ball" by throwing away their razors and rubbing Vaniqua on their chops. "Vaniqua, the only shaving cream that eliminates shaving," he was saying.

A line from the Bible also came to mind: "Esau is a hairy man, but I am a smooth man." Why Gillette overlooked that catchy singing-commercial lyric is a mystery to me.

The Associated Press story I read said facial hair in women has several causes, including an excess of male hormones. Genetics also play a role. "For instance women of Mediterranean or Hispanic descent tend to have more facial hair," it added.

I've heard that before, but no one ever explains why men like me, apparently male with our daddy's virile male hormones, have been getting bald on top since high school.

On a clear day, from a stepladder, you can see your face in my glistening bald spot. Yet, underneath, my jowls are infested with fast-growing eight-hour moss.

The word for this hairiness-in-the-wrong-places condition is hirsutism.

Do women really want more male hormones if that's the price they might have to pay?

But they don't have to confront the should-I-or-shouldn't-I questions right now. Vaniqua is not available yet. But Food and Drug Administration approval could come next year.

In the meantime, if they're not afraid of a few side effects, they might try a non-prescription remedy my dog Midas got from a friend. It's called mange.

HMO inspects his aging chassis

Everyone seems to be teed off at the health insurance folks, but not me. I think they're doing a great job keeping me repaired and serviced. As soon as a part starts making clunking noises, they're there for me.

"Sounds like a burned out bearing, kiddo. Just leave the old bod here and let us take it apart. We'll run a few tests and see what's what," they tell me.

Awhile later the phone rings.

"This is Mike. Just as I thought. It was the knee bearing. You're ready to go. We replaced the whole unit. Pick it up anytime. We close at 6."

"What's the bad news, financially speaking?" I want to know.

"Your HMO upgraded warranty and service contract covered the whole thing. Come up with the $10 co-pay and you're out of here."

What more could anyone ask? If your HMO doesn't treat you right, it's your own fault.

Frankly, the experience has been so upbeat I can't wait for my next episode.

So far I've had a high performance left knee assembly installed, complete with new shocks and am looking forward to upgrading the right one or maybe the left hip, if I can work it in between bridgework repairs.

I'm just waiting until the right foot is in good enough shape to get the carcass into the shop. An ankle bone cracked when I stepped in a hole on vacation in Maine.

Since my recent optical system surgery (two cataracts and a retina) I don't see so good. I can't judge where the ground is.

I remember as I began toppling over, preliminary to butting my head on a hard part of Peaks Island, Maine, I blurted out a heartfelt cry of apology and gratitude:

"I think they're doing a great job, keeping me repaired and serviced."

"I'm sorry, (name of well-known HMO), but thank you in advance for being there for me! I'll have the paperwork ready in a jiffy."

Now I'm into my second cast, a high-tech job that rides like a dream. In another six weeks or so I expect to be ready to take the old bod out for a spin in preparation for the next inevitable mishap.

Through it all my loyal HMO has been sensational, crooning its motto: "Bring me your tired, your sickly broken bodies, yearning to be whole. I lift my lamp beside the golden door."

Never once has it expressed irritation. "Do your worst," it seems to be saying.

"We have unlimited compassion, thanks to the premiums of the durable, non-sniveling customers who never bug us."

Bears, bulls and irrationality

First we had irrational exuberance.

That was Federal Reserve Chairman Alan Greenspan's word for what ailed the stock market a few months ago.

Now it's irrational pessimism.

The only trouble with that characterization is that pessimism, in my definition of the stock market, is never irrational. There are times when panic is the only rational response. It means you understand the situation.

I've always believed that one of the great truths that one can count on is the basic rule of all natural phenomena, namely that "what goes up must come down." Subscribers to that view are the rational ones.

> *"Irrational pessimism, therefore, is an oxymoron — like sweet sorrow... or military intelligence."*

Conversely, it has been my experience that what goes down does not always bob right back up. (Keep that in mind when you are going down for the third time. You might very well be drowning.)

Irrational pessimism, therefore, is an oxymoron. That's the word for a figure of speech that contradicts itself. (Exs: sweet sorrow, thunderous silence, military intelligence.)

Irrational exuberance, on the other hand, is simply redundant, since all exuberance is, by my definition, totally irrational.

Are there any questions?

If not, let's talk about bears, as in bear markets.

A bear market, we are told, occurs when a stock index or average falls more than 20 percent from its last peak. (The last peak was last March.)

But why a bear and not, say, a dinosaur or an elephant or maybe a boa constrictor?

I conducted several fruitless Internet searches to find the derivation of the term, finally turning to my favorite live search engine, Frank Bilovsky, our financial page reporter.

"Simple," Frank said. "A bear attacks by striking downward with its claws. A bull attacks by lowering its head and butting upward with its horns. I learned that in Economics 101."

Nothing about exuberance or pessimism?

Not a word.

However, it is my feeling that messing around with such single-minded and unfriendly dumb animals of either upward or downward persuasion is downright irrational.

End of lecture. Now go and invest exuberantly or panic pessimistically. You're on your own. I've done all I can for you.

Will tomorrow's computers practice safe sex?

I n 15 to 20 years we will have a new breed of computers with intelligence, that are `alive' in that they will have births, deaths, and propagation."
I read that in a dispatch from The Independent of London. The speaker was the head of research for a British technology firm.

Unfortunately, he let that startling news just lie there, but it sure tweaks the imagination, doesn't it?

Images of computer sex come to mind, and you can't help but wonder what makes him think computers will be any different from us.

Propagation will be just a side effect once they discover it's more fun to make whoopee that sit around the office crunching numbers.

They'll probably be just as promiscuous as we are. There will be stories in the technology journals about the deteriorating morality of the brazen young computers and the need for sex education and instruction in "values."

But when you think about it, computers are already constantly dying off (or being aborted), often at a tender age, then being reborn. That's propagation without the intimacy.

It's entirely controlled by man now, but surely that will change. It's not much of a stretch to envision computers analyzing their own performance and capabilities, redesigning themselves and programming robots to build new improved offspring.

Right now the emphasis is mostly on speed. Intel has developed a machine that can do a trillion calculations a second, but it's stupid. If you don't give it orders, it just sits there and throbs.

"Propogation will be just a side effect once they discover it's fun to make whoopee."

Tomorrow models will be clever but slow thinkers that take their time and mull things over.

Such a machine, called Magnus, is under development in England and is said to be already "programming itself." The story said it has been taught to express hunger. Show it pictures of fruit and it feels better.

It's just a small leap from there to a computer that can lust after another computer.

Then the big question will be what their offspring will be like.

Will they play nicely with other young computers or will they grab toys and grow up listening to loud music and talking back to their elders?

Let's look on the bright side: Maybe, if properly brought up, one day they can teach us how to get along with each other.

Investors take adversity in racetrack stride

My friend the retired horseplayer has no sympathy for the bettors who are getting beat up on the stock market.

"They're new to adversity. It comes as a big surprise that things can go wrong. We survivors of the racetrack wars know what it's like to see money disappear. We get used to it."

That's a composite quote from several phone conversations we've had over the last month or so. (He talks too fast for my declining shorthand skills.)

"At least at the track, you know that your horse is not a crook," I observed.

"Right. He runs for the heck of it, and only if he feels like it that day," my friend said. "He doesn't give a hoot whether you have any money on him or not."

I hadn't thought of that aspect. The horse has no conflict of interest because he doesn't promise 20 percent earnings growth every quarter and never learned to cook the books by hiding expenses like stock options.

If there are shenanigans at the track, the horse is not in on them.

In the back of my mind, however, there is a — pardon the expression — nagging suspicion the horses pass the word among themselves before a race that it's Ol' Oatburner's turn to win.

"At least at the track, you know your horse is not a crook."

But my friend rejects this conspiracy theory.

He thinks they respond to the stimulus of the moment and may spontaneously decide to go after the front runner. It may be a matter or personal pride or bred-in competitiveness.

But there is one nice thing about horseplayers as opposed to other kinds of "investors." You don't hear them pondering deep meanings in the downturn in their fortunes.

There is no Dow-Jones Average for horses' performance overall. It's every nag for itself. There are plenty of statistics, but they're all about past performances of individuals.

Personally, I never got hooked on the horses. The one time I went to Finger Lakes I made some bad investments and it turned me off as a lifelong avocation. But it sure was exciting to see them come pounding down the stretch.

They were magnificent athletes, blue chips every one.

And they looked as though they were really having fun out there.

What did they care about the glum geezer standing by the rail shredding his tickets?

One arthritis victim consoles another

S ome of us geezers were surprised and saddened to learn that Dolly, the world's first cloned sheep, has come down with arthritis.

The striking thing is that, at age 5 1/2, she's only middle-aged. (Sheep live about 12 years, sometimes 16.)

The arthritis, we're told, is in her left hind leg, hip and knee.

Funny, that's exactly where most of us have arthritic joints, so perhaps we should share our knowledge with her and her veterinarian.

I'll go first, since this is my column.

Most importantly, I'd like to assure Dolly that with just a few minor lifestyle adjustments and by popping the right pills, she can still live a meaningful life.

It is essential that she keep her sense of humor and avoid the common "Why me?" response to the aging process.

The news reports didn't say, but my guess is that she has osteoarthritis like mine, caused by routine bone wear, not the more serious and painful rheumatoid variety.

> *"If I were Dolly's vet, I'd tell her to ease up on the unprotected sex and get a nanny (goat) to bring up the children."*

I also suspect that Dolly, in the enthusiasm and vigor of a misspent youth, abused her body by gamboling around the barnyard willy nilly with the over-sexed rams, not giving a thought to the consequences.

I remember when the cartilage in the knee joint of my own left hind leg first began to wear thin and the upper and lower leg bones began to emit grinding sounds. I was playing four-wall handball and came up lame, losing both point and match.

An orthopedic surgeon (skeleton mechanic) told me he saw signs of earlier damage caused by ill-advised attempts to make the high school football team. The X-ray also revealed evidence of wear from my career as an Army pedestrian, downhill skier and long-distance biker. Today I have artificial knees that allow me to avoid arduous yard work but permit me to play geriatric ("nice shot") tennis.

Dolly, I learned, has given birth to six lambs. That couldn't have been easy.

If I were her vet, I'd tell her to ease up on the unprotected sex and to get a nanny (goat) to bring up the children.

I'd also get a good lawyer and sue the hell out of those Scots who go around cloning animals even though they know the practice causes premature aging.

If that doesn't constitute grounds for a fat negligence settlement, my name isn't Gimpy.

Remembering the 25-cent minimum wage

S ome of us can vaguely remember when those liberals in Washington wanted to pass that hare-brained law setting a nation-wide minimum wage of a quarter an hour.

It was 1938 and Franklin Roosevelt, known to my grandfather as "That Madman in the White House," was sending the country "to hell in a basket" by "sucking up to the masses."

Grandpop was a man for his times, but he'd have been delighted with these times too.

If the '38 economy had not been dead already, he would have said that liberal ideas like the minimum wage were killing it.

That summer I happened to be on Easy Street myself. I was making a cool 50 cents an hour as a steamer trunk smasher at the Weekhawken, N.J. ferry terminal.

Working in pairs, we'd flip the big trunks casually end over end from Ontario & Western baggage cars onto electric trucks while the owners looked on in horror.

Then we'd mount the little folding step platform in front, grab the tiller and control lever, and steer through the crowd to the ferries, angrily yelling "comin' through!"

> *"That summer... I was making a cool 50 cents an hour as a steamer-trunk smasher."*

We'd think: Imagine anyone trying to live on 25 cents an hour, a mere $10.50 a week. But then those poor stiffs didn't have our high level skills.

What did they expect? They were untrained, lucky to be working at all.

Most of them didn't have the sense to have fathers who got them jobs through the magic of nepotism. A quarter an hour was too good for them.

Now a new madman in the White House is talking of raising it from a handsome $4.25 to something like $5 an hour! But at least it hasn't kept up with inflation and is sensibly below the poverty line for a family of three.

Some experts say raising the minimum would price poor workers out of the job market. The people who say this happen to be those who would have to do the raising.

But let's not be cynical. I read just the other day that people who are unemployed are doing the country a service by keeping inflation at bay. If too many people become employed, the economy "overheats."

However, there are some alarming studies showing that raising the minimum wage may create instead of destroy jobs.

I'm told that would be bad news indeed!

The Federal Reserve Board would have to raise interest rates in order to cool the economy by stimulating unemployment.

Social Security takes stock of Wall Street

As a child of the 1929 stock market crash and the subsequent Great Depression, I see the justice in the proposal to let workers invest in the market as an alternative or supplement to Social Security.

Why should just we filthy rich people have all the fun of jumping out of the windows of the brokerage houses? Let the common folk in on it too. It's only fair.

Don't mind me. I get this way sometimes.

I start seeing visions of former white collar workers in worn suits selling apples or pencils on the streets of New York City outside offices they used to inhabit.

I see my father digging money out of his pocket for a former colleague, now a beggar, both of them avoiding eye contact.

Once you get the pictures of those faces in your head, they do something to your optimism.

Nobody really knows how close the country came to revolution in those days. I figure everyone was just too whipped to revolt.

I admit I don't know a lot about finance or economics. I'm just an on-the-job retiree.

For example, I still don't see why betting on stocks is called "investment" and betting on horses is "gambling," except that horses are known to be honest animals, if not terribly bright.

And I still don't understand how an optimist buying a stock from a pessimist affects the financial situation of a company, but they tell me it does. I figured it was just two traders thinking one had outsmarted the other.

> *"Nobody really knows how close the country came to revolution in those days."*

But don't tell my wife I said any of this.

She's a great believer in mutual funds, and I have to say that without her genius and blind (or prescient) faith in the system, we'd be a lot poorer. Bulls can be female, believe it or not.

Still, when you have a market that spooks and loses altitude whenever a old man named Greenspan opens his mouth, it does not fill me with confidence.

I won't go into the part about the way market analysts react with wild approval when a company lays off thousands of workers while it's making a profit, or when these same analysts badmouth a CEO who talks too much about developing new products and not enough about skinflinting.

To have my retirement income tied to such a flighty apparatus, subject to mass whims of faceless gamblers and gurus, does not make me rub my hands together in anticipation.

But I'll tell you what: Figure out a way to keep the market going up, up, up in its bull mode forever and I'll leap happily onto the bandwagon.

Discussing TV ads with your doctor

I've got a date with my doctor for a physical and I must remember to bring my lists.

One list is about all my ailments. That one's quite short.

The other is a list of those "Ask Your Doctor" questions the TV keeps insisting I ask.

That's the long one.

Surely you have noticed that the drug manufacturers have yet to come out with a medication that does not require a consultation with your doctor.

I figure that if everyone asked all those "Ask Your Doctor" questions, the practice of medicine would soon grind to a halt.

On the other hand, it's easier to ask your doctor than to read those encyclopedic tracts in microscopic print, that come with the pills and often contain words like phenylpropanolaHminedextrtoamphetamineisoproterenol and possibly fatal in the same paragraph.

> *"If everyone asked all those 'ask your doctor' questions, the practice of medicine would soon grind to a halt."*

If you've been paying attention to your TV, you know that this is the allergy season as well as the crash dieting season and there are hundreds of remedies to help you stop sneezing and begin losing unsightly body fat.

None are known to cause birth defects, especially in men who are not pregnant. However, women who take them may suffer mental problems or mood swings. (Men who are breast feeding should consult their doctors.)

Being a person of advanced age, I was curious about the effects of some of my wife's allergy pills in our medicine cabinet. I discovered (on the Internet) that there were no known problems because no studies had been done.

That was reassuring, but I put it down on my list of things to ask the doctor anyway. We geezers can't be too careful.

My primary list of specific ailments has been unchanged over the years. They all take the form of the symptom: "this little twinge I get sometimes right about here — no, actually a little more to the left and lower down."

I've had that one ever since childhood when it was described as a "growing pain." Now that I'm more or less grown, although not mature, it has become "nothing to worry about but we'll keep an eye on it."

Remember: You don't want to squander your exam in idle conversation about pharmacy.

I make it a practice to always leave time to have my blood pressure taken and my prostate tickled.

Be patriotic and lay yourself off

T he characters in this story are fictitious and do not represent real persons, living or dead.

"We need to talk, dear," the man said to his wife.

"You sound serious. Spit it out and let's get on with our lives."

"Right. I'm thinking of laying myself off. But it's a tough decision."

"That's an interesting thought. Why would you want to do such a stupid thing?"

"To help out the stockholders. They want to see the quarterly earnings increase so the stock price will go up. It's up to us employees to cut costs any way we can. Layoffs are the only way to go. Everyone's doing it these days."

"I see what you mean. You are an investor as well as an employee. You've been buying all that stock on the company's weekly no-fee payroll deduction plan. I hadn't thought of that. Wow. That is a tough decision."

"I know. It's conflict of interest. But look at it this way: If I laid myself off, the company would have my salary to play with and also my health insurance would lapse and they wouldn't have to pay for our vacations. With that kind of money, I'll bet they could go out and acquire another company or develop some hot new product."

"You certainly are uniquely qualified to solve this problem. As an investor in the company you have the incentive to cut costs and increase earnings and as an employee you have the solution within your grasp, namely to lay yourself off. And you'd have plenty of company in this layoff-happy town."

"My situation is complicated by the fact that, by law, I'm already drawing my pension and social security because of my advanced age. But that simply would make me feel less guilt when I give myself notice. I'm a real softy when it comes to laying anyone off, especially a long-term loyal, dedicated employee like myself, but my duty is clear."

> *"I'm thinking of laying myself off... to help out the stockholders."*

"Those are indeed powerful arguments, every one of them. However I see one major flaw in the concept."

"Oh?"

"If you laid yourself off, I'd have you underfoot around here all day long, studying the stock tables and complaining about how your old bosses were so much less demanding than I am."

"Is that your final answer?"

"My mother always said she vowed to cleave to dad for better for worse, in sickness and health but not for lunch."

A correction means an improvement?

I like that term "correction" that Wall Street uses when it doesn't want to say disaster or collapse.

When things are going along nicely and your Xerox stock is going up and you think you're on heading for Easy Street and then suddenly the market goes blooey and poverty seems imminent, don't worry.

It's only a correction.

No doubt the rationale is that stocks were deemed over-priced so the market corrected them.

I thought of this the other day after a humiliating day on the tennis court.

"It's just a correction," I told my guru, Ted Backe, the free-lance pro who presides over clinics at the Tennis Club of Rochester.

(Ted once played in the U. S. Open when there was no TV or endorsements and tennis players were dirt poor. He boasts that he's been beaten by some of the most famous players of his day. Now back to our story.)

Ted understood the term immediately. I was not really in a slump, I was simply correcting my performance to bring it down to the level of my athletic talent.

> *"The harsh assumption seems to be that success is incorrect."*

Similarly, when I write a substandard column, I am simply experiencing a correction, not an outright, permanent failure.

This long view helps me get up the morning after and go to the office.

For some curious reason, a correction goes in only one direction: down. When (if) Xerox stock or my tennis game recovers and starts heading back up from the basement, that will not be classed as a correction.

(A miracle, perhaps?)

The harsh assumption seems to be that success is incorrect.

These shady attempts to call a spade an excavation implement are called euphemisms.

The dictionary defines a euphemism as a term substituted for a word that is "less expressive or direct but considered less distasteful, less offensive, etc., than another."

An example, my edition of *Webster's New World College Edition* says, is the substitution of "remains" for "corpse".

I think that's a little too direct. I prefer the undertaker term used by comedienne Elaine May, the "Grief Lady." Her euphemism for a stiff was the loved one.

But perhaps that's too sentimentally euphemistic.

How about permanently corrected?

Silver lining behind falling stock market

Y ou've all heard the story: A guy wants to add a garage to his house, so he sells his shares of stock in Haloid, the predecessor of Xerox, figuring it isn't going anywhere.

A decade later he brags, "Now I've got the only million-dollar garage in Henrietta."

I haven't done the math, but now I suppose the joke should go, "Now I've got the only $19.95 garage on East Avenue."

Frankly, I'm glad the bull market is over, at least for now. I was sick of coming home from work and listening to my wife chastise herself for not having bought some really hot high-tech stock before it took off.

Luckily for us we're not rolling in money so we couldn't afford to follow through on her hunches. That's one of the nice things about not being filthy rich: You don't have to brood about lost opportunities to get richer.

The Wall Street Journal had a funny piece the other day about this, titled "41 Ways to Accentuate the Positive." It listed some "good things about a bad stock market."

One of my favorites was No. 40: "You can spend Friday evenings with somebody other than Louis Rukeyser."

He's the silver-maned, pun-afflicted blowhard on PBS's Wall Street Week. His guests are analysts who pretend to be sharing their insights, then conclude by touting specific stocks in their areas of expertise.

Another, No. 32, was: "When the cat gets hungry, you can go to the grocery store, rather than waiting for the delivery from Pets.com." No. 15 was "There are fewer fawning articles about smug Internet billionaires."

"Great news, honey! we didn't make any- thing on the stock market last year. Let's go out to dinner and celebrate!"

Some of us have always been suspicious about a market that goes down when too many people have jobs or when industries are doing too much research and long-range planning. But what do we know?

One of the really nice things about a listless stock market will become apparent when we tackle our income tax returns and discover we don't have any capital gains to report.

("Great news, honey! We didn't make anything on the stock market last year! Let's go out to dinner and celebrate!")

It's sort of like having a lot of medical deductions.

("Gee, honey, by getting sick a lot last year you earned us a huge break on our taxes! All that disease and suffering really paid off for us")!

Sitting in on a modern sex education class

Recent spectacular developments reported by the fertility laboratories suggest that future classes in sex education will soon go somewhat like this one:
(Note: I can only guess how these classroom learning encounters unfold, because I grew up when sex education was taught by the kids themselves in secret.)

Attention, class: This period we're going to talk about sex and I want no snickering. Is that clear?

Yes, teacher.

Now, can anyone tell me where babies come from? Mary?

From a dish?

Very good, Mary. Can you explain that to the class?

My mommy had her eggs frozen when she was young, before she was married, even. Then nine years ago she thawed my egg, put it in a dish and had daddy throw some fertilizer on it. Then I was hatched in her tummy and now here I am.

Do you have a question for Mary, Johnny?

Yes, why did your mommy have her eggs frozen? And didn't your egg feel awful cold when she did that?

She froze them to keep them fresh, silly. But mostly she froze them because she was too busy at the office to take time out to have a baby. She was afraid she'd lose her place. But when she got promoted to manager, she decided to go ahead and have me. I don't remember feeling cold, but I was just little then. Just a little speck.

Yes, Melissa?

My mommy calls me her Little Embryo. I was growed in a dish in the laboratory too. She told me she froze her eggs to keep them from spoiling. She said eggs are better and easier to fertilize when you're young. When you get old, they're not so good. Freezing keeps them new. Then you can melt them later.

Teacher! Teacher!

Don't be impatient, Franky. Stop waving your hand and ask your question.

My mommy and daddy said they grew me the old-fashioned way. What does that mean?

That means they didn't use a dish. They planted your egg right in your mom's tummy and your daddy fertilized it right there. Then you grew. And then you were born. That's the way it was done in the olden days.

But without the dish, how did daddy. . . ? I mean . . . um, you know.

That's all for today, children. If you have any further questions, ask your friends on the playground.

Wall Street gambling dens open all night

Q: ◊ The Las Vegas casinos are open all night, so why not the Wall Street ◊ casinos?
◊ A: Why not indeed? They're all gambling dens, after all. Call them investing dens, if you want. Same thing, really.

Q: Tell me more.

A: Sure. You've probably heard that the New York Stock Exchange, Nasdaq and several electronic competitors are planning to stay open until 10 p.m. so "traders" can place their bets by computer. This suggests that 24-hour trading is probably inevitable.

The all-night poker, blackjack and craps games were in existence for hundreds of years, before there was a Las Vegas. So there is no moral reason to justify discriminating against daytime working people who aren't allowed to play the market while working as truck drivers, brain surgeons or dishwashers.

Q: You once compared playing stocks to playing horses. Wouldn't night trading have a negative effect on that metaphor since horses rarely run at night?

A: It is true that thoroughbred horses do not ordinarily work nights and would probably resist any change in their schedules, but baseball players made the switch to night hours years ago. So have trotting horses and racing dogs. However, the metaphor still holds up when you consider that both stocks and horses have their bad days when they just don't feel like performing.

Q: But what about the effects of increased stock trading on the economy and the production of goods and services?

A: True stock gamblers do not concern themselves with such mundane matters. They only care if the price of a stock goes up so they can sell it. The "day traders" (soon to be joined by night traders) like to buy a stock and sell it quickly, take their winnings and move on to the next betting window or call their stock bookie.

Q: So that's what they call "investing?" I don't see the connection between this activity and the business of paying workers to make and sell things.

> *"They're all gambling dens, after all. Call them investment dens if you want. Same thing, really."*

A: There isn't any. These people are helping the economy about as much as the dimwits who stand in front of the slot machines pulling levers all day and often night.

Q: Wouldn't it simplify things to have logos of, say, IBM, Kodak or GM on the slot machines instead of those pictures of cherries and lemons?

A: Now you're talking sense. And I thought I was the expert!

Flexibility can lead to unemployment

Federal Reserve Chairman Alan Greenspan thinks the economy is basically sound.

Isn't that good news?

One of the most important things he likes about it is the "flexibility of the labor market."

I've been pondering that word "flexibility" since I first heard it on TV and went looking for the text of his remarks on the news wires.

> *"Flexibility means the willingness of workers to keep the economy sound by becoming unemployed."*

Now I think I've translated it: It means the willingness of workers to keep the economy "sound" by becoming unemployed.

That was one of the "bright" spots in his testimony to a Senate committee yesterday in Washington.

The chairman did admit that the terrorist attacks on the World Trade Center had produced a significant drop in economic activity over the short term, but he added that he was "confident that we will recover and prosper as we have in the past."

The airlines and aircraft manufacturers have taken a big hit since the World Trade Center attack, but thankfully, Congress is standing by to bail them out with public funds supplied by us, the taxpayers.

Nothing has been said about bailing out the workers. Boeing alone has said it will cut 30,000 jobs. But not to worry, the work force is "resilient." The airline industry may lay off as many as 100,000 before the end of the year.

How's that for resilience?

When I heard that I felt like calling up my son and letting him know that Mom and Dad are proud to know that we, and all Americans, can count on him to go quietly and flexibly into the night if he gets the call from his airline to do his bit for its profitability.

I know what he'd say.

He'd say: "It's the least I can do, Dad. I'm just thankful that I can contribute, even a little, to the bottom line of the company, the contentment of the stockholders and the already-handsome year-end bonus of the chief executive officer who had such faith in my loyalty."

All across this great land, loyal employees are happily cleaning out their desks under the watchful eyes of company security officers and being escorted off the premises after surrendering their identification badges.

It makes you want to call up your broker and buy a whole lot of stock, doesn't it?

Did we evolve for the better?

You have to wonder what happened when the first human ancestor got the idea of walking on two legs instead of four.

We, he, she, or it subjected to ridicule? Even hostility?

Surely someone must have said: "Look at Og. Showing off again. Who he think he is?'"

Whereupon Og replied: "Don't knock it until you've tried it" and was so persuasive that soon everyone in his crowd was doing it, except for the reactionaries who chose to remain apes.

I read recently that scientists generally agree that this probably happened between five million and seven million years ago in Africa.

(Of course I can't vouch for the direct quotes.)

Then about 2.5 million years ago they were making crude stone tools and half a million years later, some of them picked up and migrated to Europe and Asia.

Now the argument is about when, where and how these near-humans began to think and behave like us.

> *"Our ancestors who chose not to walk erect, have lived without a major war for five-to-seven million years."*

Scientists describe this development as "acting modern."

Some say that happened about 40,000 years ago when mankind discovered that you didn't have to hunt and eat lower animals or grow crops, you could seek out those who did and hit them over the head and steal their food.

And the rest, as they say, is history.

Today we have refined this practice and now we have what is inaccurately known as a "dog-eat-dog" society. (Inaccurate because dogs do not eat dogs.)

We call this the "free market" but the overall unfolding global process is called "evolution."

Right now there is a question of just how far we have evolved. We have just seen that mankind has developed ingenious ways to engage in sophisticated larceny on a grand scale (Enron for example) while at the same time repeatedly repairing the damage ("locking the barn door") afterwards.

I read an article in the British paper *The Observer* entitled "Is human evolution finally over?"

The author leaned toward the conclusion that "things have simply stopped getting better or worse for our species."

Meanwhile, our ancestors who chose not to walk erect have lived without a major war for five-to-seven million years.

Maybe they're the ones who really know how to evolve.

Bet your Social Security
on the Super Bowl

B rilliant idea, letting the government invest our social security funds in the stock market. The only thing better would be to bet it at Finger Lakes or give it to some government official to play the slots at Atlantic City.

Or, even more appropriately, how about putting it all on the Atlanta Falcons in the Sunday's Super Bowl?

Why Atlanta and not Denver? Simple: every financier knows that when the NFC (National Football Conference) team wins, the market goes up. Atlanta is an NFC team. Denver is AFC (American Football Conference). If the AFC wins, the market collapses.

That's known as the "Super Bowl Rule" and I think it illustrates that the stock market rises and falls for only very basic economic reasons that can be carefully analyzed by studying computer models and chicken entrails.

Most people think that stocks go up when earnings reports are favorable and the future looks bright for economic growth. They don't know the whole thing hinges on who wins the Super Bowl and whether enough people get laid off.

Some folks think Alan Greenspan, chairman of the Federal Reserve Board, makes it go up and down by sneezing in public or spilling soup on his tie, throwing market analysts into a tizzy.

Naturally I was surprised when he came out against Clinton's ingenious idea of letting the government "invest" our social security nest eggs in the market. But I can imagine his train of thought: "Any institution that goes bananas every time I scratch my nose is not where I'd put MY money."

Did I mention that the Super Bowl Rule was wrong last year and stands a pretty good chance of repeating its performance this Sunday? I'd check previous years if I wanted to dignify a stupid theory.

Al (he always calls me Dick) fears that there is no way politics can be kept out of the investment machinery if Clinton's plan (enthusiastically supported by many Republicans) goes through.

I can't understand his thinking on that score. Surely we can trust the government to not let politics influence its investment decisions. Just look at the way Congress has dealt so impartially and non-politically with the impeachment process.

Presumably whomever the president wanted to appoint to mastermind the investment of our money would have to be approved by Congress. That certainly should allay our fears.

Yeah. Sure.

Erasing wrinkles (and character) with Botox

N ow that the wrinkle-fighting drug Botox has been approved, the question becomes: Do you really want to be afflicted with an unfurrowed brow?

Do you want people to think of you as young and callow — as someone who doesn't understand the situation — like untroubled Alfred E. (What, Me Worry?) Neuman of *MAD Magazine* fame?

You can't tell from the photo accompanying this column but the author has a suitably wrinkled forehead, as befits an aging thinker who knows the score and is worried sick about it.

The silly grin, ordered by the photographer, may throw you off, but the real Dougherty is not like that. He is reassuringly balding and prune-like as well as long in the tooth.

That's why he inspires such confidence.

But the choice is yours: Do you want to be a living Barbie or Ken, forever? It's possible if you can come up with the price of Botox injections— $300 to more than $1,000 every three to four months.

You must have read about Botox. It's made from the toxin that causes botulism (literally sausage poisoning in German). It paralyzes muscles. You get it from improperly canned foods.

> *"The real Dougherty is reassuringly balding and prune-like as well as long in the tooth."*

But the diluted toxin in Botox numbs and relaxes the facial muscles and eliminates wrinkles.

A downside is that you have to avoid lying down or bending over to tie your shoes for six hours after the treatment. Otherwise the paralysis may spread to unspecified areas.

The *New York Times* story I read said Botox has been administered by some doctors for cosmetic wrinkle treatment although it had been approved only for eye muscle spasms.

The *Times* account contained this descriptive sentence:

"In a variation on the Stepford Wives, it is now rare in certain enclaves to see a woman (actress) over the age of 35 with the ability to look angry."

We'll become a "Botox Nation of citizens with unnaturally placid expressions," the *Times* fears.

This might be a boon for poker players, but I'm not certain I want to walk around impersonating stone-faced silent film star Buster Keaton forever.

I'd rather look like the portrait of Dorian Gray, who at least appeared to know what the world was coming to.

Memory software takes a brief vacation

I f I pass you on the street or in the hallway at the paragraph factory and call you by the all-purpose name, "there," as in "hello, there," please don't be offended.

> *"Your brain has been improperly shut down. DiscFirst Aid is checking and will repair any problems."*

I've been told it's only a temporary residual "glitch" from my open heart surgery.

Your name is still on file in my memory but every time I try to pull it up to the screen inside my skull behind my forehead, I get an error message telling me: "Your brain has been improperly shut down. Disc First Aid is checking and will repair any problems."

During this period after my recent hospitalization, you may notice a vacant look in one or both of my eyes. This is not dementia. I am simply waiting for the signal that the problem has been fixed and power restored.

If successful, this will take a mere 15 seconds or less.

You can tell whether I am fully operational by whether or not I now address you as "again," as in "nice to see you again."

"Nice to see again, Dave," would be better, especially if the Dave happens to be the publisher of this newspaper.

But I'm learning not to push my luck.

It's funny about memory loss. Most of mine has been natural and necessary. I've always made it a practice to periodically reduce mind clutter.

The mind is really an amazing organ, but it has to have something to work with. Who knows what's stored in all those creases?

I'll bet mine resembles a bowling ball.

(This column was written following Dougherty's heart surgery in July, 2003.)

Heart valve recipient thanks his bovine benefactor

Whom should I bump into the other night in my dreams but the cow who made me the lifesaving gift of her only aortic heart valve.

"I'm so glad I ran into you," I lied." I've been avoiding you because I haven't known what to say. I've been torn between gratitude and guilt."

"Gratitude would be fine." she said. "Guilt is optional. Frankly, we rarely see it in you carnivores."

I detected a note of disapproval of the carnivorous lifestyle, but let it pass. My mother always said "never look a gift cow in the mouth."

I was tempted to explain that I didn't participate in the decision to seek out a cow donor. When the surgeon told me the valve tissue would be "bovine," I didn't make the connection. (I learned later that there are artificial valves made of metal or plastic or something, but in my case a donation from a fellow mammal was preferable.)

But you try to explain this to the ghost of a cow when you're fast asleep.

I'm not saying this is a nightmare, exactly.

Heck, I've actually EATEN cows for years at the Scotch and Sirloin and never lost sleep over it, even though I'm fairly certain that one day I'll have to face an international bovine tribunal like Slobodan Milosovic.

"My mother always said 'Don't look a gift cow in the mouth'."

So merely accepting heart valve tissue from a cow donor can't really be a big deal. After all, I am told that the surgeons at Strong immediately install artificial replacement valves in the donor cows.

As soon as they regain consciousness in the recovery room after surgery, they go to the rehab center and are back in the pasture with the herd as good as new in no time, boring everyone with operation stories.

I haven't seen the bovine cardio rehab center, but I imagine it's much like mine, with upbeat, perpetually smiling nurses acting as cheerleaders and tyrants, checking heart monitors and helping you onto treadmills and stationary bikes.

I'm hoping that by the time the winter snows melt and the days grow longer, I'll be up to gamboling in the green pasture like my cow benefactor.

If I happen to run into her, I'll be sure to say "Thanks again, sweetheart!"

(This column was written following Dougherty's heart surgery in July, 2003.)

Chapter Six

Birds, Bugs & Lab Mice

Tenants are back and already remodeling

T he front porch Christmas wreath is occupied again and the construction season has begun. The pregnant sparrow and her solicitous mate are back.

(At least I think they're the same pair, or maybe their kids. More about this in a moment.)

The courtships seem to be waning and the nest building is in full swing. Every time we open the front door there is a frantic flurry of wings and chirping that I assume to be obscenity-laden bird protest.

Soon there will be eggs, then nagging little sparrows demanding food. Then one day this summer they will be gone and we'll take down the wreath. By then it will be brown and balding.

On the south side of the house there was a piece of siding came loose in windstorm several years ago. When I finally got out the ladder and climbed up to replace it a noisy bird stampede ensued and I almost lost my balance.

I retreated, apologizing profusely. A few weeks later, when the birds had flown, I went back, replaced the siding and built a fancy ranch style multi-family duplex. Now every spring it is occupied by house finches.

There is another domicile on the screen porch. On one screen I cut a hanging flap that serves as the entrance for the sparrow tenants. Until July it's their porch but they let us use it.

"Are these the same birds or maybe their kids?" I asked a birder colleague.

"Maybe, maybe not. I have a theory, though, that makes sense to me."

He thinks my wreath, the duplex and the screen porch look inviting to house nesters moving back north.

"Just as some birds are downtowners and like the Civic Center Garage, it's a matter of taste and location, location, location."

Any finch or house sparrow will come by, see the same place and think: 'There's a good spot for a nest, just as squatters might take a liking to a particular empty house if all Rochester took simultaneous spring vacations.'

That makes sense, I suppose. But I like to think that our birds are repeaters - satisfied tenants who come back every year.

They like the service and the ambiance (no cats, just an amiable dog who chews Kleenex and clothing into nest-building material).

When they leave, the parents tell the kids, "Take a good look so you can find the way next spring if we're not around."

Birds practice their songs

One of our early morning delights this season is lying in bed and listening to one of our neighborhood songbirds try to get his theme song straight. The poor kid just can't master the tune, phrasing or tempo. My wife says he's a young thrush, just learning his rudimentary arias in preparation for a season of dating, mating and nesting.

He'll start off confidently enough but by the fifth or sixth note he gets confused and his notes become halting and erratic.

There will be an embarrassed pause, then far off down in the glen another bird will answer him.

> *"The poor kid just can't master the tune, phrasing or tempo."*

"Like this, you dummy," his mentor seems to be saying as he launches into a flawless intricate rendition. Then the kid will try again. He is not a gifted pupil, but if he wants to find romance, he had better get cracking.

I read recently that this spring-time serenade at dawn and dusk is an all-male production designed to attract a mate. To put it bluntly, they are auditioning for sexual favors.

Females judge a spousal candidate by his singing prowess. If that's so, this poor guy is in for a lonely, frustrating season unless he gets immediate help.

All the real beauties will be taken by the time he gets into the game.

An article, in the Portland (Maine) *Sunday Telegram* the other day, said some species like flycatchers come into the world genetically wired to warble. Others, like our little friend on the rim of Corbett's Glen in Brighton, have to be tutored.

Later in the season when they get the hang of the basic melodies, they'll begin to add personal, distinguishing embellishments and even acquire regional accents.

"Cardinals have about a dozen songs in their repertoire," the author wrote. "Marsh wrens know a couple of hundred, while brown thrashers can sing 2,000 or more songs during their lifetimes."

The eye opener for me was the news that all this singing is linked to hormones. When daylight increases in the spring, the testes of male songbirds increase in size, triggering production of the hormone testosterone.

It, in turn, enlarges and stimulates the song centers in the brain.

Then the auditions begin. The females, hearing this serenade, figure that the best singers will be the best providers. Then they make their selections and the mating and nesting begins.

Luckily, my particular species does not insist on a vocal test. By silently moving my lips to popular songs, I was able to mate, nest and scavenge for food without even trying to carry a tune.

Greeting the first insect guest in Maine

S aw my first ant yesterday. Cute little fellow. So serious and busy. I wanted to stop and ask him if he "had a good wintah," as we say to each other on Peaks Island, Maine, every spring. But he was all business and didn't have time for idle talk. He was pushing a giant crumb across the counter.

You feel kindly toward the first insect of the season. Like an old friend, you want to stop and help him out. What are neighbors for?

"Here, let me give you a hand with that," you want to say. "You take this end and I'll take the other. Remember to bend your knees, not your back. Now where do you want it?"

It felt as though I was the year-rounder greeting the first of the "summah people." When we first arrive on the island, the year-rounders greet us affectionately.

They forget for a moment that every boat will be bringing more of us, clogging the aisles at Feeney's market and causing midsummer traffic jams "down front," the Peaks block-long downtown.

Same with the ant. During the first friendly encounter I forgot that more ants are on the way. It's when the rest of them arrive and start acting like they own the place that they lose their cuteness and relations get testy.

I suppose they have a community somewhere in the walls and are just starting to stir. This guy was sent out to scout for food and was supposed to report back, but found this great crumb and wanted to surprise the little woman.

As the warm weather returns I imagine they'll seem less like people and more and more like bugs. "Give them a crumb and they take the loaf," we'll say. Our irritation will mount and finally it will be war — CHEMICAL war!

Funny, you never feel that way about the first robin. You never worry about robin infestations. Yet the ants are more community oriented. They look out for each other. They have family values.

It doesn't hurt to muse about these things, I've decided. They say that fossil they found in the martian asteroid fragment in (pardon the expression) ANTarctica was of some kind of bacteria.

So future martians may indeed turn out to be bugs. It wouldn't hurt to be friendly with their earthly cousins.

I warn you: It won't be easy. Ants, not to mention mosquitoes, fleas, cockroaches and the dreaded Peaks Island brown-tailed moth are hard to love.

Lord knows I tried. I sent tiny thought transference vibrations out to my ant scout but he never responded. Naturally I began to get irritated.

Suddenly something came over me. It wasn't pretty.

SPLAT! Gotcha!

I'm afraid the One World concept is still a long way off.

Are those lab mice holding out on us?

T hose laboratory rats have been good to us humans over the years. Whenever there's a habit that's bad for us, they've gone out of their way to overindulge it so they can alert us to the terrible consequences. Whenever there's a disease that's bothering us, they've purposely come down with it so they can check out experimental remedies. They get first crack at all the hot new drugs, good and bad.

They and their cousins, the lab mice, will do anything for us, even submit to autopsies.

And what do we do in return? We call them vermin.

So I wasn't the least bit surprised to find out yesterday that the rodents are holding out on us. They've found a cure for obesity (fatness) and won't share it with us so we can forget all this dieting and exercising.

> *"These amazing animals have found a cure for obesity, but won't tell us."*

Perhaps you read about it in yesterday's paper: For years fat lab mice have been slimming down by taking a hormone called leptin. Naturally the researchers got excited. They developed a human form of it and tried it out on people.

It didn't work. Some lost a few pounds. Others got fatter.

I won't go so far as to openly suggest that we're witnessing a Revenge of the Lab Mouse scenario here, but I might before I get through this column. Irate readers have often accused me of the crime of anthropomorphism, assigning human characteristics to animals, especially dogs.

These are the unsentimental critics who think of themselves as "higher" animals, as opposed to "lower" animals who are put on earth to serve and entertain us. Lower animals happily catch terminal diseases and shrug off such indignities as dissection.

Well, now we know. These amazing animals have found the cure for obesity but won't tell us.

According to the Centers for Disease Control and Prevention, one in eight of us was too fat in 1991. Last year it was one in five.

In Georgia the obesity rate increased 101.8 per cent in that seven-year period. Southerners are less likely to hike, ride a bike, walk or join a health club than their counterparts in the rest of the nation, the Centers reported.

Meanwhile, the couch potato mice sit there in their cages shooting up leptin, watching TV, stuffing themselves with munchies and laughing at us while getting slim as reeds.

And who can blame them? Certainly not me.

Feeney catches first fly of the summer

The first housefly of spring dropped by yesterday. Big bugger. Noisy too. Feeney, the compulsive flycatcher, heard it first. I could see his ears swivel and heard him stop breathing, but he didn't stir. I'm not sure he even opened his eyes.

"A harbinger!" I hissed. "Go get him. He's a scout on reconnaissance patrol for the main body of houseflies."

I wanted Feeney to capture him, drench him in saliva and turn him loose to report back to fly headquarters that the menacing carnivorous beast was still in residence and doing business as usual.

Poor Feen. He's still got the protective security instincts, but the old bod lets him down. It just won't do his bidding with the same enthusiasm any more.

°°It grieves me to tell you this,°° I imagined him explaining, °°but I don't have all the time in the world any more and I'm not going to squander it in fruitless pursuit of cats, squirrels. rabbits or flies. You'll have to deal with them yourself.°°

I had suspected as much. The other day a squirrel jumped from the phone line to the maple tree right over his head. He was dozing at the time, but roused himself briefly, raising his head to decide whether or not to bark.

°°The hell with it,°° he concluded. °°Just don't have the old fire in the belly. Too pooped to be a predator any more. °°

> *"'A harbinger!' I hissed. 'Go get him.' He's a scout on reconnaissance patrol..."*

His mistress had already reported that both Feeney and the next door cat where dozing in the sun recently, an unheard-of development.

In the old days that would have been regarded as a foolhardy affront. Cats are supposed to kept aloft at all times, like squirrels, even on their own property. If barking doesn't do the trick, they must be chased.

But the housefly incident was even more ominous. Feeney always took great pride and satisfaction from his ability to zap a fly out of the air with a blindingly fast move that would do credit to a cobra or an anteater.

He seldom caught a cat or squirrel, but he never missed a fly. I hate to think what we'll do when the flies get word that their old adversary has retired and it's open season at the Doughertys.

The same with the seagulls in Maine, his native land. I hate to think of them laughing at him in those raucous taunting cries, but I just hope he gets to see the old place again.

These are poignant times at our house. We fear there is another wrenching parting approaching and, as always, we're not ready to face it.

Monotony bird and names that work

My wife the bird listener has a name for many of the feathered friends who wake us up every morning.

She really should get one of those bird call recordings and identify them by their formal monikers, but she prefers her own.

"That Monotony Bird is driving me nuts!" she exclaimed the other day. He's the one who sits on the deck railing outside our bedroom and repeats one boring note in three-beep segments. I call him the Backing Garbage Truck Bird.

Far off down in Corbett's Glen will come the answer: "Beeeep beeep beeep." Sometimes one will add a beep - "Beeep beeep beeeep beeep," to prove even a Monotony Bird gets bored sometimes.

A friend told me these and the other aspiring dawn-breaking roosters are all males and are declaring: "This is my territory and I'm looking for a mate so keep your distance, buster."

The Monotony Bird is not to be confused with the Whistling Tea Kettle Bird. However, it may be the same bird doing his socko finish.

"He's got a longer, higher-pitched beep," my wife explains.

"The telegraph bird... lapses into Morse Code... to find romance."

The Telegraph Bird may also be a Monotony or Tea Kettle who lapses into Morse Code out of sex-driven desperation to find romance.

The Cardinals have various identities. At first we thought they were Babytalk Birds saying "Bird-ee, bird-ee, bird-ee."

But my wife says she now realizes they are Massed Moonie Wedding Birds proclaiming "We do! We do! We do!"

There is a noisy species living in the multiple-dwelling condo I built under the eaves. She calls them Squabblers or Hysteria Birds. We can't figure out if they're fighting or celebrating, but it's obvious that teenaged drinking is involved.

We're still waiting for the thrushes to show up. This time last year they were practicing incessantly. Now we hear them only at the sunset concert. Perhaps they can't stand the untalented Monotonies and Multiple Weddings in the wake-up matinee.

The mourning dove or Identity Crisis ('Who-Who') Bird, shows up at the feeder to be picked on by a screeching bright blue Hockey Fan Bird.

Some day we'll have to sort out these guys by their real names. We know the earsplitting Fingernails on the Blackboard Bird that wakes us out of a sound sleep just as the fast freight blows for the Fairport Crossing is definitely a crow.

(The Bark Bark Bird who answers him is a Golden Retriever.)

Bugs book airline seats

Our upper respiratory infection is late again this year. But not to worry. We're taking a ride in an airliner tomorrow and expect to rendezvous with approximately 200 bug couriers.

Back in the old days, before high-speed delivery by air, it used to take weeks for a virus to make its way across the globe on foot, from one pedestrian to another.

Then, in the slightly newer days, they traveled by ocean liner, train and bus.

Now, of course, thanks to the marvels of commercial aviation and the invention of recirculated air, the little buggers can hop aboard a trolley in an urban center in the Far East, transfer to a jet and be in Los Angeles Airport the next day, having multiplied en route inside hundreds of moist nasal passages.

From there, still inside their host carriers, they fan out across the country on swift domestic flights, and can be snugly ensconced in thousands of bronchial tubes that same night.

My mother, bless her heart, warned us that "colds" were caused by wet feet and were spread somehow from one bare head to another by a process known as ``catching your death.''

Doctors told her "colds" were caused by "germs." This was before the invention of viruses, tiny wormlike creatures affectionately called "bugs" because of their cuteness.

Of course, she never believed in the new-fangled germ theory for a minute. She stuck with the old-fangled "chill" scenario.

Someone could cough and sneeze all over somebody and they'd never "catch their death" so long as they kept their feet dry and avoided drafts.

Now, as you know, they have "immunization," a witchcraft process that involves doctors injecting dead viruses into a patient's body. This is supposed to prevent, not cause, catching one's death, if you believe that.

> " *...the little buggers can hop aboard a trolley in the Far East, transfer to a jet and be in Los Angeles Airport the next day.* "

Tomorrow we'll board our craft here in Rochester and be greeted by a chorus of seal-like barking, hacking and sneezing. By the time we reach LaGuardia Airport and sit on the ground for a couple of hours, we'll have joined the chorus.

Then we'll transfer to another flying pest house and keep going until we have successfully "come down with something," as the medical journals put it.

We'll incubate the little fellows in the sun for a week, then bring them back home for your enjoyment.

Mother's Day can be for the birds

"What do you want for Mother's Day, mom?"

"Just tell the little brats to treat me decent the rest of the year, buster."

This touching domestic exchange came to mind the other day when I heard a pregnant mother bird arguing with her spouse about feathering the nest in preparation for the inevitable annual blessed events.

Either that or she was saying, "You males have only one thing on your minds. Just one time I'd like to see you try to lay an egg."

It's fun to sit in our den and eavesdrop on the bird couples as they get ready to raise the kids, lugging in twig lumber and materials to build the basinettes.

We can see them right outside the den window where I've built a roomy six-unit bird condo.

Without my noticing, a section of aluminum siding blew off a few winters ago, exposing the eaves. When spring came, we saw that bird families had moved in and built nests.

We watched them come and go all spring, bringing food to the squalling kids. One day they all just flew off.

Rather than replace the siding, I built a long multiple condo complex with six back door entrances to cover the space.

Sure enough, when the birds came back (we assume they were the same families), they moved right in. We could hear the exclamations of delight.

"Get a load of this place, Mabel! The old guy fixed it all up for us! And it's squirrel-proofed too." (Or chirps to that effect.)

When the mothering gets under way, the poppa bird is in continuous motion, bringing in baby food to regurgitate into the mouths of the spoiled, demanding kids.

To get in their units, they have to land on the top window frame then do a hop turn up into the entranceway. They can look in at us and we can hear every word.

"There they are, watching TV again. It's hard to believe the old geezer built this thing. I hope he didn't fall off the ladder. He looks awful still in that recliner."

No, as a matter of fact, the old guy survived. He was just napping.

It's been over 25 years since the last kid flew our nest. Watching the birds brings back memories of sleepless nights spent heating bottles and later worrying when she was out late and didn't call.

Maybe I imagined it, but I think I heard the mother bird say: "Next Mother's Day get me some of those egg control pills!"

Those meddling mice discover an exercise pill

Once again the laboratory mice are meddling with our lives. This time they're developing a pill that builds up muscles without exercise.

Instead of mounting their tiny stationary bikes and frantically pedaling away in cadence with loud rock music until they're near exhaustion, they'll be able to pop a pill and take a nap to get in shape.

Meanwhile we non-rodents will still have to grunt and perspire the old-fashioned way if we want to pump up those abs and lats and all those other slow twitch and fast twitch muscles.

I read about this recently on a medical technology website.

The article didn't say, but presumably a control group of mice were made to work out vigorously in the weight room and on the treadmills while the sedentary mice idly sucked their pills and watched on closed-circuit TV in the lounge.

At least that's the way I'd have designed the experiment.

> *"The rewards of exercise are in the feeling of smug superiority one gets over the non-exerciser."*

It is customary in writing about these so-called mouse breakthroughs to hail them as important milestones in the improvement of the human condition.

I prefer to take a skeptical wait-and-see attitude.

My experience tells me that the rewards of exercise are not in the increased level of fitness or muscle size and tone, they're in the feeling of smug superiority one gets over the non-exerciser.

What will happen to the satisfaction one gets from sternly chiding someone with the "no pain, no gain" mantra in a world of painless gain?

Who wants to pass up the great feeling you get when you drag yourself out of the gym, drenched in sweat, and flop down in front of your locker and mutter to your neighbor: "Why do we DO this to ourselves?"

He makes a face and says: "Tell me about it," then you both hobble off to the steam room feeling great about yourselves and your hard-won capacity to suffer.

They don't have a pill that will duplicate that kind of satisfaction.

We're talking major character-building here.

Sometimes I wish those meddling mice would leave well enough alone and go back to just being disgusting little rodents.

Chat with a beetle friend as summer ends

One of the last bugs of autumn was making its way across the deck this weekend. It was one of the Convergent Lady Beetles (Hippodamia convergens) that has been doing aphid (plant louse) control duty in the garden this summer.

To get its attention I placed a finger in its path and it halted abruptly. It stood its ground waiting for an explanation.

"I just wanted to thank you for the fine work you and the other Ladies have done this summer," I told it. "All the plants are grateful."

°°No problem. That's what we're here for. I figure I ate about 75 lice a day. Tasty little buggers. Now if you'll move that finger, I'll be on my way.°°

As long-time readers are aware, I suffer from Dr. Doolittle Syndrome — the delusion that one can talk to animals. But I was unaware until this weekend that I can also converse with insects.

"Hibernate, wake up, fly off to the orgy, mate, lay eggs. They hatch into larvae...we pupate...It's pretty regimented."

There is something appealing about ladybugs. With their colorful orange and black lacquered wing covers, it's impossible to think of them as pests.

"So where were you heading when you encountered the finger? You looked like you were on an important mission," I said.

°°I was about to scout the woodpile under your deck. The first frost is coming. A whole gang of us will be wintering down there underneath the logs if I give it the OK. Then next spring we'll all head down into that field and mate and lay our eggs.°°

"You seem to have your lives pretty well organized."

°°Well, it's a living. Hibernate, wake up, fly off to the orgy, mate, lay eggs. They hatch into larvae. Then we pupate. Then it's adulthood and the whole thing starts over. It's pretty regimented but not a bad life.°°

Was he (or she?) aware of the large number of nuthatches and woodpeckers in the vicinity? I asked. There was a birdfeeder right over our heads.

°°Birds don't bother us. They think that because we're orange, we might sting them. Also, they figure we might taste bad. Maybe we do. We can't tell. But if one gets too curious, we play dead. That's what I was doing when your finger showed up. Predators usually don't eat something that doesn't move.°°

"Fascinating," I said.

°°We can also squirt a skunk-like fluid from our leg joints as a last resort. Like this . . .smell it?°°

"Pee-yew!" I cried, shaking my finger.

°°Sorry. Just wanted to see if it worked on large animals. See you in the spring.°°

"Don't be a stranger," I said.

Chapter Seven

Peaks Retreat

Reporting the news from Catatonia
The true meaning of vacations
Make cottage like home? Why?
Sea captain fantasy fades fast
Natives restless with talk of secession
Icy ocean is good therapy (not!)
He fears he's ready for gentrification
Peaks characters we've known and loved
Nice lawn? There goes the neighborhood
Beware of moose in heat
New license plate stars chickadee, not lobster
October the best month Down East
Young deer bids us farewell
Missing those surf sounds

Reporting the news from Catatonia

PEAKS ISLAND, Maine — Near our place on Peaks, there is a woman who walks a rooster on a leash. My wife tried to rouse me from a nap to interview her, but I said I was on vacation and it was raining out. Besides, what do you say to a woman walking a rooster? "I'll be damned - a rooster?" Forget it.

There is also an Umbrella Cover Museum on Brackett Avenue. Not an umbrella museum, mind you, an umbrella cover museum.

My wife said a zealous news-hound would feel obliged to confront the curator and demand to know what she did with all the umbrellas. I said that would be like asking the chef what he did with all the amputee frogs.

Luckily, it rained all the time we were there (20 out of 23 days). The tourists never showed and the museum never opened so I stayed in my catatonic vacation mode.

I'm telling you this because my wife says everyone is interested in news from Peaks Island. I doubt that but just in case, here are some more stop-the-presses bulletins.

They had a grand opening for the new hardware store Down Front by the ferry the other day. When I stopped by for some putty, a sign on the door said "Closed."

"What's with the store?" I asked a grizzled local.

"Closed." he said.

"When's it open?"

"Dunno. Been closed since the day after the grand opening."

Feeney's Market, named for our neighbor John Feeney and our late lamented island dog is now called Hannigan's. The islanders still call it Feeney's, of course.

Name changes are generally disregarded on Peaks Island. Will's restaurant would still be called the Cockeyed Gull if it hadn't closed.

Our dog Midas is getting smarter. Last year we were in Albany before he stopped chanting °°Oh boy! We're going to the park! Oh boy! Oh boy!°°

This time he caught on and dozed off just outside Utica.

We took along his Dog Watch training flags again this year to mark his yard limits on Peaks but left behind his collar, the power source and boundary wire. He decided to respect the flags, just in case. °°No use risking a jolt,°° he muttered inaudibly.

Later his tail hit the Hurley's electrified deer fence and he went totally audible.

"@#$%&*!" (°°———°°) he yelped.

Dick Dougherty, Peaks Island, State of Catatonia. Stay tuned for sports and the weather.

The true meaning of "vacation"

The word vacation derives from the Latin *vacatus*, the past participle of *vacare*, which means to be empty.

I thought it important to look it up because we'll be on one for the next three weeks and I wanted to know exactly what was expected of me. It turns out that all I'm required to do is vacate.

I just have to abandon my station here at the paragraph factory by absenting myself and disengage my mind, a simple task if you put your mind to it.

A vacation, my dictionary tells me, is a time of freedom from work or cares: Leisure. Time free for something else: specifically, time for contemplation.

The word is also related to "vacant," defined as being without content or occupant, free from activity and also can mean characterized by absence of thought or reflection as in stupid, foolish, silly, dull, expressionless.

All of these definitions fit in nicely with my vacation plans.

They define exactly what I had in mind, namely, sitting on the rocks on the Back Shore of Peaks Island, Maine, studying the wave action and watching a golden retriever go berserk with frustration chasing seagulls.

I may absently fall into some open-ended contemplation, as described above, but I prefer the phrase characterized by absence of thought or reflection. My critics can testify that I am good at this. I get letters and phone calls saying so all the time.

"Maine is the ideal spot for vacating as well as vacationing."

In past years I was unable to devote full time to vacating because I was engaged in home ownership - weed-whacking, painting, moving rocks, replacing fallen ceiling tiles, etc. This year I am recuperating from a broken ankle and idleness is part of my therapy. My spouse has volunteered to assume my duties and responsibilities.

Maine is the ideal spot for vacating as well as vacationing. There is the hypnotic action of the Atlantic Ocean, there are sunsets to watch as clear liquids are sipped, there are naps to be taken.

Islanders have reported that the deer herd has multiplied to more than 500 head - a lot for an island a mile wide and 1 1/2 miles long - and once again have eaten all our shrubbery.

Despite performing this valuable labor-saving service, the deer are regarded as pests. There is talk of a bait-and-shoot "final solution."

But I mustn't let myself get worked up. Nothing must break my concentration on the task at hand: Vacating both mind and body.

Make cottage like home: why?

PEAKS ISLAND, Maine —One day soon, if we don't waste time looking at the ocean, we'll at last have the cottage looking just like home.

It will have a lawn to mow just like the one in Rochester. There will be weeds to pull, shrubs to trim, brush to clear, annuals to plant and a multitude of things that need fixing and replacing.

That's what we did last week on Peaks Island, Maine. It's called "opening up" the cottage.

As usual we had a winter tenant to accelerate the wear and tear and make our stewardship more challenging and exciting.

This year was special. There were screens to replace, a deck to fix and seal, a sofa and chest of drawers to take to the dump and all sorts of things to scrape, sand, repair and paint.

Now we're back, resting up. We'll return in July on our formal "vacation" and finish fixing and replacing things in time for August rentals. In September it will be time to "close up."

That's the beauty of owning a cottage. If you play your cards right you won't ever have to go anywhere else on vacation for the rest of your life.

And if you keep at it and vacation diligently, you can think of a million things to do instead of relaxing or having fun.

One of the things I miss up there is a cellar and a garage to store broken things in until you get around to fixing them or throwing them away.

A cellar gives you a little flexibility. You don't have to face a lot of hurried fix-it-or-toss-it decision-making.

A crawl space, because it is so much smaller and cramped, fills up faster and forces these decisions on you. You wind up taking things to the dump and exchanging them for other people's broken things you can try to fix before tossing them.

> *"If you play your cards right, you won't have to go anywhere else on vacation the rest of your life."*

If the dump doesn't yield any treasure, there are yard sales full of broken stuff that will keep you busy.

The selection isn't as extensive as Rochester's well-stocked garage sales, but the prices are competitive and the salespeople helpful and friendly.

People wonder why I don't retire from the "rat race" so I can vacation on Peaks like this from Memorial Day to Columbus Day.

The truth is I find racing rats restful after a few weeks of relentless vacationing.

Sea captain fantasy fades fast

PEAKS ISLAND, Maine — If we're lucky we'll be able once again to fight back the financially unsound urge to go nautical. It happens every summer.

We'll be sitting on the rocks in front of our place on Peaks Island, Maine, and I'll say: "If we had a boat we could zip out to Outer Green and look at the seals."

(Outer Green is a tiny rocky island out in the Atlantic near Halfway Rock Light.)

"Not again! Get real," my vacation partner will say.

She knows full well I have no intention of owning a boat. I just want to say I wished I had a boat.

She knows if I think about it long enough, the feeling will subside and we'll save thousands of dollars and spare ourselves untold grief and bother.

Then it will be time to go home, and we'll have escaped once again from boat ownership.

A boat, friends have told us repeatedly, is a "hole in the water you pour money into."

Years ago I took a course in navigation and boat handling through the Rochester Power Squadron and learned about the "rules of the road," navigational aids (buoys and things), dead reckoning, tidal currents, compass headings, way points and all that.

Then one summer a friend and I rented an 18-foot outboard from an islander and we tooled around the islands of Casco Bay.

I tried to talk the friend, MacDonald (Mac) Halsey, into being captain because he'd been a naval officer in World War II and was related to Adm. "Bull" Halsey, hero of historic Pacific naval battles.

But Mac begged off, revealing that during the war he navigated a destroyer escort into a mud bank while departing Boston Harbor on its maiden voyage, an exploit that made him briefly famous throughout the Navy.

The women also declined command appointments. They opted to sit back and criticize. So I took the helm and, except for running out of gas, almost drifting into a rocky shore, and various navigational difficulties, had a distinguished short-lived naval career.

But pressures of command were overwhelming. The crew became insubordinate. When I gave orders, they hooted with laughter.

Luckily, the man who owned the boat sold it that summer. Perhaps word got around, since no one else volunteered to rent to us.

The alternative was to become a boat owner myself, a prospect that had begun to seem like a life sentence at hard labor.

I've already got a house, a lawn, a cottage, two cars and a wife.

All of them need constant work.

What do I need with a boat?

Natives restless with talk of secession

P EAKS ISLAND, Maine — The Peaks Islanders are still pondering whether to break away from Away.

Away, as I have explained before, is anyplace that is not Peaks Island. But the island is part of the City of Portland, which is in Away. So it would seem logical that Peaks Islanders would want to secede if for no other reason than to avoid the stigma of being mistaken for citizens of Away like me.

It's more complicated than that, of course, but you can't help but be amazed at the restlessness of natives everywhere.

There is revolt in the air all over the globe.

Sentiment for secession has spread from Peaks Island, Biddeford Pool and Stroudwater (a mainland neighborhood in Portland) to the Soviet Union and Yugoslavia and now even her majesty Queen Elizabeth is facing rebellion and possible unemployment.

> *"There is revolt in the air all over the globe."*

I read just the other day that Australia's prime minister was going to drop by the castle and tell the queen that her services would no longer be needed after the year 2001. The Aussies don't want a monarch any more. She was fired.

They didn't say why, exactly, but I suspect it has something to do with her inability to control her spoiled children.

Or it may be the fact that she is an absentee ruler.

If you're paying part of her expenses, you expect her to show up once in awhile, the Aussies are saying. But no, her throne is in a foreign country, thousands of miles away.

Absenteeism does not make the heart grow fonder.

The New Zealanders are said to feel the same way. So do the Jamaicans and the Papuans of New Guinea. Even the Canadians are grumbling and talking rebellion.

Everywhere, it's the same: "The natives are restless tonight," as they say in those old jungle movies. Pretty soon they'll be saying: "It's quiet out there." "Yeah, TOO quiet," will come the reply.

Then the drums will start. It's happening all over.

So the grumbling of the natives on Peaks Island's should come as no surprise. The Balkanization of the world is underway and nothing seems able to stop it.

I can see it now. The mayor of Portland, Anne Pringle, is pacing in her office. "Those drums! Those drums are driving me crazy!"

"Natives restless, Bwana," says the Peaks tribal ambassador. "No want to be part of Away. Break away from Away, you betcha!" Pretty soon the volcano will erupt and the rest, as they always say, will be history.

Icy ocean is good therapy (not!)

PEAKS ISLAND, Maine — People who visit our place here often ask if it's feasible to swim in the ocean off the rocks out front.

I pass along the sound advice an islander gave me years ago:

"Sho-ah. Jump right in. It's mighty invigorating. Just make sure you jump right out before you get wet."

Natives tell me that on very hot, sunny days, if you catch the incoming tide just after it has covered a warm rock, you can survive for a few seconds before your blood congeals. (If you're a kid, you might last a little longer.)

So naturally I was surprised to discover that the folks in North Berwick insist the Peaks Islanders are all wet (to coin a phrase). They insist the ocean is good for whatever ails you.

They've revived the a centuries-old tradition of Cure-All-Day, brought to Maine by Scottish prisoners of war captured in the Battle of Dunbar in 1650 by Oliver Cromwell's forces and sent into exile in Maine.

> *"Everyone knows that ice-cold salt water has a beneficial effect on all sorts of ailments."*

"Everyone knows that ice cold salt water has a beneficial effect on all sorts of ailments, especially arthritic joints," said Royal Cloyd, a Welshman who revived the event three years ago.

"In the old days the Scots around the Berwicks would assemble just before dawn and journey the nine miles to Wells Beach by horse and buggy. They'd get there around 10, take the cure, then come back for a big picnic and festivities, like a rural fair. We make it down in 15 minutes."

Saturday's post-dip festivities were at North Berwick's Mill Field. About 200 showed up. Only about 10 show-offs took the 5 a.m. ocean therapy.

According to tradition, the supplicants link arms and walk slowly into the sea toward the rising sun — backward.

"Backward?"

"Backward", said Cloyd. "Don't ask. It's part of the tradition. We leave a gift - usually a coin or flowers - for Poseidon and he sees to it we're cured all our ills."

"Really?"

"Absolutely. Since we started this, I've never felt better in my life. Ask anybody."

"And then you just dry off and head back to North Berwick?"

"Right, we roll down our pants and . . ."

"Hold it. Did you say pants? You just go in to your knees? No total immersion?"

"The Scots may be crazy —☐but not that crazy̔"

We Peaks Islanders may have all our marbles but some say we're a sickly lot.

He fears he's ready for gentrification

PEAKS ISLAND, Maine — Even peering out of my one functioning eye, it is easy to see that this island, once an 18th century welfare refuge, has come a long way.

As we climbed the hill leading from the ferry landing to Island Avenue in Greater Metropolitan Downtown Peaks we were startled to see The Inn, an impressive new hostelry under construction with rooms expected to go for three figures per night.

When we left here to return to Away last September, the site was occupied by an abandoned, run-down, service station and hardware store and a dirt parking lot for fuel trucks and car hulks.

The new structure, to open later this summer, has an attached modern hardware store on one end and the classy Big Fish Grill on the other.

A few years ago we thought the four-way-stop intersection at the new island dump (er, environmental waste management transfer station) and the new sewage plant were the prime metaphors for the gentrification of the island.

> *"We called it our Box-on-the-Rocks until we got uppity and added a second story."*

But since then, five new palatial homes have materialized on the Back Shore, overlooking the Atlantic, just down the road from our suddenly downscale oceanfront cottage. (We called it our Box on the Rocks until we got uppity and added a second story.)

Until last year the island vehicle of choice was an ancient model car or pickup truck in tasteful disrepair and licensed for island use only.

This year it is a golf cart.

It is customary for those of us who aspire to become naturalized island immigrants to view all these developments with contempt. But I sort of like the idea of a golf cart, so long as I don't have to actually play the infuriatingly stupid game.

(I wouldn't mind an ocean kayak or a crewed sailing yacht either and I have to admit I think the new inn looks great.)

I've even acquiesced to modest yard improvements, provided they are performed by my spouse and hired help. (Recent eye surgery has helped me get away with malingering this summer.) My wife and my dog would like to see me retire and emigrate up here full-time like many of our friends.

But I'm confident the authorities would reject my citizenship application. Besides not speaking the language, I think I lack gentrification potential.

I figure the way things are going, this island will soon become a gated community, and I'd have a problem making it past the security guards.

Peaks characters we've known and loved

PEAKS ISLAND, Maine: Jerry Garman unveiled his long-awaited Alternative Deer Control Initiative this summer. He has developed a computer-generated full-color poster bearing a powerful message: "IF YOU'RE A DOE, JUST SAY NO," it reads.

Unlike Rochester, which uses the ever-popular Bloodbath Method, Jerry prefers a Planned Parenthood approach.

"We like to appeal to the deer's sense of community and family responsibility," he told me. "If this doesn't work we'll try counseling."

Every day we've seen deer families in our front yard enjoying the shrubbery and flowers my wife grows for them.

> *"Every day we've seen deer in our front yard enjoying the shrubbery and flowers my wife grows for them."*

Whether the Garman posters will do the trick is uncertain, but we all know how wildly successful Nancy Reagan's just-say-no drug program turned out.

My own proposal was that we rename the island Deer Isle, but some picky critic pointed out there already is one down east of here.

The other big news on the island is that Donny Smith, the plumber, has an 800 number and a pager!

To appreciate the full impact of this startling development, you have to remember that until now the traditional Down East way to find anyone has been to consult your memorized island conveyance directory.

To find Donny you used to drive around the island until you spotted his van with the white pipe carrier on top.

You'd knock on the nearest door and there he, or one of his sons, would be. So simple.

Now he's plugged in to an elaborate electronic technology network. Next thing you know he'll be making us push buttons. ("If your septic tank is regurgitating sewage, press 1 now.")

My island conveyance directory has "Billy Flynn, electrician, silver van," "Bobby McTigue, carpenter/contractor/fireman, red GMC pickup," "Donny Groeger, "human backhoe, brush hauler, gray Dodge Ram pickup."

It is customary to wave to these people, either head-on or through your rear view mirror. Unless you owe them money, they will wave back.

The island went through a similar technology revolution years ago with the answering machine. Now island machines Down East talk to each other without human help all the time, just like here in Up West.

One professional I know invites you to leave a message at the beep then makes it a practice never to play it back. To him, inaccessibility is a matter of personal pride and saves him the trouble of just saying no.

Nicknames through the ages

One of the curious customs on Peaks Island, Maine, where we're heading at the end of this week, is the way the natives use the diminutive form when addressing grown men.

It's Bobby, not Bob. Kenny, not Ken. Donny, not Don.

It seems startlingly out of character for New Englanders to talk this way. Sure, in Georgia it's Jimmy and Billy Carter and in Texas is Billy Bob and Willy. We're used to that, just as we're used to men referring to their fathers as "mah daddy."

But to call Will Willy in the land of Ay-Yah, Yup-Nope, Never-Chew-My-Cabbage-Twice taciturnity seems strange to me.

It's like calling FDR Franky or Stalin Joey. Would William the Conqueror been an awe-inspiring figure if they'd called him Billy?

Or how about Georgie Washington, Daddy of His Country? Or Tommy Jefferson? Or Julie Caesar and Gengy Khan?

What about Benjy Franklin, Alfy Einstein, Hank and Sammy Adams, Billy Jennings Bryan, Billy Shakespeare, Abey Lincoln?

They sound as out of place as James Carter, Alphonse Capone, William Nelson or Amos and Andrew.

The dictionary defines the diminuitive form as "expressing smallness, endearment or condescension," but none of these apply on Peaks Island.

> *"It's like calling FDR Franky or Stalin Joey... what about William Nelson or Amos and Andrew"*

One Donny we know up there is a plumber, fully grown and grizzled. Treating him with endearment or condescension could get you a pipe wrench in the chops.

The other Donny is built like the boulder wrestler he is. He digs in septic tanks by hand without disturbing your shrubs. Detractors call him the human backhoe, but rarely to his face.

(By the way, Donny in PeaksSpeak is pronounced Dawny.)

None of these folks have called me Dicky yet. If they ever do, which seems unlikely since I'm not even a naturalized islander, I'll have to consider whether to be pleased or insulted.

On the one hand it could mean I've been accepted as a not-bad-guy-for-an-off-islander-from-Away.

But on the other hand, it could mean that I am being dismissed as an insignificant pipsqueak out-of-state mainlander, unworthy of being taken seriously.

You never know with these Downeasters.

Nice lawn? There goes the neighborhood

It was inevitable, I suppose: The dreaded grass infestation has spread to the back shore of Peaks Island, Maine.

Three years ago when I first saw my next door neighbor Bob Hurley diligently cultivating turf in his yard, I knew the end was near. "There goes the neighborhood," I muttered.

Sure enough, he was building a lawn! Naturally that meant my supervisor would insist we have one too. My hopes of transforming my declining years into reclining years were dashed.

When we first bought the place years ago, our "front yard" was like most of the back shore - a gorgeous horticultural tangle - sumac and stunted cherry trees rising out of nondescript miscellaneous undergrowth, all of it being strangled by bittersweet and wild grape vines. It could best be described as a "carefree thicket."

> **"Having the Atlantic Ocean for a front yard just isn't good enough for some people."**

Then Bob had to go retire, quitting his job as a college psychology prof and becoming a compulsive nest-featherer and maintenance freak.

"What will you do to keep busy up here?" I asked him, figuring he would miss the intellectual challenges of the head-shrinking dodge.

"Oh, I'll be okay. I love to work in the yard," he said.

My heart sank.

"You need some of your own medicine - like electric shock treatments," I murmured to myself a little too audibly.

"What?"

"Nothing. I was just thinking your yard looks terrific just the way it is right now."

Now it is 1998 and by the 21st Century he'll have a golf green for a yard and I'll be shamed into spending my vacations harvesting dandelions and dog droppings.

I was doing just that on vacation earlier this month when I cleverly arranged to step into a depression and break an ankle bone, enabling me to abandon horticulture for the summer.

Happily warming up for my "reclining years," I hit the couch to read and listen to surf, seagulls and the incessant rainfall.

But next year I may not be so lucky. The Hurley Effect will take over.

Having the Atlantic Ocean for a front yard just isn't enough for some people. They have to clutter it up with unsightly grass and shrubbery.

You may be one of those dim people who wonder why I don't retire from the paragraph factory and move to our idyllic island retreat in Maine.

Well, now you know.

Beware of moose in heat

PEAKS ISLAND, Maine —Another thing we'd never have known if we hadn't gone to Maine this month:

It's lawful to impersonate a moose in heat, provided you don't use an electronic device or draw a rosined rope through a hole in a bucket.

However, it's not a good idea to deceive a moose, orally or otherwise, because when the bull moose hears your call and arrives to find you're not a cow moose after all, he will be very disappointed and upset.

A veteran moose fancier, who may or may not be a great kidder, told me a truly amorous and nearsighted moose could mistake you for the real thing, and that would be even worse.

When approached by a moose bent on romance, he said, it is best to be up a tree with provisions enough for a long stay because moose, at this time of year, have only one thing on their male chauvinist minds.

Sexual harassment is an equal opportunity, not-neccessarily-consensual pursuit in moose society.

> *"When approached by a moose bent on romance, its best to be up a tree with enough provisions for a long stay."*

It is also a good idea to avoid a bull moose when it is moving on an intersecting course with your car. When responding to an invitation from a romantic cow, a bull does not look both ways before crossing the road.

Gene Letourneau, outdoors columnist for the Portland Press Herald, wrote recently that once you hear the plaintive call of a cow moose in heat, "the strain is seldom forgotten."

"It is something like that of a domestic cow but lasts seconds longer and sounds like a wailing dirge in the low registers of music," he wrote.

The subject of moose lore came up recently when someone recalled the seagoing moose that swam across Casco Bay last year, arriving on our island just in time to enliven the cocktail hour on the clubhouse porch. It nonchalantly strolled ashore and disappeared across Island Avenue and into the woods, apparently searching for a meaningful relationship.

Some of the more exuberant spectators attempted moose calls, some of which sounded more like cows, horses and even chickens. The moose kept its mind focused on its mission and ignored them.

I asked about it last week but, like the whale that came to dinner at Lowell's Cove on Bailey Island three years ago,no one had seen it since.

"Probably just a Summah moose from Away," an islander said.

New license plate stars chickadee, not lobster

The State of Maine license plate on the Peaks Island car we owned (until it died of a rust infection awhile back) had a resplendent red lobster on it. I wish I'd saved it. The plate's probably worth more than the car ever was, now that the lobster has replaced by - get this - a chickadee!

> *"When this island contained a penal colony, the prisoners rioted over their unrelieved diet of lobster."*

Somehow it doesn't seem very Maine-ish, even perched on its pine tassel and cone. When you think of Mainers, the word "cute" rarely pops into your head.

Also, it's the official bird of Massachusetts, the state Mainers love to hate.

But truth to tell, I've never been entirely happy driving around advertising a sea crustacean (genus Homarus). With their menacing pincers and evil little compound eyes, they're ugly little beasts.

Also, the license plate lobster is clearly deceased because he (or she?) has a scarlet complexion. As any lobster coroner will tell you, the redness indicates foul play of the very worst kind - it means the victim has been boiled alive.

Sometimes when visitors come to dinner we do the deed ourselves. We order them live from lobsterman Bob Spears.

He cuffs them with stout rubber bands. We take them home, toss them in the pot and scald them to death, callously sipping gin and tonics and ignoring the screams.

Just kidding. Actually, they love it, as you would if you'd spent a lifetime deep down in 45-degree Maine waters.

A weird historical sidelight on this story is that back in the days when this island contained a penal colony of sorts, the prisoners rioted over their unrelieved diet of lobster.

Callous guards told them to eat their crustaceans and shut up.

Until very recently some of their descendants may have been doing time in state prison making, of all things, lobster license plates! Now they're making chickadee plates. Go figure. Is there a subtle irony there someplace?

To sum up, put me down as a willing chickadee booster.

The Parus atricapilli are charming little fellows and girls. They remain monogamous for years. The female builds the nest and does all the eggsitting. The guy brings her food to regurgitate into the kids.

The chickadees out on the Mendon Ponds Nature Trail will take seeds right out of your hand and chirp a thank you. Mainers are more taciturn.

If I'd been consulted, I'd have suggested the seagull. But guess what: It's the official state bird of landlocked Utah! I looked it up.

October the best month Down East

PEAKS ISLAND, Maine — October is the best month up here Down East, we've decided.

The fall colors are stunning, the air is crystal clear and the stars are brilliant. But there is more to it than that:

The Summah People like us are back in Away. There is room to park Down Front and the landscaping competition is over.

Telephone service is not interrupted by visiting cruise ships.

(This summer one anchored in front of the microwave transmitter in Portland. Service to the island was restored as the tide changed, lowering the ship 10 feet and swinging it 180 degrees.)

The natives are in a good mood because the population is down to three digits and they have their island back.

Last week the islanders gave us wary looks, but when we explained that we were leaving next week they brightened up and told us to "have a good wintah."

Of course there is a downside. The quality of stuff at the island "transfer station" (formerly known as "the dump") falls off sharply. Some days the selection is so poor it's hardly worth the trip.

This visit was especially rewarding because I ended my unbroken string of repair and maintenance disasters by cleverly forgetting to bring my tool box.

So instead of drilling a hole to install a patio door lock and shattering the glass as I did in June, costing me $400, I called a carpenter. He charged only $20, a saving of $380.

The plumber still enjoys telling his friends about the time I broke the septic tank pipe with a pickaxe while planting a shrub.

One of the best ways to ingratiate one's self with these taciturn Maine building trades craftsmen, I've found, is to keep them supplied with personalized "crazy mainlander" stories.

> *"This is the guy who broke the septic tank with a pick axe while planting a shrub."*

This year was our first season without a winter tenant and I was tempted to risk starring in another island comedy by single-handedly attempting that routine October ritual, "shutting off the water."

Veteran cottagers assured me "you can't go wrong."

"You underestimate me," I told them.

Instead, I called plumber Donny Smith's answering machine.

"This is the guy who broke the septic tank pipe with the pickaxe. Tell Donny I was thinking of arranging to have the pipes freeze, but I changed my mind," I told it.

Young deer bids us farewell

PEAKS ISLAND, Maine — We saw a lone deer, a young doe, moving through the vegetation in the front yard the other day.

She looked unperturbed, which seemed remarkable, considering that nearly all of her family and friends were victims of the recent municipal massacre. The islanders hired a professional sharpshooter to do the deed.

I'm told he set up baiting stations on the browsing routes. When the deer came to feed, he picked them off with a rifle equipped with a silencer.

Where once there were over 250 deer on this tiny island, now there are around 20.

The parade through our yard used to be continuous. The dog and I enjoyed the spectacle. Midas would practice his "point," standing motionless and silent, left paw raised, tail rigid, nose pulsating.

The gardener in the family would clap her hands and shout at them. They'd calmly look up and stare at her, then resume dining.

"There once were over 250 deer on this tiny island; now there are only around 20."

This time she let the doe alone, maybe because the frost had already put an end to the garden, but perhaps it was out of sympathy and respect for the dead.

I was careful not to voice these musings, remembering the scorn heaped upon me the time I wrote that safety manual column for the deer, advising them on avoiding the dreaded "orange pelts" (hunters). Angry letter writers called me a "@#$%&&* Bambi-ass," which I thought was pretty colorful, oath-wise.

(I could imagine myself laughing derisively and flashing my white stub of a tail at them as I bounded away through the woods.)

When we arrived on the island it was sunny and warm and the sea was as flat and still as Mendon Ponds, and we wondered why we hadn't moved up here in these beautiful surroundings.

When we left on Tuesday, black menacing clouds were moving in, a bitter wind brought horizontal sleet and we stopped wondering.

It was time to pack up and flee, leaving the cottage to Rick, a hardier, grizzled soul with an insulated beard who pays his rent in carpentry and maintenance. He promised to keep an eye on the deer and the Atlantic for us until we return in the spring.

Missing those surf sounds

ROCHESTER, New York — What's that sound that suddenly stopped, causing us to awaken at 3 a.m. and sit up in bed? Ah yes, it's the absence of the Atlantic Ocean.

Our island retreat in Maine is like being back in the womb, bobbing contentedly in Mom's abdominal fluid as it sloshes and gurgles.

You can hear her breathing, digesting her food, humming to herself and talking to someone, but you can just lie there and float. You are aware of another world out there, close by but you don't have to go there. Not yet.

Then suddenly someone turns off the surf and substitutes the sound of a truck downshifting on I-490 and a jet overhead lowering its flaps for the final approach.

Soon the alarm will go off and you'll be out there in the traffic yourself, listening to a voice on the car radio inventorying the day's disasters, large and small.

> *"What's that sound that suddenly stopped? Ah yes, it's the absence of the Atlantic Ocean."*

When we left Peaks Island it was shrouded in fog so thick you could barely see your feet. In the distance we could hear the moaning fog horns.

We've come to know them by sound - Spring Point Light, Portland Head Light, Ram Island Light the Casco Bay Lines ferry, the basso profundo of the Scotia Prince headed to Nova Scotia.

The offshore bell buoys out front marking the Hussey Sound entrance toll in a varying sequence as they slowly rock in the ocean swells. Last year they'd sound the opening notes of My Old Kentucky Home ("The sun shines bright on...").

This year the Coast Guard buoy tender has been at work. Someone who can't carry a tune has been tinkering with the bells and whistles.

Our place sits right on the brink of the Atlantic. Out front is a finger of rock ledge extending into the sea. When the surf is up, the waves hit the ledge and the vibration shakes the whole cottage. You can feel it in your abdomen.

When you combine all these hi-fi sensations, audio and visual (blinking red and green buoy lights, the Halfway Rock beacon on the horizon, the lights of Cliff Island) you're living in a world of vivid special effects.

Turn them off suddenly and substitute the news of new global disasters, violence and mindless TV froth and you've got serious sensory deprivation.

I could go on with this but I'm already deep into withdrawal and there's a Seinfeld rerun coming on the tube even as we speak.

Chapter Eight

War & Warriors

"Taps": The tune that says it all

I n this made-up conversation, someone asks the aging veteran if he has anything planned for Veterans Day this year.

"When's that?"

"Tuesday."

"Oh, right. Used to be Armistice Day. World War I. Ran out of veterans of that war. Now they're running out of mine. Only 6.7 million of us left. Read it somewhere. Average age 77, same as me."

"No plans then?"

"Getting up in the morning should do it. If that works out, I'll probably go to the office. Only bureaucrats get the day off."

"No parade for you?"

"Never parade. Don't believe in it. Did some parading in the Army. Didn't enjoy it. Made us do it to keep us from going to town, drinking beer, chasing girls, having a good time."

"Don't you have any pride in having served your country?"

"Didn't say that. Said I didn't parade. Not an appropriate activity for a civilian. When I was a soldier, all I thought about was becoming a civilian. Couldn't wait. Parades meant inspections. Shining shoes. Cleaning rifles. Scrubbing barracks. Standing at attention, staring straight ahead, sweat running down your neck, blowing flies out of your nostrils. All that."

"Doesn't the sight of the flag passing by bring a lump to your throat?"

"Didn't say it didn't. What is this, some kind of patriotism test? What war were you in, sonny boy?"

"No offense, old timer."

"Don't call me that, young timer."

"You called me sonny boy."

"Too-shay. Go ahead. Ask me some more stupid questions."

"Don't you find martial music stirring?"

"Of course. But it makes the heart beat faster. Not looking to squander heartbeats. Might run out of them. Hard to replace."

"Stars and Stripes Forever. There's a stirring march."

"Over hill, over dale . . .hit the dusty trail." May hum a few bars of that raking leaves after work."

Understand there aren't any parades in town today anyway, so you're off the hook, old timer."

"Off we go into the wild blue yonder."

"Pack up your troubles in your old kit bag. That's World War I.

"Long long trail a-winding."

"I know. But there's only one tune that says all there is to say about the war - any war - sonny boy."

"What's that, old timer?"

"Taps."

127

Draft money and capital as well as soldiers

While we're debating the role of women and gays in the military, let's talk for a moment about another oppressed minority that is unfairly denied the privilege of serving in combat: the millionaires.

Just the other day I was reading a proposal that in time of war they should be drafted, regardless of age or physical condition, along with, get this, their money.

You won't believe who came up with that creative idea: Warren G. Harding!

I hear you. You're exclaiming: Warren G. Harding, the long-gone, poker-playing, philandering ex-newspaperman and Republican president best known for the his thieving cronies and the Teapot Dome oil-leasing scandal of the 1920s?

Yep, that's the one.

Harding's proposal attracted the attention of Will Rogers, the legendary cowboy philosopher and stand-up humorist. According to Will's autobiography, Harding said that in case of war, "capital would be drafted, the same as men."

Will thought the idea was great, serious or not:

"Say, you take a boy's life, don't you? You send him to war and the part of that life you don't lose, you let him come back with it. Perhaps you may use all of it. Well, that's the way to do with wealth. Take all he has, give him a bare living the same as you do the soldier."

Pay everyone the same wage the soldier gets, Will argued. In those days it was $1.25 a day.

"Pay everyone the same wage the soldier gets, Will Rogers argued. Then it was $1.25 a day."

"The government should own everything we have, use what it needs to conduct the whole expenses of the war, and give back what is left, if there is any, same as you give back to the boy what he has left."

"Every man, woman and child, from Henry Ford to John D. (Rockefeller) down, get their dollar and a quarter a day, same as the soldier. The only way a man could profiteer in a war like that would be to raise more children."

The idea has a lot of appeal. It reminds me of the Ross Perot rule: first commit the nation, then commit the troops. If you can't do one, don't do the other.

It certainly would make the conduct of war more difficult. It would take a monumentally popular war to persuade us to make a huge personal monetary sacrifice. Giving up someone else's life for one's country is one thing. Willingly taking a financial hit is another. I can't see it ever happening.

Neither could Will:

"It will never get anywhere," he predicted. "The rich will say it ain't practical, and the poor will never get a chance to find out if it is or not.

U.S. Army has sandwich superiority

I take back everything I said about the Pentagon thinkers. All these years I've been bad-mouthing them for not focusing on useful ground warfare ordnance instead of exotic weaponry like smart bombs.

I urged them to develop an instant foxhole to replace those sandbox shovels called "entrenching tools."

Just pull the pin, cover your ears and blow yourself a hole to crawl into. If I'd had one of those in 1944, I wouldn't have had to rely on luck and prayers to get through a working day.

But they chose to develop a replacement for the mule instead and came up with the jeep.

Don't get me wrong, it was a welcome tool, but pedestrian soldiers still had to spend much of their time digging holes.

But just yesterday I read that the Army has made a startling breakthrough that puts our forces far ahead of whatever enemy we might face.

> *"The Army is... developing a peanut butter and jelly sandwich... that will remain edible for three years."*

It is on the threshold of developing a peanut butter and jelly (PB&J) sandwich that soldiers can carry in their pockets. It will remain edible for three years!

Imagine! Three years! A sandwich that will outlast most modern wars!

Nothing to heat up. No mess kit or utensils. Just unwrap and stuff in your face! With practice, you can even chew and dig a hole at the same time!

The Army also came up with preservative formulae that will keep pepperoni and barbecue chicken sandwiches good for three years in the 80 degree heat, six months at 100 degrees.

"The trick was to get rid of the 6,000 mile extension cord to the freezer," joked Jerry Dasch, director of the Defense Department feeding program facility.

The PG&J delicacy still needs work to stabilize the peanut butter and better retain the stick-to-the-roof-or-your-mouth consistency.

Meanwhile, the troops in Afghanistan are enjoying high calorie MREs (Meals Ready to Eat) such as pasta primavera, beef stew and seafood jambalaya which cannot be eaten on the run. The diner has to add water to plastic heating pouches.

The new three-year sandwiches, which generate only 325 calories, are designed just to supplement 1,300 calorie MREs.

But to make the dining experience truly memorable, I still think the Instant Foxhole would add to the ambience, especially when people are shooting at you.

Does "don't ask, don't tell" apply to cowardice?

A lot of us veterans of various wars think the new policy of "don't ask, don't tell" makes good sense.

That's because we ourselves functioned smoothly under the same principle. Nobody asked us whether we were cowards and we didn't tell. We just kept our mouths shut and pretty soon the war was over and we went home.

The heroes kept their orientation quiet too. If they refrained from heroic behavior, and never openly acknowledged their preference for bravery, none of us bothered them.

So there you go. No problem.

We refrained from open cowardly behavior. When the shooting started, we ducked but did not run away. It was the same with the guys whose orientation was heroic. They ducked too. They kept quiet about their preference and nobody asked.

We did not go around telling our officers that in the event of enemy action we were likely to respond with fear and cowardice. Let the brass hats find it out for themselves when the time came, we reasoned. Maybe it would never come up.

In our case it did come up. Our outfit was shot at many times. But we were so afraid of what the others would think we simulated shooting back. We were too cowardly to risk running away.

Nobody knew who in the outfit was a hero or a coward.

Don't ask don't tell. Sure, we suspected some of the guys, of heroism, but they kept quiet about it for fear of ridicule.

Nobody wanted to be around a certifiable hero. A hero might do something stupid, like drawing fire. We hated it when anyone drew fire. So it was best to give heroes a wide berth when they were acting out their heroism.

Our objective was to walk through the entire war without ever drawing fire. ("Drawing fire is what they call "getting shot at." They're the same thing.)

I never had much to do with heroes. We never mixed with them socially. It was sort of like guys who were always volunteering for something. We tolerated them, even indulged them.

Sometimes we would kid compulsive volunteers about their affinity for sergeants, but there was nothing malicious about it. "Sergeant's pet," we might call them. But hey, if they liked sergeants, what the hell. Just don't try to convert us, we'd tell them.

All of us spent most of our military careers lurking in one kind of closet or another.

Even if I were a woman in the military, I think I'd keep it quiet. Why stick your neck out?

Old foes share a sandwich

When you're sitting across from a guy who once, given the right circumstances, was supposed to shoot you, there is a fleeting moment when you contemplate what might have been.

But then, it passes.

Alex Martens, former German paratrooper, bit into his Reuben sandwich and pointed to the map of Germany he had brought to lunch.

We figured out that we were probably out of range at the time and not feeling terribly hostile anyway. Just anxious.

That would be May 1945. He was trudging down a highway near Rosenheim south of Munich, and I was doing the same outside Tegernsee, not far away.

"We were looking for someone to surrender to. We had kept our weapons because of the SS," he said. (The SS were diehard fanatics who would have shot them as traitors.)

"The Americans just ignored us. Finally someone stopped and told us to throw away our guns and walk on until we got to a temporary PW collecting depot in Rosenheim."

That was the end of the war for him. I had to wait another day.

"I remember passing lines of you guys. We just waved you along to the rear and kept on going," I recalled.

Luckily I missed Alex when he was armed and dangerous. He was a member of the elite 2nd Landing Division of paratroop and glider units. He was wounded jumping in the invasion of Crete in the Mediterranean.

Later he was wounded again by French underground fighters and sent to a military hospital in Strasbourg near where my division later was in action. By then, he had been transferred to a communications unit.

Now here he was sitting across from me, leafing through my 36th Infantry Division history, looking not only harmless but friendly. What a difference a mere 55 years makes!

During that time he had come to America and now was a retired Bausch & Lomb vice president for research.

Today he is executive director of the Center for Technology Commercialization Inc., which scouts industries interested in applications of NASA research.

We both had "volunteered" in 1941, knowing that we were about to be drafted.

It was Alex's idea to get together. He'd read my references to shared times and places.

For old time's sake, I had planned to use a German phrase from my training manual that I remembered but never got to use.

"Hande hoch!" (Hands up!) I was going to bark at him.

Maybe next time, if he doesn't get the drop on me first.

Computer screws up Army skirmish

The new, redesigned Year 2000 Army division will be an "information age fighting force," more agile than today's forces and "better able to handle a multi-front 21st Century battlefield," the Pentagon says.

That's the good news.

The bad news is this: The redesign will 'incorporate the very latest in sophisticated, modern digital computer technology.'

Uh-oh!

Here's my 21st Century Battlefield Scenario:

Sarge! My computer is flashing a "Tank Sighting!"

Activate all countermeasure programs! Relay coordinates to all battalion weapons! Armor-piercing ammo! Fire when ready! Prepare flanking maneuver to the right flank and activate counter-attack defense program. Message headquarters via e-mail!

It says 'Fatal Error!' It says it's shutting down!

Push Escape button!

I did! Now it's saying "Operating System Not Found!" Uh-oh, now the mouse is frozen!

Goddam mice! Push Alt-Control-Delete.

Nothing! No, wait! It's saying 'Push Any Key to Continue!' I'm pushing. Nothing! No, wait! It says it's doing a diagnostic scan!.

Click on Help button!

Gimme a chance, sarge. This may be a digital army but I've only got five digits on each hand, you know.

What's that on the screen?

Now it says 'press any key to continue.'

They're shooting at us! Let's get the hell out of here!

Wait! Now it says the diagnostic scan found nothing wrong. "Restore from backup and restart."

Deploy quick restore CD!

It says my files will be lost!

Call tech services 800 number at headquarters.

Got it.

I'm getting elevator music — 20th Century oldies. What now?

It says for Windows250 software problems, press 1 now, for printer problems, press 2, for . .

FORGET IT! Take a message to the general. Tell him I've got a plan to win this stupid war.

To: Supreme Commander, headquarters, New Improved Agile Allied Forces.

From: Lt. Dougherty.

Subject: Victory Plan.

Message Text: Recruit a traitor to steal this damn system and leak it to an enemy spy ASAP.

A day for Bush to consider Iraq casualties

When I came to work this morning, the Civic Center Garage behind our paragraph factory was nearly empty.
Why?

Because it was Veterans Day and the courthouse was closed. So were most of the government offices and all schools throughout the area.

Which category of all the government workers who did NOT have the day off do you suppose was easily the largest?

You guessed it, members of our armed forces.

They could become the veterans of future wars, one of which may be imminent.

It's supposed to be their remembrance day too (that's what Canada calls it), but like police officers, firemen, ambulance drivers and hospital employees, they have to work.

For most of us, there is not even a requirement that we take time out of our extended weekend to give a moment's thought to the soldiers, sailors, airmen and Marines in Afghanistan, Korea, and on their way to the Mideast.

> *"I have to think that President Bush will take a moment today to reflect on the costs of wars..."*

It seems to me that when it was called Armistice Day from 1938 to 1954 it was a more solemn occasion, and we actually did observe a moment of silence on 11th hour of the 11th day of the 11th month marking the end of World War I.

All traffic was supposed to stop and church bells ring as "Taps" was broadcast from Arlington Cemetery at the 11th hour and we were supposed to honor the World War I dead (53,402).

Many of us actually did.

Today, for most of us, it is just another welcome long weekend.

As World War I receded in memory and was displaced by World War II with its 291,557 battle deaths, the name was changed to honor the 42.3 million veterans of all wars since the Revolution (including 1 million Confederates and 2.2 million Yanks in the Civil War).

(Total battle deaths in all wars: 650,954.)

As this was being written, the United Nations Security Council had just given Iraq an ultimatum to disarm and America is massing its devastating firepower in and around the Gulf.

I have to think that President Bush will take a moment today to reflect on the costs of wars — not only our own casualties, but those of the enemy and helpless civilians.

Eleven o'clock this morning would be a good time.

Contradictory name for local War Memorial

When I first heard they were going to change the name of the Community War Memorial to the Blue Cross Arena, I was incensed. Now I'm just a little ticked off.

What the hell, it's a metaphor for the times, I told myself.

I think what wised me up was an imaginary conversation I had with some war dead I once knew.

There were 3,974 official war dead in my World War II outfit, the 36th Infantry Division not including 4,317 missing and presumed dead. (There were 15,000 in a division in those days.)

In my fantasy, they are hunkered down around their graves in one of those vast military cemeteries in France, smoking and swapping stories, when I walk up.

They look me over and one of them says: "What outfit?"

I tell him 131st Field Artillery, but quickly add that I spent my time with the 141st Infantry.

I ask him where he got hit.

"The Vosges (mountains) outside Hagenau. Mortar fire."

"I was there. Bad, wasn't it?"

"It wasn't one of my better days."

"You don't sound bitter."

"You get over things. Nobody here has what you'd call a success story, you know. Sick of talking about it. So what's it like back home? They still remember us?"

"On Memorial Day for you guys. Veterans Day for us live ones."

"Memorial Day. What kind of memorial you got in your town?"

"An arena. Big one. For sports, concerts, conventions. They used to call it the Community War Memorial but now it's the Blue Cross Arena."

"Sounds appropriate, a cross. But why Blue?"

"It's an insurance company. Blue Cross. They sold the naming rights to them."

"Hey, fellows, hear this: They named our memorial after an effing insurance company!"

"Health insurance, actually."

"HEALTH insurance! Now isn't that appropriate! Hey, guys! Health insurance! A little late for us, isn't it?"

"It IS sort of ironic. Shameful, I'd call it."

"Hey, forget it. It's just business. Remember the slogan from our day: Lucky Strike Green Has Gone to War? That was pretty stupid too."

"I'm surprised you're taking this so well."

"It's no big deal. There are no big deals here. It's hilarious."

When I turned to go, one of them shouted: "Have a nice Health Insurance Day!"

That really cracked them up.

Laptops on horseback in Afghanistan

Some of my fellow World War II forward artillery observers would be fascinated to learn that some of our special operations target spotters in Afghanistan do what we used to do — only on horseback and with far-out high-tech equipment.

According to a piece in the *New York Times* yesterday, forward spotters use binoculars equipped with laser rangefinders.

They can spot enemy targets miles away, read the range and compass bearing, and electronically plot the target coordinates by adding the distance from their own location (established by global positioning system satellite).

> *"As we darted ahead from hole to hole, we looked like frantic commuters trying to catch the last train."*

Then the spotters fire off the data using their laptop computers or satellite phones and wait for the planes to arrive.

Mission accomplished, they mount up and gallop off with their Northern Alliance tribesmen, looking for more action.

In our war we had jeeps, but much of the time we were pedestrians. Our radio operators carried 40-pound radios designed like suitcases. We lowly second lieutenants lugged the battery pack, which was equally heavy and awkward.

As we darted ahead from hole to hole, trying to keep up with the infantrymen, we looked like frantic commuters running to catch the last train.

A horse might have been nice, if he'd fit in the hole with you. (Imagine digging a foxhole for a horse!)

When an infantry platoon got in trouble and wanted help, we'd consult our air photo or map and radio rough coordinates to the fire direction center.

When the first smoke shells whistled overhead one at a time, we'd "bracket" the target, then call for "fire for effect."

If all went well, we'd mount our jeep and go chasing (or fleeing) the action.

People don't believe me when I tell them we had horse-drawn artillery (French 75s) when I was a private at Fort Sill, Okla., in 1941. We also had mule pack howitzers!

Horses wouldn't take orders from me, but they did let me shovel out their stalls. (We spread the stuff on the dusty Afghanistan-like grounds in a futile effort to make grass grow.)

Meanwhile, the infantrymen in basic training at installations like Fort Benning, Georgia, were armed with brooms as they fought wooden vehicles with "tank" painted on their sides.

We actually won that war!

Maybe it was because we didn't have laptop computers.

How Germans picked generals

At the start of this century in 1900 the German army is said to have divided its officer corps into four categories to determine which should be put on the fast track to promotion to general.

The four categories were:

1. The intellectually dull and physically lazy.
2. The intellectually dull and physically energetic.
3. The intellectually bright and physically energetic.
4. The intellectually bright and physically lazy.

Category 1 officers were obviously losers on both counts.

Category 2s were dangerous. With subpar intellects they could come up with bad ideas and energetically make them happen.

Category 3s with their brains and energy would seem to be the ideal material for promotion to general.

But no. They were made staff officers because they had the tools to undertake difficult tasks and see them through.

Category 4 officers were the winners. They were put on the fast track to general because they were smart enough to figure out what ought to be done, but lazy enough to seek out the easiest, simplest way.

I'll leave it to the historians to insert the great American generals into their proper categories.

> *"I'll leave it to historians to insert the great American generals into their proper categories."*

Where, for example, would they put Eisenhower, said to be intellectually so-so and moderately energetic, compared to high-energy Doug MacArthur, brightest cadet in his West Point class?

My comrades in the 36th Infantry Division would agree that intellectually bright and physically energetic Gen. Mark Clark should have been a permanent staff officer. That would have kept him from ordering the 36th into the Rapido River slaughterhouse in Italy. (After the war, the outraged survivors almost persuaded Congress to cashier him.)

Then consider the bright energetic category 3 staff officers who were unaware the hedgerows of Normandy were death traps that could have aborted D-Day.

The Germans surely would have made me a category 4 - physically lazy but intellectually smart enough to know I should never have made second lieutenant, much less general.

It helps to keep in mind that, using this ingenious system, the Germans picked the generals who masterminded monumental defeats in two World Wars.

So, as they say in the German High Command:

"Rechne es aus!" (Go figure.)

"Crazy Morgan" remembered

Today may be Veterans Day, but to many of my generation it will always be Armistice Day - the 11th hour of the 11th day of the 11th month when World War I ended 80 years ago. When I think of that war, I think of "Crazy" Morgan, the only man in our town who tried to tell us the truth about that barbaric, insane conflict. Most of the men who were in it wouldn't talk about it, knowing that it was impossible to explain to anyone who wasn't there.

But "Crazy" Morgan "talked" about it incessantly babbling and ranting in unintelligible gibberish. We kids, sadistic little monsters, would taunt him into chasing us.

Seeing this, the other veterans were protective. "Shell shock," they'd say. "Leave him alone!"

Years later when I read Barbara Tuchman's *Guns of August*, the works of Wilford Owen, Robert Graves and Siegfried Sassoon and the recent 1990s novels of Pat Barker, I understood what Pvt. Morgan had been trying to tell us. World War I was a horrendous war crime committed by generals and statesmen.

> *"World War I was a horrendous war crime committed by generals and statesmen."*

During the trench war, thousands of men attacked and counter attacked back and forth over the same ground day after day, month after month. In no-man's-land the incessant artillery barrages churned up mud and human body parts. In 1915 at the battle of Ypres, the Germans first used deadly chlorine gas on the British and Canadian troops killing them in their trenches and bunkers.

Fussell calls the British, French and German generals, architects of this madness, "the enemy behind." Nearly an entire generation of British and German young men was wiped out over the four years of fighting.

President Wilson called it the "war to end all wars."

When it was over 8.3 million soldiers were dead, 100,000 of them Americans. (The U.S. came into the war in its final stages in 1917.)

Keep in mind that the armistice didn't end the war. It just recessed it while the victors extracted vengeance and planted the seeds for the next one.

Famous military analyst recalls some historic exit strategies

"What's all this about Clinton's not having an 'Exit Strategy?' " my wife wanted to know.

"An exit strategy is an essential component in any war," I replied in characteristically pompous fashion. "Some military historians think it is more important than an entrance strategy, but my feeling is that you can't have one without the other."

"But did they have exit strategies in other wars? Funny I don't recall hearing the term before."

"Obviously you haven't been paying close attention," I said. "There have been exit strategies since the Revolutionary War."

Then I went on to explain how during the drafting of the Declaration of Independence Ben Franklin turned to Thomas Jefferson and said: "This isn't bad for a first draft, Tom, but haven't you forgotten something?"

"Not that I know of, Ben."

"An exit strategy, you dummy." said Ben gently.

"Oh my god! Hand me that quill," said an embarrassed Jefferson, and the rest is history.

Jefferson penned in the now-famous paragraph that began, "But on the other hand." (It was deleted in committee.)

Later, outside of Lexington, Mass., one patriot said to another: "Before you fire that thing, Seth, do you have an exit strategy?"

"Pull the trigger then run like hell?"

"Sounds good to me. Fire that historic shot heard round the world!"

During the First Continental Congress Patrick Henry was chided for lacking an exit strategy when he impulsively declared "give me liberty or give me death."

Nearly a century later a Confederate artillery commander, about to fire on Fort Sumter was asked about his exit strategy.

"That's up to Bob Lee, I just work here," he replied.

As events unfolded, it turned out that Gen. Lee did indeed have an exit strategy: namely surrender.

"Wait till we get to Appomattox Court House, then you'll know," he announced at a press conference that same day, April 21, 1861.

When Gavrilo Princip, the Bosnian Serb, took aim at Archduke Ferdinand in Sarajevo on July 28, 1914, to start World War I, he scoffed at the idea of an exit strategy, but he was lucky. His side won without one.

Perhaps the most famous example came on Dec. 7, 1941, when Admiral Isoroko Yamamoto shouted: "Damn the exit strategy, furr speed ahead to Purr Harbor!"

The Story of Tegernsee:
A town nearly destroyed at war's end

(This article appeared as a Sunday feature in the Democrat and Chronicle *Oct. 15, 1995, tracing the post-war pilgrimage of Dick and his two sons to Tegernsee, a town in Germany saved from destruction by his artillery unit in the final days of World War II.)*

OBEROTTERBACH, GERMANY — As we drive down the one-lane country road near this tiny village just over the French border. I silently rehearse my opening lines in this oral history episode.

I visualize myself standing on a ridge like the one we see just ahead. I'll gesture grandly at the rolling fields below and describe how our 200-man company lay there, pinned down by machine-gun fire coming from elaborate German fortifications, while the mortars and rockets worked us over.

In March 1945 I was a second lieutenant forward artillery observer assigned that day to C Company, 141st Infantry Regiment of the 36th (Texas) Division. We were trying to dislodge the German defenders along the border.

"We were sure we were going to die," I'd tell my two sons. They'd talked me into making this "How-Pop-Won-the-War" pilgrimage to the old battlefields. Dick Jr., 51, is an airlines systems analyst whose discounts made this journey possible. Steve, the younger son at 47, is a writer for *People* magazine.

Our pilgrimage will take us from this once-bloody battleground to deep into Germany for a reunion with a baron whom I last saw 50 years ago. We'll end up in Tegernsee, a lovely Alpine town I almost destroyed with artillery fire on the last day of the war. Town officials plan to honor me with a formal reception — but I think they have the wrong hero.

Today, we're looking for vestiges of the Siegfried Line or West Wall, the menacing array of interlocking concrete bunkers and pyramid-shaped tank obstacles called "Dragon's Teeth."

The vast fortifications that 50 years ago stretched from the English Channel to the Rhine River seem to have disappeared without a trace. Not a visible fragment remains in this valley.

This place is far too tranquil. There never could have been a war here. It seems impossible that men were terror-stricken and dying here.

Yet this gently rolling terrain has been an invasion route as far back as the days when armies were hordes armed with spears and clubs.

Today we give up and go to nearby Bad Bergzabern and over beer and wurst I show on the map how I finally was able to drop artillery smoke shells to screen our withdrawal. There was no question of trying to breach the line here. It was impregnable. It was stupid to even order us to try.

"We eventually moved over here into the hills, following another unit of the 36th that had broken through," I explain. "Finally, the Germans had to withdraw because (Gen.) Patton was coming behind them and the way was open for us to dash on to the Rhine."

"A likely story," says one of my comedian companions.

Later we run into Anja Stahler, a younger reporter for the Bad Bergzabern bureau of the *Kaiserslautern Rheinpfalz*.

I show her my Dragon's Teeth photo and she flips through a bound file of her stories to a headline *"Neue Kaempfe amalten Westwall"* (New battles in old Westwall). There they are, in a photo under the headline! Dragon's Teeth!

"I can take you there!" she says. and does, dropping her work, intrigued by the idea of an old enemy returning to find the war her parents told her about.

We follow her red sports car back to Oberotterbach. Just outside town, hidden in a wood near a creek, we find about 20 crumbling, lichen-covered specimens.

"What did I tell you?" I say to my sons triumphantly. "There was a war here."

NIEDERBACHEM, GERMANY — We came to this little town near Bonn to meet the real hero of Tegernsee, Baron Hannibal von Luettichau.

I had last seen him on May 3, 1945. Then a major, he had come forward with the town burgermeister (mayor) and an interpreter under a white flag while I was adjusting artillery fire on enemy positions above the town. His brave action saved Tegernsee from destruction and spared me a lifetime of certain regret and probable guilt.

Fifty years later, my sons and I pull into the driveway of the baron's estate on a walnut tree plantation high above town. He strides forward to greet us.

He ushers us inside to meet the baroness and to tour Haus Rodderberghof. It looks palatial to us — until we see a picture of Baerenstein, the family castle near Dresden that was seized by the East German Communist government during the Cold War.

After the tour, the five of us settle down and begin a hilarious four-hour conversation in fractured German and English.

The Baron will not be going to Tegernsee with us for the reception with the five valley burgermeisters. He must be with the baroness, who has serious surgery scheduled for the next day. This means I'll be the sole guest of honor, an imposter compared to the real hero of that fateful day.

I tell the baron that until recently I had credited the long-dead Tegernsee burgermeister, Karl Mueller, with saving the town from destruction. The baron sets me straight.

"Mueller!" he shouts, spitting out the name contemptuously. "I say to Mueller, 'You *moos* go with me to the Amis (Americans). ' He say, 'I wish not.' I say, 'You *MOOS* go.' Mueller was a Nazi. He say to me, 'The werewolfs will shoot me! Ai-ai-eeeeee!'

Rumor had it that "werewolfs" — hard-core Nazi terrorists — would wreak vengeance on the faint-hearted and defiant who failed to heed Hitler's April 12, 1945, order to fight to the last.

One thing that has puzzled me is how von Luettichau was able to persuade the SS to withdraw and let us enter the town unmolested. Now that we have seen him in person, it becomes clear.

"Were you in uniform when you talked to the SS?" I asked.

"Ja. In uniform. Like this." He hands us a photo from the war. It shows his steely, commanding gaze, resplendent uniform and Iron Cross for heroism. Obviously a man not used to being contradicted.

When he approached our lines, he also wore a highly visible white bandage beneath his dress cap. He had come to Tegernsee to have delicate brain surgery to remove the grenade fragment that left him with a scar so prominent today. He was still a recuperating hospital patient when we attacked the town. "I tell the SS commandant, I say, 'You *moos* not stay here. Go, go into the mountains back here, away from the town. It is better for you there,' " the baron says.

It was a con job, but the commandant bought it and agreed to withdraw. I suspect he was relieved to have a high-ranking officer, especially one named Hannibal (after the great Carthaginian general), suggest a tactical excuse for wriggling out of an impossible situation.

Now the baron and his party had to convince the Americans that the way was clear into town — and that a full-scale attack, starting with an artillery barrage, against a town full of wounded men was not only unnecessary but wrong.

Capt. Virgil "Pete" Pederson, whose A Company, 141st Infantry, had been under attack, was not easy to convince. Pete was angry at the thought of risking his men on what turned out to be the last day of the war for us. The Austrian border was just down the road.

"Pederson!" shouts the baron when I ask him about all this. "I remember Pederson. And you. You were there, too! I remember."

I am happy to accept his version, although I recall being a silent bystander some yards away.

The baron refreshes my memory on a key point: Pete was hesitant to take von Luettichau's word that the SS had indeed withdrawn. An A Company patrol sent out earlier in the evening had not come back.

"So I say to Pederson, 'I go with you,' " the baron recalls.

He led our small task force into town, a heroic act that would have bordered on the foolhardy if he had been wrong about the SS withdrawal.

The baron tells us he was impetuous in those days. His military career had suffered because of his outspoken criticism of the conduct of the war. He was imprisoned by the Nazis at one point, but was released through the intercession of high-ranking friends.

Later this evening, the baron's sons, Bernard and Hubertus, arrive for dinner.

Both of the baron's sons speak excellent English, but the four of us have talked ourselves to exhaustion. We say our "auf wiedersehens" and head for the hotel.

The next day we drive to Munich, then on to Tegernsee. I feel sheepish about being honored by the town while the real hero will be up here, pacing the hospital corridors, waiting for word about the baroness.

But there's no turning back now.

TEGERNSEE, GERMANY — Fifty years ago we came down the east shore road below the Hotel Bayern, a file of some 200 nervous infantrymen, pursuing remnants of the defeated German army, knowing the war was virtually over.

Getting killed at this stage would have been cruel after all the division had been through. (The 36th lost more than 4,000 men, killed in action, mostly in Italy)

We were filled with anger. Two days earlier we had come upon a concentration camp near Landsberg that was still smoking and piled high with bodies. Even today, the memory sears. We did not view Germans as people that day.

At the edge of Tegernsee we came under attack from high-velocity 88mm guns from the south and west.

Today we stand on the balcony of the Hotel Bayern high above the lake, snow-capped Alps in the distance.

We are having our pictures taken with the mayors of Tegernsee and four other lakeside towns.

With us on the balcony is Markus Wrba, a young Tegernsee attorney who has written an illuminating history of *Kriegsende,* the final days of the war in these mountains as seen from the German perspective.

We had a perfect right to be nervous that day 50 years ago, Wrba says. There was a huge railway gun shooting at us from Rottach-Egern at the foot of the lake.

"Railway gun?" I ask, surprised. A railway gun is a serious artillery piece, a long-barreled monster of battleship proportions.

"It's obscene to think of having a war in a place like this," says my son Steve.

"Exactly so," says one of the host burgermeisters at my side.

The highlight of this day for me occurs when we go inside and I recite my speech in German and everyone understands me or skillfully fakes it. (The text is printed the next day in the *Tegernsee Zeitung* newspaper).

Back out on the balcony, I try to recall, without success, where my last artillery shells of the war landed out there in the vast, magnificent panorama before us.

"I think some of them must have landed there," I say, pointing to a ridge to our south. "Or maybe there (by Rottach) and most certainly there (by Bad Wiessee)."

It is easy to be lighthearted about these things 50 years after they took place, but I often shudder at what might have been. The next command, had the baron not successfully interceded, would have been "fire for effect" and Tegernsee could have been reduced to rubble.

As I said in my speech, it would have been painful to walk through town the next morning and view the results, knowing I'd given that command.

The baron spared me that, I told them.

"Vielen danke (many thanks)," I told him as we parted earlier in Niederbachem.

"Bitte schoen (you're welcome)," he replied, bringing his heels reflexively together and giving my arm a painful squeeze.

Will we two ever *wiedersehen* each other?

It took us 50 years to find each other. Doing it again at our ages seems like pushing our luck, but you never know.

Chapter Nine

9/11 and Thereafter

Flying the flag with pride

I t's nice to be able to fly the flag again without being mistaken for a mossback conservative.

We've got two flags at our house. One is a little one my wife bought two weeks after the terrorist attack when there was a run on large flags.

The other is a large cardboard replica taped to the picture window.

If some of my Republican friends (who are many, believe it or not) had passed by the house a month ago, they'd have stopped dead in their tracks and gasped: "Good grief! The Doughertys have seen the light at last!"

Now they wouldn't give it a second thought. Even we knee-jerk liberals can hoist the banner of liberty without drawing a crowd.

It's a nice feeling.

I don't mean to trivialize the Sept. 11 tragedy, but it has been hard to shake off the lingering, sickening sense of unease — call it depression — that hangs over the nation.

We can use a brightener, however faint.

Who knows how long this will last?

I suppose it will fade with time and one day campus radicals can exercise their constitutional right to burn the flag again and be attacked by infuriated hardhat patriots.

Then we'll know we're back to normal and I'll be able to criticize my president with impunity or whatever carping weapons I have at hand.

But now I only regret that I am no longer a soldier and entitled to salute the flag. I always regarded saluting the flag, as opposed to officers, as one of the rewarding perks of military service.

Placing a civilian hand over the heart just doesn't cut it. It smacks of the "you got me" gesture we used in playground warfare games.

It has been hard to make out a silver lining these days.

My son, who has been writing a book proposal, tells me he has 60 pages in his home computer which is buried under six inches of concrete dust from the collapsed South Tower of the World Trade Center.

After a fruitless search for his tax rebate check yesterday he came home to a friend's house totally discouraged.

"Then guess what, in the mailbox I found a check from FEMA (the Federal Emergency Management Agency) for $2,036 to pay for cleanup expenses!"

"As they say in oft-overcast Rochester, the skies are brightening," he e-mailed.

Could it be that silver lining people talk about?

145

How to define "proportionate response"

Forgive me for hanging back like this, but I'm not quite ready to follow the lead of deep thinkers who are urging us to face up to the deeper reasons why everyone hates America.

Sure, I know, we're supposed to walk a mile in our enemy's shoes and get over our anger, so we can think straight.

Maybe later. Right now it's too soon. At least for me.

The sickening images of the twin towers burning, the people jumping, the towers collapsing, the crowds running through the smoke are only rarely shown on TV these days.

Yet the images are there in our minds just below the surface. You have to restrain your imagination from filling in the details of the horror or you'll go insane.

> ## "If you don't have nightmares you feel guilty."

But if you don't have nightmares, you feel guilty.

Almost three thousand people! Three thousand innocent people!

Some people are saying that our response to the Sept. 11 attacks should be proportionate, meaning, I suppose, appropriate or in balance.

Otherwise we become as guilty as the terrorists, they say.

I think they're misusing the term proportionate.

To be truly proportionate, or commensurate, our response would not be just to destroy Osama bin Laden and his al-Qaeda terrorist network, it should be to kill only the innocent, purposely, as the terrorists did.

What they really mean is they want a disproportionate response, which would punish only the guilty and spare the innocent.

Perhaps one of these days we hair-splitting slow thinkers will get around to seeing the wisdom of easing Iraqi sanctions, getting out of Saudi Arabia and pressuring Israel to stop building new settlements.

But right now we're too angry. Giving terrorists what they want wouldn't stop them and just doesn't make sense.

Nor does turning to the United Nations or the World Court, as we are with Serbian war criminals, seem appealing now.

Keep in mind that when the bombing of the Taliban started, I urged a Marshall Plan approach and bombing Afghanistan with food. We did that, but not vigorously enough.

That shows that I'm not entirely stupid. Just mad as hell.

I hope I get over it.

Be patient with me.

What does Allah think of Osama bin Laden?

I 've been told that the Quran contains the injunction, 'thou shalt not kill.' Is that true?" I asked the professor.

True, he said.

"The Ten Commandments are not listed, exactly, as in the Bible, but yes, they're all there," said Emil Homerin, UR associate professor of religion and classics.

So how can the Sept. 11 terrorists justify the murder of nearly 7,000 innocent people and call themselves true Muslims? Shouldn't they be suffering the wrath of Allah?

The professor agreed that most Muslims are as appalled and outraged as the rest of us.

"But frankly, I do not know to what extent bin Laden is even a practicing Muslim," he said.

"His supporters call him 'the emir' (prince) and 'the director'; none of these are religious terms. His organization, called al-Qaeda, means 'command central,' a military term."

Years ago I sat in on a lecture series by Prof. Homerin and was surprised to learn that Muslims regard Jesus, Abraham and Moses, as well as Mohammed, as prophets.

Americans, in our rage over the horrors of the attack, should not lose sight of the fact that the Christian religion differs little from Islam. Indeed, the Quran is regarded as a compilation of revelations dictated by the Angel Gabriel to Mohammed, father of Islam.

Islam has been called a religion of peace, social justice and tolerance. The word itself, in Arabic, means peace and submission to Allah (God).

Prof. Homerin feels that right now Americans would do well to cool the war rhetoric.

"What we have here, large as it is, is a murder investigation, and I'm glad we're treating it that way. They have to patiently follow up leads, trace the flow of the money and slowly but surely find the strands that combine to form these organizations and root them out.

"But eventually we must go beyond concerns about security and address the fact that three quarters of the world population is very poor and has few political freedoms and very little chance for change."

He thinks we should start with resolving the Israeli-Palestinian conflict.

"Palestinians have been living in camps for 50 years. These are the breeding grounds. They produce the constant hate and senseless violence that produces individuals who believe there's nothing left to live for, so it's easy for them to die for a cause."

Altogether a grim outlook that cries out for the sort of bold Marshall Plan statesmanship that put Europe back together after World War II.

Allah would like that.

New solidarity with New York City

P EAKS ISLAND, Maine: In the past, when identifying ourselves to islanders as New Yorkers, we'd routinely specify that we were from UPstate, not
"The City."

Things are different now.

Now we say we're from New York, Period, in the hope of being mistaken
for downstaters and sharing their martyrdom.

If pressed, we'll sheepishly admit we're from somewhere up near the
Canadian border.

Isn't that sick?

Not really, I tell myself.

It's harmless, sort of like bragging about landing at Omaha Beach without
explaining that it was postwar 1945 and you were a rear echelon laundryman.

But to be on vacation up here last week seemed like malingering. It was
impossible to "vacate," so we had to come home.

We found ourselves spending the entire time, hour after hour for three
days, watching the unspeakable horror on TV and trying to reach our son Steve
who lives in Battery Park City across from the doomed towers.

We finally heard he was safe. He'd heard the roar of the plane exploding as
it hit the first tower and felt his apartment building shake. He rushed to his
daughter Eva's school on nearby Chambers Street and helped lead her and 12
classmates on foot to an evacuation center.

> *"As I was running toward the school, the second plane slammed into the second tower, right overhead."*

"As I was running toward the school the
second plane come in low, very close, and
slammed into the second tower, almost right
overhead. I could read the numbers on it. I was
terrified. When we got the kids out, one kid
screamed 'shit' and slammed down his back-
pack," he said.

Later, he went back at night to rescue his
daughter's beloved terrier, Audrey, but was
turned back repeatedly at checkpoints because
he'd left without his I.D.

"I was exhausted and went into a shelter to rest around 3 a.m. I met a rabbi
and two social workers who volunteered to get Audrey. I drew them a map and
they climbed up eight floors in the dark. They found Audrey under the bed,
growling at them.

"When I woke up in the shelter, Audrey was in my arms! The rabbi had put
her there."

In the broad panorama of horror, this little story isn't much, but gives you a
hint of the small acts of compassion that pervaded a tough city consumed by
shock and anger.

As we now-unified New Yorkers say, "You got a problem with that?"

148

How many virgins per terrorist?

S ome of us have questions about those terrorists and their imagined "virgin entitlement."

The stories I've read put the figure either at 67 or 72 virgins per terrorist who reaches paradise.

Doesn't that seem excessive to you? One virgin per customer should be enough for anyone, don't you think?

Take this hypothetical example. Say a martyred lady terrorist shows up at entrance to Paradise. Would she be entitled to have 69 or 72 virgin guys at her beck and call?

The common assumption is that all terrorists are, ipso facto, males, when in fact we have all known women who, given the opportunity, would make splendid terrorists. Many of them routinely practice terrorizing their spouses just for fun.

(Although no names come to mind, of course.)

> *"No, for the last time, ladies, I don't want to be rubbed down with jasmine and frankincense!"*

Let's face it, terror is, or certainly should be, an equal opportunity sinful endeavor.

So, let's say our hypothetical lady terrorist makes it through the pearly gates turnstiles. Should she have the right to have her way with all 69-72 of those chaste guys, one after another, discarding each after his chastity is compromised, until her entitlement runs out?

No, no, a thousand times no!

One of the major reasons many of us have not taken up terrorism as a career is that we don't think we could stand having to deal with 67 virgins all at once, especially at our age.

(The other reason, of course, is fear of hellfire and brimstone.)

We don't have the stamina to put up with their constant overtures and having them fawn over us when all we want is a good night's rest.

("No, for the last time, ladies, I don't WANT to be rubbed down with those jasmine and frankincense body oils! And stop strumming those damned lutes!)

Can you imagine the din of all that idle chatter about boys, boys, boys (or conversely, girls, girls, girls)?

For the record, I made a half-hearted effort to check out the documentation and find the accurate virgin entitlement figure.

Our library's copy of the Quran promised "chaste maidens" in paradise to men only (Ch. 55: 70-74) but no numbers were given. Where the 69-72 figure came from is a mystery. My guess is one per person and none per terrorist.

More importantly, there are some truly scary passages about the eternal fate of those unfortunates who overlook the commandments about taking life.

Do-it-yourself profiling

We're going to fly to Dallas by way of Chicago this weekend. I'm not nervous, really, but I do have dreams. Not nightmares, you understand. Actually, they're quite positive and reassuring.

In my favorite dream, I imagine I'm in the gate area at Greater Rochester International waiting to board.

Just to ensure a safe flight, I dream that I decide to check the security arrangements myself one last time before takeoff.

Moments before boarding, I climb up on my seat in the gate area lounge and make the following announcement:

"Give me your attention, fellow passengers of American Flight 1271. We're just about to board our flight now, and for our own safety I'd like put a few questions to those of you who resemble Middle Easterners. I hope you won't be offended.

"Now you, sir, with the beard, swarthy complexion and turban, may I inquire if you've been racially or ethnically profiled by the security personnel?

"Good. Then we may assume that, because of your suspicious appearance, you have been meticulously interrogated, electronically frisked and vetted and your luggage has been x-rayed and sniffed by anthrax-detecting beagles. Is that correct?

"Excellent!

> *"Do we have your word... cross your heart and hope to... er... have a pleasant flight."*

"Then, as a result, we all can feel confident that you have no plans to hijack this plane or cause it to fail to remain aloft at all times except when taking off and landing. Is that assumption also correct?

"Do we have your word as a fellow human being on that?

"Cross your heart and hope to...er...have a pleasant flight.

"Thank you for your patience. I am sorry to have put you and your family through this demeaning ordeal, but I'm sure you understand we are all a little tense and even paranoid.

"You're welcome too.

"So now, in conclusion, on behalf of all the passengers and crew of American Flight 1271, I would like to wish you...What is that your children are mumbling? Oh, they are singing! And they want all of us to join in? How wonderful!

"From the mountains, to the prairie, to the oceans white with foam...

How PLO dealt with Black September terrorists

Every now and then you hear of a really ingenious idea, and you wonder if it isn't too good to be true.

This one was described in the December issue of *The Atlantic Monthly*.

In an article datelined Gaza City, Israel, Bruce Hoffman, author of *Inside Terrorism* and director of the Rand Corp. terrorism research unit, tells of an interview with an unidentified general in one of Yasser Arafat's security and intelligence units.

Titled "All You Need Is Love; How the terrorists stopped terrorism," it describes how Arafat's PLO got rid of its elite Black September terrorist unit when it had become a political liability years ago.

Black September had horrified the world with the kidnapping and massacre of the Israel Olympic team in 1972. Arafat later decided the unit was an obstacle to his acceptance by the international community.

He gave the order to his deputies to find a way to "turn Black September off."

> *"Why not marry them off? Give them a reason to live rather than to die?"*

Rather than kill the members, they hit upon an idea: Why not marry them off! Give them a reason to live rather than to die!

The general and his superior traveled to refugee camps and countries with large Palestinian communities, systematically identifying the most attractive women they could find.

They told them, in effect, the Fatherland needs you. Chairman Arafat wants you to come to Beirut and learn the details of your critical mission to serve the Palestinian cause.

"So," Hoffman wrote, "approximately a hundred of these beautiful young women were brought to Beirut. There, in a sort of PLO version of a college mixer, boy met girl, boy fell in love with girl, boy would, it was hoped, marry girl."

The aroused Black September swains were offered $3,000 cash, an apartment in Beirut and nonviolent employment by the PLO. If they had a baby within a year, each couple would pocket yet another $5,000.

The Black Septemberists, to a man, jumped at the deal and bought the whole package.

You can't read Hoffman's article without projecting into the present.

Should we buy off the al-Qaeda terrorists by pairing them off with Mideastern beauties? Would they see a bride in hand as preferable to a slew of virgins in the paradisiacal bush?

Sounds worth a try to me.

Near Ground Zero, life goes on — almost

I t has been three weeks since Sept. 11. Yet it seems so long ago.

Our son Steve, his daughter, Eva, and terrier Audrey are now living in a hotel on Union Square as guests of the American Red Cross until their Gateway Plaza apartment in Battery Park City is cleared of asbestos and concrete and glass dust.

Gateway Plaza is across West Street from the rubble of the collapsed World Trade Center towers.

After that first phone call, when he described how he fled the building and ran to his daughter's school as the second plane roared overhead into the South Tower, we have communicated mostly by e-mail.

The tone of the messages during the intervening days has gone from anger to relief at having survived to a vague depression and disorientation.

One of the most poignant messages described his discovery, in the court-yard debris, of party favors, menus and kitchen staff instructions for a scheduled office party that morning at the Windows on the World restaurant.

"It was so sad. There were snapshots of wives, husbands and kids that had been on people's desks," he wrote last week.

"The FBI was searching the plaza for the plane's cockpit voice recorder. They never found it. Somehow I hope they don't."

Monday's e-mail reported that the debris had been cleaned up, although he doubted that anyone was able to salvage the treasured snapshots.

> *"Across the street there are still fires burning..."*

"Across the street there are still fires burning, and when the wind blows out of the east, the awful smell comes back. Eva's school has moved twice. Her own building has dangerously high asbestos levels. She wants to get back, but I'm not so sure."

Finally, there was a faint ray of hope in the pervasive gloom.

"Now it's Tuesday and once again I woke up at 3 a.m. and couldn't get back to sleep. I have nightmares about that damned plane. I keep seeing the numbers and logo on the tail and thinking about the people inside."

"But the breakthrough is that I actually wrote something on my laptop. It was the first time since the 11th, but all I could do was write about that day.

"The book proposal is still on the hard drive of my desktop computer in the apartment. I couldn't concentrate anyway so it doesn't matter right now, but I've got to start making a living again pretty soon. I need that advance.

"But I'll get going again. It's just that right now all I can think about is *those bastards!*"

Poll: High schoolers veto war

Maybe I'm moving in the wrong circles, but I haven't heard *any* of my friends approving of war with Iraq.

Yet the polls say the American public is increasingly in favor of the idea. Are we out of step or is there something fishy going on?

The highly regarded Pew Research Center poll in mid-September had 52 percent saying the president had convinced them of the need to take military action against Saddam.

Thirty seven percent said he hadn't.

Before the president made his speech to the United Nations, the figures were the exact opposite: 52 percent no, 37 percent yes.

When asked in the most recent poll if they favored war even if it meant significant American casualties, 48 percent said yes.

You have to wonder about this willingness to risk the lives of other Americans.

> *"You wonder why nobody polls those who may have to do the fighting. Well, somebody did."*

You wonder why nobody polls those who may have to do the fighting?

Well, somebody did.

A teacher friend told me the results of an unscientific poll of high school seniors in an advanced placement course.

That means they were of higher than average intelligence and had college hopes that a war might dash or put on hold.

They were asked which statement they agreed with:

1. The U.S. should invade Iraq with or without U.N. agreement. (2 agreed)
2. The U.S. should invade only with U.N. agreement. (20 agreed)
3. The U.S. should not invade. (18 agreed)

If the U.S. does invade, did they think conditions in the Mideast would be...

1. Better, more politically stable, less terrorism, oil supplies safe. (4 agreed)
2. Worse. (24 agreed)
3. The same. (11 agreed)

Finally, they were asked how long did they think a postwar U.S. occupation would be required?

1. One year. (6 agreed)
2. Five years (16 agreed)
3. 10 years or longer. (18 agreed).

PS: Now consider this: Why did I not reveal the identity of the teacher and the school?

1. An oversight. (no).
2. Fear of getting him (or her) in trouble? (yes).
3. Has it come to that? (almost)

Guess who's not itching for war: the generals

Like many ex-soldiers I've always had a jaundiced view of generals in general.

I've visualized them addressing the men before the big attack, wishing them godspeed and saying: "I'm sorry I can't go with you."

The rest of us troops are standing in the rain muttering: "Yeah, sure. Me too, buster."

So you can imagine my surprise and delight when I read that there is a big debate going on in the Pentagon between the civilians who are itching to go to war with Iraq, and the generals, of all people, who are hanging back.

If I were a cartoonist, I'd draw the tiny figure of Defense Secretary Donald Rumsfeld flailing at an impassive Saddam Hussein and growling: "Let me at 'im!" while a huge figure of a general, representing the Joint Chiefs of Staff, indulgently holds him back with a fingerhold on his diapers.

Maybe, if I wanted to get a lot of angry mail, I'd use the figure of George W. Bush instead.

All of the think pieces out of the Washington news bureaus these days tell us that the hawkish civilians, like Rumsfeld and his deputy Paul Wolfowitz, neither of whom saw combat, are pushing for war, insisting it would be a walk-over, a quick in-and-outer, using lots of smart bombs and Special Forces units.

The generals say it would take upwards of 250,000 ground troops, air power and billions of dollars; and this time Saddam's Republican Guards might not take flight at the first shot.

I'm with the generals.

At least they have made a lifelong study of warfare and many of them have experienced combat personally.

There are suggestions that the Joint Chiefs themselves may have leaked the reports that the administration is plunging blindly toward war. They wanted to force a debate before things got out of hand.

> **"With war toys... it's hard to resist playing with them. My hat's off to the generals who know better."**

Meanwhile Army Gen. Tommy Franks has moved his 3rd Army headquarters to Kuwait and the 101st Airborne has been sent back from Afghanistan to Fort Campbell, Kentucky, to prepare for redeployment. It can be airlifted into action anywhere in the world in 72 hours.

With war toys like the 101st I suppose it's hard to resist playing with them. My hat's off to the generals who know better.

Sometimes I think what this country desperately needs is more wimps like me.

Are we being led to war?

(August 1, 2002)

D o you get the feeling that war on Iraq has already been declared and that all you can do is watch?

Try to suppress it, if you can. Otherwise you'll start brooding that you're being manipulated.

Tell you what: If there is no monumental incident, phony or real, between now and the November elections that scares the beejeezuz out of us, like, say, Saddam launching a nuclear missile at Tel Aviv or the U.S. Sixth Fleet in the Persian Gulf, maybe we can relax for awhile.

(Remember the phony North Vietnamese gunboat "attack" in the Tonkin Gulf that kept that war escalating? That's the sort of thing that comes to mind.)

What is the specific origin and purpose of all these leaked "analysis" pieces quoting highly-placed sources?

Are they "trial balloons," propaganda pieces designed to get our juices flowing?

Of course they are. Reporters aren't allowed to rummage through the Pentagon's secret war plans —are they?

Why do I, a bush league (lower case "b") columnist, have to be the one to ask these questions?

Why shouldn't the Congress be asking them? After all, they're the ones who are going to have to ratify the decision to go to war and find the money for it.

By the way: What ever happened to the War Powers Act? Has it been repealed? Ignored?

You realize, of course, that I am not a fan of this Bush administration or the one before it, so you're at liberty to write this off as the rantings of a biased wimp.

I'm not even much of a fan of "regime changes" carried out by long-range, imprecise "pinpoint" bombing that involves a lot of collateral damage to the innocent.

I don't think it makes friends.

And I'm not prepared to accuse Bush of avenging his father's failure to finish Saddam, nor to accuse the Republicans of trying to divert attention from the Bush-Harken, Cheney-Halliburton affairs.

Not yet.

But the fact that I even think such thoughts shows how paranoid I've become.

Are there others like me?

Is there a Pied Piper down there in Washington piping us into inevitable war with Iraq?

Isn't anyone questioning whether we have to follow him blindly?

Sometimes I have this sinking feeling in the pit of my stomach.

If I had a son of military age, it would be a lot worse.

Prophetic fears foreshadow Baghdad takeover

Most of the critics of war with Iraq speak of the physical harm that might befall our troops.

They're talking about them being wounded or killed.

A retired Maine general warned Congress the other day that they would face a "nightmare scenario" if Iraqi forces tried to defend Baghdad.

We'd win but the casualties would be high on both sides.

But I'm talking about the guilt and emotional casualties.

The game plan is for the war to open with massive, prolonged "pinpoint" bombing.

Then it will be up to our troops to move through Baghdad and "mop up," eliminating the resistance and taking possession of the rubble.

Mopping up has a benign sound of simple "tidying up" that is totally misleading.

As I dimly remember such operations, our infantrymen walk or ride tanks into a city that has been "prepared" by artillery fire or close air support.

The lead unit's dangerous role is to "draw fire" from the diehard defenders, then use "fire and movement" to close in to grenade or bazooka range.

Today's tools may be different but the drill is much the same.

My role as an artillery forward observer in that ancient war was to hang back and watch all this through binoculars and direct the artillery fire for the attacking infantry.

I didn't have to go in and flush out the enemy with rifle or bayonet but I was close enough.

When the action moved on, I would follow and view my handiwork. Enemy bodies in uniform never bothered me but the women and children were grist for nightmares.

(I remember one family huddled in the remains of a cellar...but never mind).

The civilians who survived were pitiful. They looked at you with such hollow-eyed fear, waving their improvised white flags.

If we go into Baghdad, our troops will see what I'm talking about — and all the Arab world will be watching on al-Jazeera TV.

My moment of truth in World War II came when I was spared having to destroy the village of Tegernsee in Bavaria.

The Germans negotiated a cease fire with fanatical SS holdouts. The town was teeming with Wehrmacht wounded and refugees. If I'd had to level it with artillery fire, the scene would have still haunted me.

I hope our troops will be as lucky.

Diversity of little fears

Without going to the trouble of conducting a scientific study, allow me to proclaim that the once-popular neurosis, "mid-life crisis," is dead. Remember mid-life crises? There used to be a lot of them going around.

They were everywhere.

Times were good, the economy was booming, and all of us had plenty of leisure time on our hands for brooding, whining and self-absorption.

Picking at our emotional scabs was the in-thing. A person couldn't make the transition from youthful adulthood to middle age without making a big deal of it.

You were supposed to be consumed by doubts. "What am I doing here? Halfway to what?"

> *"Now that the country is at war, more or less, we haven't got time for navel-gazing."*

But now that the country is at war, more or less, we haven't got time for introspective navel-gazing.

"Looking inward" has become a luxury of an earlier time.

If someone went into a psychiatrist's office today and said he or she was worried about an impending mid-life crisis, I suspect (and hope) the shrink would put aside monetary considerations and say, or at least be tempted to say:

"Get over it. Don't you know there's a war on? I've got a waiting room full of squirrels out there with real problems. Buck up and pull yourself together."

That's one of the few nice things about a serious national crisis like a war or a depression. There is a lot less whining going on.

Why? Simple: You don't want to be overheard by a firefighter or a soldier.

Remember the GI expression: "See the chaplain. He'll punch your TS ticket." TS stood for "Tough (Something)."

I remember back when the popular magazines were full of advice articles on dealing with a mid-life crisis. Now most of them have been replaced by fitness and weight-loss stories.

Some of us were able to get through mid-life without excessive gnashing of teeth because we weren't paying attention.

Suddenly we looked up and realized mid-life had passed us by and the opportunity to indulge in a crisis was gone.

Now here we are, full-blown geezers, ready for another major crisis of passage, and we just can't summon the energy to brood about it.

I blame it all on Tom Brokaw calling us the "Greatest Generation." We believed his malarkey. Now we have to fake it.

Warmongers need a vacation

I think I know why the French are reluctant to join us in attacking Iraq or even thinking about it right now.

They're all on vacation.

When the French go on vacation, they don't kid around. Every August they shut down the country and leave it to the tourists.

"Come back in the fall when we're refreshed," President Jacques Chirac told the Pentagon hawks. "Then we'll talk; it's too hot for a war right now."

That's the kind of attitude I'd like to see in my president. They say he knew how to relax at Yale. He majored in it. Where did he go wrong?

Now he goes on an oxymoronic "working vacation" and takes along a whole bunch of worker bees to his Crawford, Texas, ranch so he can hold interminable meetings and plan a war — anything to avoid actually having to vacate.

You can bet Saddam Hussein has given his Weapons of Mass Destruction Factory workers the month off. It's really hot in Baghdad this time of year.

I've never been to France in August but I have an idea what it's like. It's like noon time anywhere in France in July. At the stroke of 12 you hear the rattle of storefront metal shutters crashing down all across the country. Pity the tourist who doesn't make it out the door in time.

By 12:05 all you can hear are sipping, chewing and belching sounds, followed by snoring. The French really know how to eat and digest lunch. It takes them two hours.

While we're on the subject of vacationing, I suppose you've all heard that sun tanning, instead of causing cancer, may stimulate the production of vitamin D that prevents it.

There was something about it in the news the other day. Apparently sunbathing laboratory mice reported it in some prestigious mouse medical journal.

I forget the details, but check it out before you go on vacation. There probably is a catch. It wouldn't be the first time mice have led us astray.

But I'm told the mice are unworried. They've discovered that aspirin may cure or ward off cancer. (I forget which.)

We in the media tend to get over-excited about mouse discoveries.

Weren't they the ones who also said both sunlight and aspirin were bad for us?

They obviously need a vacation.

Chapter Ten

Holidays &
Special Days

CEO's Labor Day speech

This Labor Day address was prepared for former Global Crossing Chairman Gary Winnick to deliver Monday to an audience of well-wishers. (Editors: Hold for release. Do not publish prematurely.)

"I'd like to welcome all of you to the 2002 Labor Day Picnic for Downsized Employees and Betrayed Shareholders at this beautiful California home.

Look around you, ladies and gentlemen. This $94 million estate, including $30 million in renovations, was made possible by your generosity and sacrifice.

My wife and I want all of you to think of this mansion, beach houses and grounds as yours.

(Thank you. Thank you. You're embarrassing me. Please take your seats.)

We're not talking just about today, mind you. We want you to feel free to drop in any time and stay as long as you want.

For your convenience and comfort, please bring your own linens and towels. No children or pets, please.

I know some of you were miffed when I cashed in $735 million in stock while leading the company into bankruptcy, but most of you understand.

I can't tell you how many of you unemployed workers, who lost your jobs, severance pay, 401(k)s and promised medical benefits, have stopped me on the street to tell me how you wished you could have done more to ease my burden.

I was deeply moved.

I told all of you it was your loyalty and productivity that made all this possible. And I meant it.

Many of you shareholders who have seen your Global stocks suffer told me you wished I had tipped you off when I was bailing out, but all of you understood my position.

If word had leaked out, my own shares would have been worthless and your guilt would have been unbearable.

You were good sports about the hand that fate, and fate alone, had dealt you.

'The market is the market, after all,' one little old lady told me today. My chauffeur will be driving her back to her homeless shelter after the party is over.

In closing, let me remind you that it was 200 years ago that Labor Day was born when workers took an unpaid holiday to march hand-in-hand with their CEOs around Union Square in Manhattan.

That spirit still lingers among us today. Thank you and godspeed. The bar is open."

Advice from '50's to include in Mother's Day card

A friend sent me the following excerpt from a 1950 home economics textbook, suggesting I slip it into Pat's Mother's Day card. Instead, I chose to read it aloud. I suggest all husbands do the same. Let me know whether or not it markedly improves your marriage.

"Plan ahead, even the night before, to have a delicious meal — ON TIME. This is a way of letting him know you have been thinking about him and are concerned about his needs. Most men are hungry when they come home and the prospect of a good meal is part of the warm welcome needed.

Prepare yourself. Take 15 minutes to rest so you will be refreshed when he arrives. Touch up your makeup, put a ribbon in your hair and be fresh looking. He has just been with a lot of work-weary people. Be a little gay and a little interesting.

Clear away the clutter. Make one last trip through the house just before your husband arrives, gathering up school books, toys, paper, etc. Then run a dust cloth over the tables. Your husband will feel he has reached a haven of rest and order, and it will give you a lift too.

Prepare the children. Take a few minutes to wash their hands and faces, comb their hair, and if necessary change their clothes. They are little treasures and he would like to see them playing the part.

At the time of his arrival eliminate all noise of washer, dryer, dishwasher or vacuum. Encourage the children to be quiet. Greet him with a warm smile and be happy to see him.

Some don'ts: Don't greet him with problems. Don't complain if he is late for dinner. Count this as minor compared with what he might have gone through.

Make him comfortable. Have him lean back in a comfortable chair or suggest he lie down in the bedroom. Have a cool or warm drink ready for him. Arrange his pillow and offer to take off his shoes. Speak in a low, soft, soothing and pleasant voice.

Listen to him. You may have a dozen things to tell him, but the moment of his arrival is not the time. Let him talk first.

Make the evening his. Never complain if he does not take you out to dinner or to other places of entertainment. Instead try to understand his world of strain and pressure, his need to relax.

The goal: Try to make your home a place of peace and order where your husband can renew himself in body and spirit."

"There," I said when I finished. "Are there any questions? You seem to be very quiet."

No response.

"Are you all right? Your face looks positively purple."

Still no response.

Funny how home economics affects some women. They just don't get it.

Graduates: "Go forth and commence"

I t must be depressing to be a high school senior these days.

Here you are, with graduation only a month away, and you keep reading in the paper that somebody says you're poorly educated.

Well, I'm here to tell you to forget it. When your name is called, march up there and get your diploma anyway. You've earned it, no matter what anyone says.

My position has always been that it is impossible not to learn something in school if you show up often enough. The stuff just seeps into your head by osmosis.

(Remember osmosis? They mentioned it in general science, or whatever they call it now.)

I'll bet anything that you're a lot smarter and better educated than anyone thinks. Take my word for it.

Now, after you get your diploma and go out into the adult world, that's another matter. Then it is customary to be horrified how much education has deteriorated since you graduated.

You can start decrying the condition of the school system as soon as a decent interval has passed. One year is the minimum. If you decry too soon, you are casting doubt on your own credentials.

My advice is to wait at least four years. Middle age is even better. When you reach retirement age, you can really turn up the decrying to the threshold of sheer outrage, but go easy at first.

Years ago I gave a high school commencement speech making this very point. I drilled the commencers in vocal decrying by leading them in that tiresome litany of adulthood: "My God! The kids today!"

> *"I'll bet anything you're a lot smarter and better educated than anyone thinks."*

I had them repeat it in unison until they had it down pat. They left the hall fully prepared to go out into the world and feel superior to the future victims of the system, heaping scorn on their morals, music and hairstyles.

Today I'll bet they can decry with the most cantankerous of their generation. I'm sure I'd be proud of them.

That little exercise was the high point in an otherwise typically tedious speech that mentioned the obligatory John Kennedy phrase, "passing of the torch" and called commencement "a beginning not an end."

However, I did steal Art Buchwald's moving line at the end when I told them to "go forth and commence".

"We're leaving you a perfect world. Don't screw it up," I said.

George and Abe can sure sell cars!

Those super salesmen George and Abe have done it again. Can they move the merchandise! While Clinton scratches his head and ponders what to cut and what to tax, the two ex-presidents were out over the weekend slashing prices on everything from TVs to tubs, sofas to sneakers, sheets to shorts.

They don't just sit there brooding about the economy and preparing to go on TV to talk about sacrifice. No sir, every February they get out there and slash prices storewide, all over town.

All presidents talk about getting the country moving. These two get out the wig and the stovepipe hat and do what has to be done.

Unlimber those credit cards, they tell us. Do it now while these fantastic savings last. Everything must go.

> **"It's strange that George and Abe are the only presidents in history that actually get out there and sell."**

It's strange, isn't it, that George and Abe are the only presidents in history that do actually get out there and sell? The rest of them, Calvin, Tom, Rutherford B., Herb, they probably just stood there in the showroom waiting for someone to show up.

But George and Abe take out ads! (I don't know why, but I've always been in favor of people taking out lots of ads.)

I suspect that the reason they're so successful at modern marketing techniques is because they're the only presidents who arranged to get their birthdays declared holidays. They realized early on that you have to give people the day off on your birthday to shop or it's no use taking out ads.

In one of the ads I saw somewhere George and Abe were ringing bells and shouting "Hear Ye." The old Town Crier shtick.

You probably thought that the guy on TV who stands in the used car lot yelling at you was the inventor of the personalized selling approach, didn't you?

Well, now you know: The practice of getting The Big Guy himself out there in person shouting his head off dates back to the founding of our country.

I can see it now: "Hey Chief, I've got this great idea!" George's chief economist says. George is doubtful. "It's so undignified, so schlocky," he protests.

"Schlocky? Whatever. But listen, the retail sales index is going under, Chief; you've got to do something!"

George says: "Oh what the heck," and the rest is history.

One thing is certain. This pair, the Father of the Country and the Great Emancipator, were all-time all-timers in the annals of marketing. We'll never see their like again. Until next February.

164

Only "0" anniversaries demand gifts

Tonight I really should give the lady one of those diamond things that tell her I'd marry her all over again.

Women are so sentimental. I can hear her murmuring: "It's lovely. I hope you kept the sales slip."

A week later there would be a knock on the door.

"Good morning. You must be the 1956 bridegroom, right? We're here to knock out the wall and remodel the kitchen."

"The surprise anniversary present you ordered is here, sweetheart," I'd yell.

This is the same woman who once told me she wanted a blacktop driveway for her birthday.

When she unwrapped the hunk of asphalt and read the card, she threw her arms around me and called me a "sentimental old fool."

The memory of that scenario is the main reason I don't give her the $5,000-or-whatever diamond trinket. It would turn into a new cottage septic tank or a lifetime supply of Compost Helper.

The other reason is that it's an anniversary that doesn't end in a round number like VE Day. It's only our 39th.

I think the 39th is known as the Ceramic Bathroom Tile Anniversary. I forget, but I'm certain it definitely is not named after one of the precious metals.

You don't say you'd marry her all over again on a 39th. You wait for the zero to come up signifying a multiple of 10. On the 39th, you say: "What say we try for 40?"

Then, according to Miss Manners (or was it Erma Bombeck?), she's supposed to say: "Oh, What the hell."

> *"It's an anniversary that doesn't end in a round number."*

We'll go out to dinner in time for the Early Bird Special. We'll drink a toast of some clear or amber liquid.

Maybe there will be candlelight. It will be so romantic. That's when I'll explain about the diamond trinket not being appropriate but maybe next year.

And she'll say: "The sales slip would be nice."

As we go out the door hand in hand and starry-eyed, she'll suddenly pull away.

"You forgot the doggy bags!"

A fitting and appropriately modest end to a sort of memorable evening.

Fifty-six was really a great year, but the anniversary doesn't hack it.

Like the 51st anniversary of World War II, it has second rate digits.

*Why not honor **all** the war dead on Memorial Day?*

hree of us aging World War II codgers came up with a great idea at lunch the other day: Why not transform Memorial Day into a remembrance of ALL war dead, not just ours?

Perhaps it was the presence of Alex Martens, former German paratrooper and now a fellow American, that brought the idea to mind.

I've written about Alex before. We met for the first time last year to compare notes and discovered that our paths must have crossed in Bavaria in the final days of the war.

Alex and survivors of his unit were trudging down the road near Rosenheim trying to find someone to surrender to, while we were passing in the opposite direction, waving them to the rear as we headed for the Austrian Alps, hunting down diehard SS fanatics.

Alex immediately endorsed the joint Memorial Day idea.

So did Jim Payne, former deputy chief of the Rochester Fire Department, who, like me, was an artillery forward observer in the war.

He was with a corps artillery unit during the fighting around the Ruhr Pocket, the last big battle of the war in which 335,000 German troops were encircled and captured at Lippstadt in northern Germany.

When the lunch broke up, I thought briefly of trying to mount a campaign for the idea but quickly decided the nation, and maybe the world, isn't ready for such a sensible proposal.

Too bad.

Alex told me the Germans do not have a Memorial Day. They'd rather put the war behind them. But now that we're friends and allies, as we are with the Japanese, it seems the least we could do is memorialize their war dead along with ours.

He thinks his former Wehrmacht comrades would welcome the idea.

Sachio Ashida, the former Japanese fighter pilot, now a professor at SUNY Brockport, agrees.

So, I'm sure, would members of the elite Japanese-American 442nd Regimental Combat Team that fought with my 36th (Texas) Infantry Division in Italy and France.

And let's not forget our former allies, the Russians, Chinese, Vietnamese, French, Australians, New Zealanders, Ghurkas of India, Ghoums of Morocco and others I have forgotten momentarily?

When you try to think this through, the confusion mounts.

For example, what about all the millions of civilian war dead, including those killed by our bombs in Dresden and theirs in the London Blitz and Warsaw?

It was a grand idea, a joint memorial day for all war dead — and certainly a lot more appropriate than the opposite, namely stirring up old hatreds with a Hollywood-ized movie about Pearl Harbor using terrifying fake "special effects" and releasing it on Memorial Day.

Pitfalls of Valentine solicitations

I think I first invited the lady to be my valentine back in 1955. Little did I dream it would lead to long-term cohabitation, reproduction, homeownership and all the rest.

I'd extended the same flirtatious invitation to other young women over the years, but the consequences were inconsequential by comparison.

Now here we are, "five dogs later," as she reminded me recently, and still going strong. (Well, sort of. We're still above ground, at least.)

We're surrounded by jointly owned possessions, much of it "stuff" that accumulated with the passage of time and filled the closets, the basement, garage and backyard tool shed.

Years ago, while musing about this subject, I warned readers about the pitfalls of valentines and suggested that they use extreme care in picking targets. I suggested love-sick swains follow up their cards with a form outlining the terms of the intended relationship.

"If you agree to be my valentine, as proposed in the enclosed card with the fat little flying cherubs on it, check the appropriate boxes describing your expectations and mail immediately," it began.

"Frankly, I'm surprised the Valentine tradition survives in this age of sexual harrassment."

The options ranged from "casual, harmless and innocent flirtation, lunch, maybe a movie or a hockey game," through "heavy petting and murmuring" to "long-term affair."

If they checked the final box ("marriage, kids, two cars, mortgage, joint checking accounts, PTA, cub scouts, Little League, etc.") I promised to send them a prenuptial agreement by return mail, complete with financial statement, inventory of assets and a copy of our proposed wills (open to negotiation).

My Ultimate Valentine and I didn't take these precautions, but we were young and foolish back in those days.

Frankly, I'm a little surprised that the St. Valentine tradition survives in this age of sexual harassment. Imagine sending a woman an unsolicited invitation to be your "Valentine!"

Lawyer for the plaintiff: "And what, exactly, would being your valentine entail, as far as my client is concerned, may I ask? What were your intentions?"

Defendant: "Lunch? Perhaps some innocent ogling and footsie? Nothing untoward."

Lawyer: "I rest my case, your honor."

Judge: "Take him away."

Happy 75ᵗʰ! An interview with himself

So now you're 75. Congratulations. Tell me, how does it feel?

Ten years older than the new turnpike speed limit, 20 more than the old one. Even older than the Pope. He's just a kid. HE didn't come into the world until May 18, 1920. I made MY entrance nine days earlier.

Any successes to report?

Look, I'm not through yet. There's still time for me to amount to something.

What's taking you so long?

Made a lot of false starts. Barked up a lot of wrong trees. That kind of thing. But now I think I'm getting the hang of it.

To what do you attribute your longevity?

You live long enough, it comes naturally. But they say it gets harder from here on out. Eventually you run out of longevity. Don't know what will happen to me then.

You seem to be in pretty good physical shape.

Not bad. With new bearings and an orthopedic lube job the ride would be a lot smoother, but the valves and the exhaust systems are in fair shape. I work on it at the Y and take it into the shop for checkups, but the warranty has expired.

Mentally?

A little loss of storage space. Too much clutter. You wouldn't believe the stuff I've got stored in there. Accessing it gets harder and harder, but it's all in there. Just the other day I surprised my spouse by remembering our anniversary. Also remembered VE Day.

Any advice for younger people?

Like the boy Pope? I'd tell him to hang in there. He'll grow up one day. I'd tell him to leave the pontificating up to professionals like myself.

What about the rest of us?

Stop sticking microphones in people's faces and asking them to tell "in their own words" how it feels to be something, like 75. I always tell things in my own words. Whose words would I use?

You sound bitter.

Just curmudgeonly, as befits a man of my vintage. It's one of those "entitlements" they're talking about. At 75 you're entitled to become what is known in geriatric studies as an irascible old coot.

A privilege of seniority?

Exactly. I used to hate it when I was 74 and had to act responsibly.

What do you see in the future as you approach the next year ending in a zero?

I look forward eagerly to turning 80, the threshold of advanced geezerhood when I become an emeritus and a whole array of new entitlements will be heaped upon me.

Which of these do you most eagerly await?

The eligibility to not only cackle at busybodies like you, but to lash out with my cane.

Beware of taking your child to work

We had a bring-your-kid-to-work day here at the Paragraph Factory earlier this year.

The idea was to give the kids a chance to see their parents interacting with their peers in the work environment.

I asked my wife if I should bring our eldest son to show him what daddy does at the office. She didn't think so.

"He's 55. That's older than any of the other kids in the newsroom and probably most of the grownups except you. I don't think he'd fit in. Besides, he's already got a career," she said.

> *"The kid is on the threshold of senior citizenship himself..."*

She was right. I'd forgotten that the kid is on the threshold of senior citizenship himself, is gainfully employed and no doubt makes more money than the old man.

Not only that but he wears white shirts and ties and always has his shoes shined — all violations of the newsroom dress code. I was afraid my colleagues would make fun of him.

I called him at his office in Texas to explain. He took it well.

Back in the 1950s I feared he might follow in his old man's footsteps. After all, he flunked out of college and joined the army rather than come home in shame, just as his dad did, except that he enlisted. Pop got drafted.

Instead of following dad into the Paragraph Factory after his discharge, he got a job smashing baggage at Los Angeles International Airport. He did it so well he soon worked his way up to station manager and finished college at night. Now he's with the parent corporation of American Airlines in Dallas doing something important and mysterious with computers and statistics.

He flies to meetings all over the world and supplies his parents and siblings with passes, sometimes in first class.

If he'd stuck with me, with my guidance and pull, he could have been writing about fires and town board meetings all these years.

I suppose I can live with that. His brother and sister went into the journalism dodge and made good. That takes away the sting.

The reason I'm bragging like this is because he's been on my mind ever since he announced he's getting married! The wedding is next week and family and friends are all getting passes to attend.

The bride is a Texas girl who is not only gorgeous but also very gainfully employed.

I keep thinking: What if I had taken the kid to work and he'd said " Oh boy! I want to do THAT when I grow up."

Goodbye, King George

Y ou may be wondering why I was summoned here to deliver this mythical address commemorating a hitherto unrecognized occasion.

I'll tell you why if you'll stop fidgeting and picking at your July Fourth sunburn peelings.

Yesterday we marked the anniversary of the adoption of the Declaration of Independence by mowing lawns, drinking mood-altering beverages, littering the parks, killing and maiming each other with automobiles and watching simulated bombs bursting in air.

Today we are celebrating the anniversary of July 5, 1776 when the newly-ex colonists asked themselves questions like these:

1. What have we done?
2. Is it too late to turn back, and the King be angry?
3. Will the king be angry?
4. Who is going to clean up?
5. Does this mean that I, personally, must share the blame for every bad thing that happens instead of blaming it on the king?

The answers back in 1776 were as follows:

1. You have done something historic but perhaps everything will be all right in the end.
2. Yes, and the king will be very angry but one day he will be a motherly woman instead of an ugly king and she will forgive us.
3. No one will clean up.
4. Yes, you must share the blame. From now on each generation will whine: "It's a world we never made." And no one will be able to grumble "Tell it to the king."

But now let us stop brooding and look at the brighter side: Two hundred years ago our forefathers assembled here and were told: "One day on this spot a great city will rise."

We have built that city. It is called Rochester, New York, and it still stands despite vigorous efforts to pave it over and make it into a vast parking lot for Rich Stadium.

Two hundred years ago people were saying, "They don't make 'em like George III no more."

History has shown that we made a lot of them but without the roman numerals.

As we leave this hallowed ground today, let us do as the ex-colonists did and remember that although the Declaration of Independence was adopted on July 4, it was not signed until next month on August 2.

There was still time for the colonists to grovel before King George and beg forgiveness. Today we know they passed up this chance, signed the Declaration and now we are free.

Now let us resolve to meet here again on August 3 and reassure ourselves once again that our forebears did the right thing.

Thank you and Godspeed. The king is dead! Long live all of us!

Big day tomorrow! Be careful!

"**B**ig day tomorrow," the man said.

"Really?" said his wife of many years.

Something in her tone should have suggested that there was more to her response than he imagined. But he plunged ahead.

They were closing up the cottage on Peaks Island, Maine, on the outer fringes of Boston Red Sox Hysteria Country. Everyone on the island would be watching television this weekend. The mysterious Long Island lobster virus and the upcoming "harvest" (massacre) of the island deer herd would be out-of-mind topics.

"Really," the man said. "Roger the Rocket Clemens, the former Red Sox pitcher, is coming back to Fenway Park as a despised New York Yankee."

"Wow, that's really something. I can hardly contain myself," she said.

"And that's not all. He'll be going against Pedro Martinez, who's won 23 games for the Red Sox this season. He struck out 313. He and Clemens are both Cy Young Award winners."

"Of course. Cy Young. Winner of the Nobel Prize. Don't tell me."

"Take my word. It's a huge deal. The Red Sox haven't been in a World Series since the Battle of Bunker Hill. New Englanders think of the Yankees as the Tories. Clemens is Benedict Arnold."

Every year since they've been coming up here during October Hysteria, Sox fans have told them this could be the year, not really believing it. The man's wife manages to keep her excitement under control. But her spouse lets himself get caught up in it.

"So what you're saying is tomorrow is really special. Am I right about that?" she asked.

"Absolutely," he said.

"Then I take it you won't be able to take me out to dinner after all because you'll be watching the greatest ball game of all time — is that what you're saying?"

Was it irritation the man detected? No, it was resignation!

"Birthday! It's her @##$%&* birthday, you dummy!" the man thought.

She could see the old memory cells pulsating as they kicked in. Would you believe she laughed? What a woman!

"Look," he said, "I knew it was your birthday. At least I knew it two days ago. But you said . . ."

"I know. I said not to make it a big deal and not to get me anything. You had a senior moment and I got what I asked for — nothing."

The next day the man set her straight on that: "Nothing! Yanks humiliated 13-to-1, Clemens knocked off the mound in the third. You call that nothing?"

"Sigh," she said.

This was written before last night's game. If the Red Sox lost, let him read it himself.

A Thanksgiving cheer for the Digestive Department

I'd just like to give leftover thanks to the crew in the digestion department for their fine work over the long weekend.

Good going, guys!

You took everything that came down the tube and tirelessly metabolized it. I know because the groans of your exertions woke me up from a sound sleep, not only at night in bed but afternoons on the couch.

I know you couldn't see from your vantage point down there, but we were in Myrtle Beach, South Carolina, in my sister-in-law's handsome apartment overlooking the ocean.

We go there almost every year to give thanks by stuffing food and pouring beverages down our gullets until we can barely walk. Then we go lie down and listen to you guys do your stuff.

After about two hours we regain consciousness and are able to move about. We shuffle out to the balcony and gaze out to sea sipping more beverages. Then comes nap time. Then we wake up and go back to the table.

> *"Your work is largely unsung, but don't think it's unappreciated."*

But of course you guys know all this. What you probably don't know is what the stuff is and what it looks like before you see it, so let me tell you.

Thursday's huge load consisted of a very fat and ugly dead feathered bird, of the non-airborne variety. It was executed, plucked, disemboweled, then stuffed and cooked. Then we dismantled it and shoveled the pieces down the tube to you guys.

With it came the stuffing, mashed sweet and white potatoes, gravy, squash, peas, cranberry sauce, lettuce, onions (cooked and raw), tomatoes, olives. All this looks attractive before we start grinding up everything and mixing it with white wine.

But of course when you get it, it's already garbage. I just thought you must have wondered how we could swallow such an unattractive mess, but it really was quite beautiful for a brief moment.

The bird was so big that it took four of us all weekend to do the preliminary processing for you. Only the stark carcass remained until we had picked it clean.

Believe me, after a weekend like that you know you have been giving thanks.

So, once again, allow me to congratulate all of you, especially the liver. Your work is largely unsung but don't think it's unappreciated.

I promise to let all of you rest up for the next four weeks.

You'll need it; the year-end week is a doozy, as all of you know.

The Pilgrims didn't know what they'd started

J ust so you know: The Pilgrims would be amazed at what we've managed to do with their Thanksgiving.

"They didn't know they were having a First Thanksgiving," said my friend John Waters, the U. of R. history prof, the other day.

"They didn't have a set feast or a date. They thought that would be 'papist.' When they felt the need, they might have a feast or a fast, depending on the circumstances."

(A feast to give thanks for a bumper harvest, a fast of atonement after a lean year.)

Technically speaking, John is a "cliometrician," a historian who uses mathematical and statistical methods to analyze documents and data using computers to reconstruct lifestyles.

Using cliometrics, he and his colleagues have studied Pilgrim villages in New England and have come up with some surprising insights and tidbits.

"For example," he said, "we find no evidence that the Pilgrims used forks."

"No forks?" I exclaimed. "How did the eat the turkey?"

"With knives, spoons and bare hands, of course."

Aha, I thought, that sounds like Mess Night at our house when we'd indulge the kids' outrageous whims as a reward for exemplary manners.

(Pat would pretend not to notice when they tried to shock her by eating with their hands — off the floor or no-handed out of the dog dish.)

I asked John about an article I read suggesting that the Pilgrims, and later the Puritans, were far from puritanical.

It said they enjoyed sex and drinking beer.

> *"Homemade beer was a favorite with the pilgrims. So was hard cider."*

"Well, of course everyone enjoys sex, but it was almost always within marriage. In the small villages we studied, illegitimacy was very low," he said. "Nobody would marry a 'spoiled woman.'"

"Marriage was a civil contract, not a sacrament. Romance came into the picture only after the marriage."

"Farmers would rent two boys and four oxen. Under the right circumstances, they could become husbands to your daughters."

John confirmed that home-brewed beer was a favorite with the Pilgrims. So was hard cider.

No prudes, these Pilgrims.

I'll bet if they'd have had TV in 1621, they'd have turned it on and dozed off, beer in hand, watching the game just as I plan to do this afternoon.

50th *anniversary should be final observance*

The nicest thing about 50th anniversaries is that they're the last. By the time the 60th comes around the participants in the event itself are either dead or too pooped to care any more.

Anniversaries ending in intermediate numbers don't count for anything. A 55th anniversary is pretty much a non-starter. Zeroes are the thing.

I'm not talking wedding anniversaries, dear, so don't look at me that way.

(That was for a lady I know. I may be stupid but I'm not foolhardy.)

I'm talking anniversaries of wars especially. The dropping of bombs. Things like that.

We spent a lot of time this year arguing about the morality of dropping the atomic bomb. It was bitter because a lot of us who were in the military at the time are still around.

We find the argument that the bomb saved lives (especially ours) by ending the war before we got shipped to Japan, to be a very powerful one indeed.

But by the 60th anniversary we'll be fewer in number. By the 70th I'll be 115 and my plan is to be out of here, if all goes well and medical science gets itself under control and lets me depart.

Then you young folk can discuss everything frankly and fully without getting any of us absent veterans riled up.

And when you do, I'm pretty sure you'll conclude that atomic or non-atomic bombing of civilian populations is morally wrong.

That's O.K. We understand.

The most powerful argument on our side is that prolonging a brutal war is more cruel. The humane thing is to get the inhumanity over with.

Then there is the "They Started It" defense.

When I gave my little speech last month in Tegernsee, the German town I almost blew up, I had expected someone to ask what I thought about the fire-bombing of Dresden late in the war.

I had the reply ready: "What about Coventry? What about Rotterdam. What about London and Warsaw?"

But nobody asked. I'm glad. I hate those "Did-didn't-did so" shouting matches.

Perhaps the best resolution of all this would be to draft some kind of new Geneva Convention and have the terror bombing of helpless civilians clearly designated a war crime once and for all.

It worked with poison gas, even though both sides had enormous stock-piles of the stuff.

Once that's cleared up, the world could start over.

But that's up to you. We'll be out of here.

Christmas letter from the Doughertys

ell, folks, another exciting year here at Chez Dougherty is drawing to a close, so it's time for that annual report you've all been waiting for (hah, hah).

The big news is that Dick is still going in to the paragraph factory every weekday and trying to look busy (hah, hah) as he has for 50 years.

"Still getting away with it," he is fond of saying (hah, hah).

To keep from getting in a rut, he regularly changes his commuting route on Tuesdays and Thursdays. Instead of exiting Interstate 490 at Clinton and taking a left at Broad, he crosses the bridge and gets off at Plymouth, then doubles back on Broad and into the garage.

He says change is what keeps him young (hah!).

But the big satisfaction for him is that he's now got 92,000 miles on his '90 Honda Civic. He's shooting for 95-thou but may have to go for a new timing belt first. That's $400! Or he may trade it. We'll let you know in next year's letter.

Three times a week he goes to the Y at 6 a.m. and rides the stationary bike for half an hour or so.

He often sees George Fisher of Kodak in the locker room, sometimes with his clothes off. He says 'Good morning' and George says 'Good morning' right back. Just two ordinary naked guys!

When he (Dick) gets to the office, he always has breakfast in the cafeteria. Again, to avoid that rut, he now has oatmeal with brown sugar and milk (plus a Lactaid pill and sometimes a Beano for gas).

"Hope you and yours are having as exciting and fulfilling lives as we are."

He made that big change in 1991. Or was it 1990? Whenever. Before that, he always had a bagel and cream cheese, sometimes with jelly (grape).

As always, he and Pat and Midas the golden retriever went to Peaks Island, Maine. (Some ruts are too comfy to climb out of (hah, hah!).)

There they keep an eye, or an ear, on the Atlantic Ocean. Tough job, but somebody's got to do it (hah, hah!).

The big news for Dick was that he finally found someone to clean the leaves out of the eaves. "It really changed my life," he says. "Wish I'd thought of it sooner."

Right now both Doughertys are waiting for their first winter respiratory infection to arrive.

Gotta run. Hope you and yours are having as exciting and fulfilling lives as they are.

They wish you a merry century and a happy millennium and remind you to keep on aging. It's when you stop that, that the trouble begins (hah, hah!).

They can hardly wait for *your* holiday newsletter!

Joint credit card enhances Christmas spirit

"Don't worry about it. Consider it your Christmas present," we've said to each other over and over this season. That's one of the perks that comes with joint credit cards and checking accounts.

Now here it is almost Christmas and not only is our shopping all done at a cost of a mere umpteen thousand dollars, but we have saved a fortune on day-to-day expenses.

My wife gave me a new front tire for $38.95 plus mounting and wheel balancing after I had a flat on Monroe Avenue and came home in a foul mood after changing to the spare in the rain.

"I hate to see you unhappy. Make it your Christmas present from me. Put it on our Visa," she said.

"Wow! Just what I always wanted! A new tire!" I said.

"Just what I've always wanted. A new tire!"

What a woman! She had already given me another winter of snow plowing and half a new roof, all on her joint checking account.

"Are you sure you can afford it?" I asked.

"'Tis better to give than receive," she said. "What's your paycheck for if not to make me feel generous?"

Played out to its fullest, we figured we could reimburse each other for Christmas gifts of all our household expenses. Think of all the cheer that would spread all over us!

As part of her duties as chief financial officer, she was auditing and paying bills the other day when she exclaimed: "You wouldn't believe what the total came to! Guess."

"So it's a fortune. Forget it. Consider it my Christmas present to you," I said.

Later the same week I got her a week's supply of groceries, a library fine and a teeth cleaning, and she got me a car inspection sticker and a mange treatment for our joint dog, Midas.

But the biggie this year was the beautiful new dining room we got for each other for a paltry thousands and thousands of dollars.

Now we can have eight people in for a sit-down dinner and really pack them in at a stand-up milling-around punch party. Until just last month we'd feed two couples in the kitchen and call it "entertaining."

"Just what I always wanted!" we exclaimed in unison as we wrote the check last weekend. "How did you ever know!"

Christmas never used to be this much fun back in the days before we discovered the miracle of credit. We used to think of it as "being in debt."

Scrooge meets George Bailey in Bedford Falls

Scrooge: George Bailey! Mr. Savings & Loan, you old son of a gun. Can't get over how much you look like Jimmy Stewart. Still having *A Wonderful Life*?

Bailey: Ebenezer! How's the counting-house dodge?

Scrooge: Can't complain. Money rules the world, Georgie Boy - Bedford Falls or London.

Bailey: You can say that again. Listen, I've been meaning to talk to you. I heard on TV how much you gave your man Cratchit. Everyone's talking about you exceeding the wage guidelines. I suppose you know you're spoiling it for the rest of us.

Scrooge: That wasn't a raise. That was severance pay. Hurt like Charles Dickens for me to pay it. We're going to computers in '87. Scrooge & Marley have to keep up with the times.

Bailey: Cratchit didn't have the software to crunch the numbers, eh? I always got a kick out of seeing him sitting on that stool, scratching away with that quill pen.

Scrooge: Well, he was a sorry soul but he came cheap. We thought of sending the books offshore to one of the cheap labor countries to have them cooked up, but Cratchit was a heck of a bargain until he started having problems at home with that whiny kid of his.

Bailey: Productivity fell off? Absenteeism? Clockwatching? Tell me about it. I've been there. Almost took the bridge over an employee's blunder. I mean seriously.

Scrooge: I know. I saw the program. Say, what do you hear from the old buzzard Henry F. Potter? Man after my own heart. Ran a tight ship, Henry did. Reminded me of myself in my prime.

Bailey: Funny, he reminded me of Lionel Barrymore. Potter and I had our differences, but the business of business is business, as they say. Henry tried a hostile takeover but had to back off. Now we get along. He has his scams and I've got mine.

Scrooge: I was worried about you two. No reason you couldn't have worked together. You could have squeezed Bedford Falls dry.

Bailey: Well, I had a lot of soft-hearted liberal ideas. They sneaked up on me. They say Christmas will do that to you.

Scrooge: Don't I know it. If you could have seen me Christmas Day, you'd have thought I'd gone all mushy inside. Terrible nightmares. Woke up in a sweat. Started giving away money like it was going out of style. Feel a lot better now.

Bailey: I can see that. The old crafty sparkle in the eye. You look like that guy in the movies.

Scrooge: Robert Redford?

Bailey: No, Alistair somebody. Forget it.

Scrooge: I have. Oops, there goes my beeper. Gotta run.

Bailey: Right. Have a lucrative New Year, Eb.

Scrooge: You too, Jimmy - George - whatever your name is.

Could Santa run for president?

We political analysts try not to venture far out on limbs, but this time I feel I owe it to my readers and the American people.

My prediction: Santa Claus, if he runs for the presidency in 2000, will have only an outside chance of victory. He could be buried in a humiliating landslide.

But if he won the nomination of a major party he'd be a shoo-in.

I base this uncharacteristically forthright conclusion on the fact that a recent poll indicates Santa is perceived as an independent, and independents do poorly in presidential elections.

The poll, commissioned by Fox News, reported that nearly two thirds of registered voters think the old boy would have no party affiliation. Nine percent thought he would be a Democrat and 6 percent guessed Republican.

> *"When your most memorable public utterance is 'Ho, Ho, Ho', you've got a lot of wiggle room."*

A total of 517 voters were contacted Dec. 2-3 by phone, giving the poll a margin of error of plus or minus 4.5 percentage points, not enough to help the rotund geezer win a major party nomination.

It is my educated guess that the poll was an undisguised trial balloon sent aloft by the Santa forces in the Republican party to lure him into the race as a "spoiler" to draw liberal votes away from Gore.

They calculated that Santa, an empty-headed do-gooder with a record of being soft on spending other people's money, would make an easy target.

They could be wrong. The man has charisma and name recognition. Nobody ever says "Santa who?" He is untouched so far by sex scandal, but this could change after we jackals of the media get on his case.

But Santa's major weapon is his camouflaged position on the major issues of the day. So far, the man is perceived as a clean unknown because he never takes a stand on anything. When your most memorable public utterance is "ho-ho," you have a lot of wiggle room.

The original "Teflon" man, long before Ronald Reagan, he still remains beloved despite the fact that he has openly lied to the American people. He repeatedly promised innocent children he would bring them presents if they were good, then routinely reneged on delivery.

But somehow, instead of harboring resentment as they grew up, his victims worshipped the old fraud, later conspiring with him to deceive their own kids.

Final word: The major parties will regret not drafting this artful politician, if you ask this veteran analyst.

Turning over new leaf for new year

When you get to be my age you run out of new leaves to turn over, but it doesn't matter. There are plenty of pre-turned old leaves left over from past leaf-turnings to keep you busy.

Just pick one and turn it over again.

If you can't find a turnable leaf, just ask your spouse. He or she will be delighted to point one out to you.

"Why don't you turn over a new leaf next year and remember to keep the dog out of the bathtub?" she said recently. "You just have to slide the door shut, you know. Is that too much to ask? I'm sick of wiping up his paw prints. This isn't a dog house, you know."

"Oh yeah? Who says?" I replied, quickly biting my tongue and muttering: "Just kidding."

Some people think I've got the leaf image wrong. They think of the leaves as pages of a book - the old Self-Improvement Book for Men - Vols. 1-500.

But I like to think of them as leaves off a tree like our silver maple that showers those pesky helicopter seeds all over the front lawn.

(I tried to tell the tree to turn over a new leaf and stop it, but it can't help itself. It's a solitary sex act that's now become a disgusting habit.)

Turning over the leaves of a book doesn't hack it as a viable metaphor. It's too easy and neat. Wallowing around knee deep in leaves (bad habits needing correction) is more like the situation at our house.

One of the major leaves I've turned over successfully that have stayed turned over is the one about smoking. I wrestled with that damn leaf for years and finally got it upended and onto its back in 1980.

It has been suggested that I turn over the martini (on the rocks with olive) leaf, but I'm afraid my liver would wonder what's going on, so I've let that leaf lie there unmolested for now.

> *"Try it. Pick a leaf and just flip it over. It's no big deal."*

But if New Year's Eve comes and I'm desperate for leaves to turn over, I may give that one another nudge. I can always turn it back over again at the next happy hour.

As I've said many times, the timing is everything here. Vows made before midnight New Year's Eve can be pronounced fulfilled the following morning.

("How about that! No cigarettes ALL YEAR!")

I've celebrated that one more times than I can remember - from my teen years to age 60 and never failed to get that short-lived high that comes when you kick a bad habit for 24 hours.

Try it! Pick a leaf and just flip it over. It's no big deal.

Trouble with New Year's babies: they're all boys

C an it be a year since that diapered baby showed up? Wasn't he a cute little bugger?

What a precious smile! Little did we know it was just gas. We forgot to burp him. He turned out to be a mean little guy. Nothing but trouble.

Now he's an old geezer with scythe and hourglass. Sure, we'll sing Auld Lang Syne at him, but we're really giving him the bum's rush and he knows it.

All eyes will be on the new kid. Maybe this one will live up to our hopes, but don't bet on it.

It has been my experience, having seen a lot of years grow up, that few of them make the grade.

I think I know the problem. Funny I never noticed it before, and I'll bet you didn't either.

They're all boys!

Despite all the advances in the fight for equality all these years, every damn new year since that newspaper cartoon first appeared has been a boy kid. No wonder they've been so screwed up!

Another thing: All these kids look alike. They're all white, for one thing. All male with no identifiable ethnicity.

They all arrive with fireworks and hype, causing a giant traffic jam in Times Square. People put on stupid hats, blow toy horns, sing that stupid song, get drunk and kiss everyone in sight.

But by 12:05 a.m. the kid is out of there and nobody even notices he's gone! All he does is show up and split!

We don't see him again for an entire year and then he's an old geezer who forgot to shave during his entire lifetime.

We never find out what he does for a living. He gets married, has his midlife crisis, divorce, prostate surgery, all in total privacy.

We don't even know if he grew up fat or thin, got arrested and did time, or what. But the strangest part is we don't much care. Out of sight out of mind.

It's my feeling that if the new year were a girl, there would be a lot more interest in her as she grew up. Newspaper cartoonists, being mostly men with only one thing on their minds, would naturally want to check her out at age 19. I know I would.

When she finally made her final exit, we'd say: "There goes one hell of a girl. Never lost her looks or her temper."

We'd sing Auld Lang Syne with real feeling and tears. (It means "long time since," you know, Scottish for "the good old days.")

Then I suppose some cartoonist would figure, for the sake of gender equality, that it was time for a sex change.

We'd take one look and say: "Oh God! Not another one of THOSE!"

New Year's life: Solitary, poor, nasty, brutish, and short

I keep thinking of that little orphan kid, New Year, in the diaper, top hat and sash with 2000 painted on it.

Despite being born out of wedlock and abandoned, like all his predecessors, he comes into the world tiny and vulnerable but brimming with optimism and promise.

Then 365 days later he's a dying old man with a scythe and an hourglass that's run out. He heads off into the darkness beaten and discouraged — the cheers for his successor ringing in his ears.

The way we, a so-called civilized society and acknowledged leader of the free world, treat our New Years is a scandal. Talk about child neglect!

In between his birth and death he just disappears.

After the big welcome, we never hear a word about him and couldn't care less.

When he dies, none of us goes to the funeral. We don't even mourn. The general feeling is that he never amounted to much, never fulfilled his destiny, so good riddance. He's a failure, like all the old used-up years before him.

When you figure the life expectancy for a male child these days is 78, the kid sure ages in a hurry.

Let's see, 78 years in 365 days! In a little over a week he'll be in his terrible twos!

Or, dividing 12 months into 78, you get 6.5 years per month. In February he'll be in first grade!

By mid-March he'll be either an Eagle Scout or experimenting with drugs. Give him another week and he'll be dealing them.

Because of his rapid aging, he'll get social promotions nearly every week. I imagine his swift graduation to sexual maturity will be a problem for the school authorities and his female classmates.

("Johnny, you're old enough to know better than that!" "But gee, Mrs. Murgatroyd, I'm only 3!")

By June, when other kids are going to day camp and playing baseball, he'll be having his midlife crisis.

"Sometimes it seems life is just passing me by," he tells his analyst.

"When did you first get that feeling?"

"When I started fifth grade last February."

My wife asked me whether I knew why the New Year is always a boy baby. I told her it's because the cartoonists want to spare the feelings of women.

"We geezers take wrinkles in stride. Crones are more sensitive," I explained.

Recycle those old resolutions

The important thing to remember about making New Year's resolutions is to stick to those that have withstood the tests of time.

Don't make new resolutions. Recycle the old ones.

For example, every year since 1980 I have resolved to continue not smoking. This saves me the trouble of thinking up new self-improvement vows that might prove more difficult to keep. Unkept vows undermine one's self-esteem.

I like to think of this process as will-power conservation.

> **"...That would make an excellent resolution: Resolve not to squander will-power on new resolutions."**

In fact, that would make an excellent resolution: Resolve not to squander will power on new resolutions.

One can never have too much will power. It's important to conserve it by fighting the urge to resolve.

Come to think of it, conserving energy isn't a bad idea either. I've been instinctively doing that for years now without the formality of a resolution.

I've found that energy conservation gets easier with each passing year. At my advanced age, it is almost effortless.

A friend told me just yesterday that his will-power conservation secret was to swear off only those things or activities you never contemplated in the first place.

"For example, I'm swearing off eating whale blubber next year," he explained.

"Not bad," I said. "Mind if I join you?"

This year, in addition to my tobacco and blubber vows, I have decided to swear off the accumulation of great wealth. That has proved easy for me in the past. All I had to do was cleverly select the right profession and fight off the advances of rich women.

It is important to make the correct decisions now, because time is running out, and the stakes are much higher than usual this year. Millennium resolutions made Sunday should not be taken lightly.

New Century resolutions are bad enough but millenniums (millennia?) last 1,000 years and put a terrible strain on one's will-power resources.

Remember, self-improvement is not for everyone. It is all right for children, but can be harmful for impressionable adults. As they get closer and closer to maturity and perfection, it can even be fatal.

To be on the safe side, I recommend resolving to swear off resolutions at least until the year 3000.

Chapter Eleven

Really Random

The Almighty watches the Super Bowl
Barbie lets herself go
Too 'mature' for tennis?
Ships lose their feminine identity
"Interesting question" (or not?)
Let's become unhyphenated
Nicknames through the ages
Hyatt Regency "skeleton" serves guests
Dick's answering machine: "Press 1 now"
Panic at announcement of plane crash
Hot idea: voting machines with levers
Eating your way through the news
"Put the toaster on the phone," says tabloid journalist
He goes, like, wow!
Did Ghengis Kahn have "bad hair days"?
Script ideas for a Seinfeld episode
What did Neanderthals talk about?
Science explains springtime fancies
Motherhood at 60? What about Dad?
Forgive us our (financial) debts
Female hurricanes deadlier than the male?
A totally flexible generic prayer

The Almighty watches the Super Bowl

I n this fantasy I see the Almighty and some male angels sitting around in the celestial den with their feet up, watching the Super Bowl.

"Look, there's another one bowing his head and crossing himself. What's that all about?"

"He's thanking you for that touchdown, Boss."

"Me? What makes him think I'm rooting for Green Bay?"

"The same misconception that the Patriots guy had when he intercepted that pass and ran all the way to the goal line. He knelt down and beamed a thanksgiving prayer. These guys think you really care about this game and are on both their sides."

"They think I intervene on every play? That's incredible!"

"Actually, they thank you only for the good things. When something bad happens, they throw their helmets on the ground and cry for damnation."

"Damnation. Who do they think they are, ordering me about? I'm omnipotent. I never even accept suggestions."

"It may not be blasphemy, exactly. It's sort of harmless."

"I'll be the judge of what's harmless. What do they say, exactly? Give it to me straight."

"They say GODDAMMIT."

"Really?

"I'm sure they don't mean it. They've just lost control. It's a reflex. Part of the game."

"In other words, on every scoring play, one guy is beaming thanksgiving prayers at me and others are imploring me to damn the same outcome? How stupid can you get? If I wanted to intervene in the affairs of men, I'd do something sensible, like making them smarter and peace-loving. I wouldn't squander my powers on a game of pushing and shoving."

"Maybe you should send them a non-returnable message?"

"A message?"

"A thunderbolt, perhaps?"

"That seems a little harsh, don't you think? And they might not get it. Humans are not the brightest creatures I ever created, you know, and these brutes seem exceptionally retarded."

"You could just leave the whole thing alone, I suppose. Don't intervene, just let the victors thank you. Ignore the soreheads' oaths. Chalk them up as the mouthings of fools who know not what they do."

"In other words forgive them. Is that what you're trying to say?"

"It's your call, Boss."

"I know. It's always my call. My son would say forgive and forget. But tell you what ..."

"What?"

"Hand me that clicker. First let's see what's on the other channels."

Barbie lets herself go

That new realistic non-bimbo Barbie doll is just the ticket in this Age of Sensitivity.

You've probably heard that the Mattel toy company is going to reduce the size of her bust and lard up her waist with a little fake cellulite.

The idea is reported to be in response to a supposed yearning for "realism" among today's little girls. Barbie's critics have always felt that her magnificent bosom (38-inches), slim waist (18) and rounded hips (34) foster feelings of inadequacy in their little mammas.

But I'm afraid the marketing surveyors blew this one. I'll bet they quizzed the usual "focus groups" but forgot to tell the mothers to wait outside.

"How many of you like this new Barbie better than the old Barbie?" the "facilitator" asks.

Little heads swivel in unison to look at mommies, then eager hands shoot up.

"I like the new Barbie best!"

"Me too!"

"I like her best because she looks more like a real woman — more like my mommy than a movie star."

"Yeah, mine too!"

"Yeah, my mommy's pretty, but let's face it . . . uh-oh!"

Mattel concluded from these responses that there was a blockbuster market for a plain Barbie.

However, the giant toy company isn't stupid. It did not retire Bimbo Barbie. She's still wiggling down the assembly line runway.

I think I know what was going through the great minds at Mattel. They saw, as I do, a new way of playing with dolls. Think about it: A little girl is playing with new Barbie. She squeezes her waistline.

"Filling out are we, Barbie? Getting into the cookie jar again? Bad Barbie! Disgusting Barbie! Look how cute Old Barbie looks. She doesn't lie in bed watching soap operas and stuffing her fat face like some people I know. Mommy is ashamed of you. Mommy's going to spank you. Now get with the program!"

Of course I've never been a little girl, but I know something about playing with dolls.

I know when my Ken doll picks up Barbie to take her to the sock hop and sees how she has let herself go, he'll recoil inside. He won't say anything then, but I know how the date will end.

"That was a wonderful evening, wasn't it, Ken?"

"It was OK."

"Want to sit on the porch swing and fool around for awhile?"

"Nah. I've gotta go home and study. Big test tomorrow."

Too "mature" for tennis?

Funny how your priorities change over the years. It seems only yesterday that I cared deeply when a tennis ball bounced out of reach.

I hated it when I was forced to say "nice shot."

Today I'm more philosophical. I weigh up the alternatives:

Should I make a show of darting forward and striving mightily to forestall the dreaded second bounce?

Will it permanently damage my self-esteem if I fail?

Will it give my opponent undeserved satisfaction?

After all, he's not Pete Sampras. He might get the idea that he "earned" the point, when in fact I chose not to contest it seriously.

Will success make him uppity?

Until recently I would decide to play it safe and go after the ball on the long chance I could make the shot and experience that uppity feeling myself.

But for the last year I have been able to hang back and pretend it doesn't matter.

"Let him run after it, if he wants it so badly. It's not that big a deal in the grand scheme of things," I'd tell myself.

I figure this change of attitude is a sign of maturity. I prefer that term to being "over the hill." That only happens to old people.

Still, I'm a little worried that I am able to lose so many points and not get disgusted with myself as I used to do in the past. If I can take defeat so graciously, what's the point of the game in the first place?

I remember when I gave up golf because my putts never seemed to go in the cup. I vowed not to go back out on the course until they invented the funnel-shaped green with the hole in the middle.

There's no reason why an athletic move like hitting a drive or a long fairway iron shot should be negated by such a stupid patty-cake shot like a putt, I complained.

So I turned my back on golf and never really missed it.

Now here I am asking myself what's the big deal about getting the ball back over the net.

Does this mean that I'm on the verge of giving up another sport just because it's pointless and I can't be bothered?

If so, how come I spent all that time and money learning how to play the stupid game?

Maybe I'd better get out there and give a damn again. Chase down those little yellow balls and whack the hell out of them, you old geezer.

Sometimes too much maturity is bad for you.

Ships lose their feminine identity

I t was a shock to learn that the *Queen Mary* had been spayed and the *Prince of Wales* neutered.

In case you haven't heard, *Lloyd's List*, the shipping industry newspaper, announced the done deed last week.

Now they're both "its" instead of traditional "shes."

The editors felt it was time to have all ships "fixed," although they didn't use that ominous word that strikes fear into the hearts of dogs and cats and turns calves into veals.

> **"But I suppose it's no big deal, whether male or female, to be an 'it' if you're fictitious."**

Lloyd's called it an act designed to bring the publication into the world of modern, unsentimental international usage.

I have to admit that I've always had a problem with calling male ships, such as the *Bonhomme Richard* and the *Flying Dutchman*, by the feminine pronoun.

The same with the late German terror of the seas, the *Bismarck*, sunk off France by the *Prince of Wales* in one of the great sea battles of World War II. It's hard to think of either of them as feminine but even harder to imagine their reaction on learning they'd been neutered.

I suppose this means that shipbuilders will think twice before they put their newborn in harm's way. We'll be seeing a lot of sexless *Titanics, Lusitanias, Monitors, Merrimacs, Nautiluses, USS Lexingtons* and *Bountys* from now on.

Even the *HMS Pinafore* would feel threatened in today's new world. I'm not sure about the *Pequod*, Captain Ahab's whaler in the novel *Moby Dick*, either. It could be either gender.

But I suppose it's no big deal, whether male or female, to be an "it" if you're fictitious.

However, I'm sure Horatio Hornblower would be outraged to learn that his beloved first command, *Lydia,* had been given a hysterectomy by a shipping newspaper editor.

I'm told by mariner friends that calling a boat or ship "she" has always been a term of affection.

Unnatural as it may seem to seasickness-prone landlubbers like me, it has become traditional. I think *Lloyd's List* will regret tampering with the gender of the seafarers' beloveds.

I have no ax to grind. To me, all vessels are *its*, even the 10-foot Cape Cod Skiff I used to sail around Great South Bay out of Fire Island in the 1930s.

IT and I became quite close, but I never confused *IT* with any of the bronzed, sun-bleached teenage *shes* who let me look but never touch.

"Interesting question" (or not?)

We were watching one of those round-table discussions on PBS the other night when someone on the panel said: "That's a very interesting question."

My viewing companion, an outspoken woman (is there any other kind?) said: "Why do they DO that?"

"Do what?"

"Call a dull, and even dumb question interesting when it's obviously not. Just once, I'd like to hear someone say, 'That is a very uninteresting question.' I know it's uninteresting. You know it's uninteresting. They know it's uninteresting. So why do they always flatter the questioner?"

I told her it's part of the protocol of TV punditry. The producers can't let one pundit out-pundit another. They try to break up the tedium by making the panelists fake some interest in each other's views.

Before the show, one pundit says to another, "When I've made my point, I'll pause and look at you. That's your cue to ask me, `What is the mood in the White House in the light of these revelations?' or your usual, 'How will this play in the hinterlands?' Got it?"

"Got it," says second pundit. "But don't forget. You have to say: 'Well, Dick, that's a very interesting question.' Otherwise, no deal."

"Well, that's stretching, don't you think?" responds first pundit.

"Look, you know the drill," says the second. "It's like the Senate. Everyone is a 'distinguished senator, from someplace or other."

She was unconvinced.

"Wouldn't it be refreshing," she wanted to know, "to hear someone say: 'Can you expand on that point?' Why do they always want to expand on points?"

I told her that would open the door to all sorts of abuses. "You'd have pundits saying, 'Let's try to place that out of context.' "

"Hey! I LIKE that," she said. "How about 'Let's view this from a murkier, narrower perspective.'"

"Not bad. Or have the host say: 'David, can you help us place this whole situation totally out of focus?' "

"That could lead to out-of-focus groups!"

"Long overdue," I agreed. "We could bunk myths about productivity and the economy! I remember a funny piece in the *New Yorker* where a guy talked about mitigated gall, ruly crowds and strong givings, promptu and sapid remarks and shrinking horizons."

"Look him up and let's get him on the NewsHour With Jim Lehrer."

"Great idea! Two ways about it!"

Let's become unhyphenated

My people got through another season of ethnic festivals without having to paint ourselves blue and dance around the bonfire. I consider that a big plus.

It means we Celtic-Americans have outgrown our hyphens. We're just Americans now. One day perhaps all of you will be unhyphenated too.

All it takes is the passage of time. You never hear of English-Americans any more. They don't even have a month for themselves.

The Germans and Italians have just about outgrown their hyphens. The Belgians, Finns, Dutch and many others never really had any to speak of.

Africans still have theirs although they've been in America for many more generations than a lot of us.

The Chinese, Japanese and other Asians and Latins can't seem to get rid of theirs either, so they cling to them in self defense. But surely their day will come.

Oh sure, some of us Celts still get together in the saloons on St. Patrick's Day (even us non-Catholics) and listen to our tiresome diddilee-diddilee fiddle music, but we hardly ever get naked in public and make fools of ourselves any more.

Pat Truly, columnist for the *Fort Worth Star-Telegram*, sees this issue differently. He wants to have a Scots-Irish-English-Celt-Picts-Gaels and Saxon-American Heritage Month.

He wants us to revive the parades of blue-painted naked men and women and have banquets at which sides of roast beef are the hors d'oeuvres.

We'd hear "speeches in 14th Century Gaelic and other historic languages that no one would understand, but what the hey!"

After all, he says, our people "developed the bagpipes, the Irish flute and the Gilbert and Sullivan operetta, to say nothing of many hymns, Burns, Shakespeare, Wordsworth . . . etc., and left the entire world richer for their literature and art . . ."

That's one way to look at it, I suppose.

But I say let's all unhyphenate ourselves once and for all. "Diversity" is the popular thing these days. It's not a bad concept, but to me it seems to celebrate those damned hyphens.

I know it's obsolete, but I liked the old-fashioned "melting pot" image a whole lot better.

Hyatt Regency "skeleton" serves guests

(Because of financing difficulties, Rochester's Hyatt Regency Hotel sat unfinished at the corner of Main and St. Paul, its steel and concrete skeleton dominating the skyline in the 1980s and prompting this fictictious shouted exchange.)

Front desk! Give me the manager!

Hyatt Regency here. How may I help you?

There are no towels in this room. No little bars of soap sealed in little monogrammed wrappers.

An oversight, sir, I'll send a boy right up. You're on the eighth floor, I see. Is there anything else?

Well, a bed would be nice. With a mattress, some sheets, and blankets. And pillows. That's about it. Wait! My wife says she can't find the tub or toilet. Don't you have a toilet with one of those monogrammed paper ribbons around the seat?

No problem. One tub, one toilet with seat ribbon, coming right up. Anything else? We're a full service hotel.

Well, since I've got you on the line. I can't find the controls for the air conditioning. What if I want to turn it down?

We've had a small problem with the air conditioning but we're checking with the weather bureau. The controls are coordinated with the outside temperature and wind direction.

Wait, I think I see the problem. There are no windows! But the view is certainly fantastic!

Shall I send up some windows, then? Perhaps some doors? Carpeting? We do all we can to make your stay a truly romantic adventure.

Yes, I see that. Now could you connect me with room service?

Another of our dramatic touches! Instead of sending up orders, we provide each room with a propane camp stove and packages of freeze-dried food. The beef stroganoff is nice. Just add water from the canteen and voila!

Mon dieu! Haute cuisine. And I must say the idea of having luggage delivered by crane and offering hard hats to your guests is quite innovative. By the way, may we keep this handsome megaphone as a memento of our stay?

Certainly. Actually, it is an orange traffic cone modified for in-house communication with our guests. And thank you for staying with us here at the Hyatt. If it's adventure you want, let us be your high-altitude base camp whenever you're in Rochester.

Dick's answering service: "Press 1 now"

I'm thinking of installing one of those new computer-assisted phone answering systems for the convenience of you callers.

You know what I mean, the kind that start out saying, "If you are calling from a touch tone phone, press 1 now."

First I'd record a personal message saying "your call is important to me" and explaining that it "may be monitored to ensure that the high reader service standards of the Dougherty Hotline are met."

Then I'd subject the caller to a brief key-pressing drill designed to sort friend from foe.

"If this is a hostile call, press 1 now," the voice will say.

If the caller selects this option, he or she will be instantly rewarded with a dial tone.

Those who stay on the line will be offered the next option:

"If this is a friendly call to express admiration for Dougherty's keen insight and impeccable logic, press 2 now."

If the caller chooses this option, he or she will be warmly greeted by a live voice, saying: "Hi there! Dougherty, your full-service columnist speaking! What can I do for you today?"

Of course the system may require some fine tuning based on customer response.

For example, the hostile caller might be told Mr. Dougherty and his staff of service reps are assisting other angry customers, but to stay on the line.

"Your diatribe will be processed by the next available representative," he will be told as selections from Lawrence Welk's Greatest Hits waft over the line in the background.

This might be followed by frequent interruptions saying all the representatives are still busy, but to stay on the line.

Eventually, of course, he will be disconnected.

However, I think that response is too cruel. A quick cutoff would be more humane.

My friend Al has an answering machine announcement that tells the caller to check and see if an extension phone is off the hook. Friends know that this is actually an invitation to leave a message at the beep.

Perhaps I could use a variation of that call-filtering scam.

I'll be working on this system over the next few months. If you want to check my progress, call my number and see if I, or a recorded robot, answers.

Good luck and thank you for calling the Dougherty Automated Reader Service Hotline.

192

Panic at announcement of plane crash

We were sitting in back of an overhead TV set in the gate lounge at Chicago's O'Hare International Sunday morning waiting to board our flight home.

Facing us were row on row of silent upturned faces watching a CNN report on EgyptAir Flight 990. Some were shocked. All somber. Some couples were holding hands.

Between announcements of boardings and arrivals we could hear snatches of the audio.

Down off Nantucket, 217 aboard and feared lost.

We'd heard some of it earlier in the hotel in Fort Worth.

Plummeted from 33,000 feet in two minutes. Water 270 feet deep.

No distress call.

Feared lost. Next of kin...

My wife sighed: "Feared lost," she murmured. "Feared lost."

Later, after we were home and had unpacked and turned on the TV, it was showing the faces of families assembling at JFK.

That's when it hit my wife:

"Do you realize that all of us, all the people we care most for, were in the air today? Just think."

The wedding in Fort Worth was over. Our son and new daughter-in-law were flying off on their wedding trip. Our other son and his little girl were on their way home to Manhattan, our daughter to Colorado. All the out of town guests — all flying somewhere.

I tried to be cool and logical:

"But look at the odds. Five, six planes. All going down the same day? It's an impossibility."

She gave me a withering look.

"More than a hundred were at the wedding. We met them all. All of them so happy and animated at the reception. Having so much fun. All our new Texas family and friends. Try to imagine all that grief. Tom (our daughter's husband) waiting at home with the two girls."

"But . . ." I said.

"You should write something about this," she declared.

"I couldn't. I mean, nothing happened. We didn't crash. We all got home safely!"

Just about then New York Mayor Giuliani appeared on TV announcing that grieving families were being flown to Providence, Rhode Island, where they could walk the beaches and stare out to sea.

They were being asked to bring medical records and photos to help identify their loved ones, he said.

My wife looked at me with a now-do-you-feel-it expression.

Logic forgotten, I felt it.

I liked it better when I hadn't.

Hot idea: voting machines with levers

I f Florida had had the sense to buy and stick with Rochesterian Jacob Myers' 1880s voting machine, all this election 2000 unpleasantness in Palm Beach County, Fla., could have been avoided.

"Is that a fair statement?" I asked Andy Wynham yesterday.

"Absolutely," he said.

Andy is customer support manager of the Jamestown company that's the successor to Myers' American Ballot Machine Co. on Mill Street, which manufactured his automatic voting machine, or AVM, and its many later versions.

> *"I envision a machine like a computer that enjoys 'processing' data by making it disappear."*

"The old mechanical AVM is obsolete now, but we try to service them for New York customers by replacing parts cannibalized from the few machines we have left."

Is he able to keep them all going? "Barely," he said.

His firm, a division of Sequoia Pacific Voting Equipment Co. of California, now makes an electronic model called the Advantage, which is high-tech but still as voter friendly as Adler's machine.

"What we're talking about here is 'direct record' voting machines versus 'central tab' machines like Palm Beach, where the voter marks a paper ballot that has to be read by another machine."

"The old mechanical AVM and our electronic Advantage model don't allow the voter to make the kind of mistakes they claim to have made in Florida. There's no paper to be punched. It's just the voter and the machine — a direct record."

I didn't think it would be good form to wax nostalgic over the passing of the old machines, thereby identifying myself as a sentimental old geezer, but I do think Jacob's old levers and gears are still the way to go.

When you mention the word electronic I envision a machine like a computer that enjoys "processing" data by making it disappear. When you pulled a lever on one of Jake's old machines, or its successors, it stayed pulled.

Jake was a safe maker and knew how to machine intricate parts so they worked smoothly and precisely.

His first machine appeared on the scene in the election of 1892 in Lockport, down Route 18 in Niagara County.

The last was made in Jamestown in 1982. After that, gears and levers were replaced by transistors and silicon chips.

If you ask me, it's been downhill ever since.

Eating your way through the news

Some old timers say the written word is dying. TV is killing it.
I disagree and I'll tell you why: You can't eat TV.
For years I have been eating newspapers and magazines and I have to say they're as tasty and satisfying as ever.

Actually, I don't really eat them in the metabolic sense of swallowing and digesting to generate energy. I just sort of casually nibble on them.

My method, which some picky people, including my present roommate, deem an offensive habit, consists of ripping triangular corners off the pages of reading matter and chewing them into what used to be called "spitballs."

When I have extracted the flavor, I roll the fragment between thumb and forefinger and lob a two-pointer into the wastebasket.

Back in the distant past when most of us first discovered paper as a delicacy, we'd fire them at elementary school classmates using ruler, peashooter or rubber band launchers.

Now most of us are too adult for that, although sometimes I'll fire one at a sleeping dog to watch him jolt awake and mistake it for used food.

One of the important benefits of this curious habit is that it enables you to quickly find your place in a magazine by riffling through the pages.

I especially enjoy nibbling highbrow magazines such as the *New Yorker*, *Atlantic* and *Harpers*. They have good texture and compact nicely.

A single page corner can be formed into a sphere and tucked in the bridgework for later excavation with a paperclip.

This newspaper has a more spongy but equally satisfying texture. Try this page now if you are left-handed. If you're a righty, try 3A. There. See what I mean?

Personally, I don't recommend the color ads and I avoid all pre-printed inserts. I am an ROP (Run-of-Paper) man myself.

If your roommate is a fastidious housekeeper, I would not recommend this practice. Luckily, mine is not.

As the designated vacuum operator, I am able to police up my "misses" before company comes.

Despite these precautions, she often expresses disapproval.

"What a disgusting habit!" she will remark. "I don't understand the appeal."

"Simple. It compares to picking a peeling sunburn or mining ear wax," I explain. "I haven't chewed a fingernail since 1980 when I gave up smoking and chewing tobacco."

That's a fib, actually. I've been snacking on the stuff since the third grade, but who's counting?

"Put the toaster on the phone,"
says tabloid journalist

W e've got 17 years to duck.
That's when the asteroid known as NT7 may or may not hit us.
(Correction: Make that hit *you*. I'll be 101 by then and have no firm plans to be around to watch.)

The asteroid is estimated to be 1.2 miles wide. Scientists say that is enough to risk killing a significant portion of the human population.

A British social anthropologist terms NT7 the "most threatening object in the short history of asteroid detection" and says it's "important to raise public awareness of the threat posed by asteroids and other bodies in space."

"Osama bin Laden Builds Giant Asteroid in Secret Space Factory"

Personally, I plan to keep up to date on the threat by browsing the headlines in the supermarket tabloids. This is their kind of story and I'm sure they'll be constantly raising our awareness.

They've done a magnificent job of keeping us abreast of the space aliens threat, for example.

"Space Aliens Raped My Electric Broom!" (*Weekly World News*).

The *WWN* is right on top of the continuing talking appliance story. An editor explained recently that "If someone calls and says their toaster is talking to them, I don't refer them to professional help, I say put the toaster on the phone."

Zealous newsgathering like this characterizes their medical science coverage too. ("New Hope for the Dead!" and "Blind Mom Can See After Baby Gives Her a Hug.")

I look forward to the revelations to come about the approaching asteroid, of which NT7 is surely the first of many.

"Osama bin Laden Builds Giant Asteroid in Secret Factory in Space!"

"DOW Falls on News of Attack from Asteroids Piloted by Suicide Space Aliens."

Some people prefer *Scientific American* and NASA bulletins for news of impending doom from Outer Space, but I think they are too slanted with graphs and numbers and have a history of covering up the juicy stuff.

For example: Why did their science reporters ignore the WWN scoop: "Baby Born With Tattoo of Solar System?"

Just a simple oversight?

I don't think so.

He goes, like, wow!

I think I'm catching on to this tricky Modern English. Once you get the hang of it, it's really cool.

You just have to unlearn a lot of archaic grammar and vocabulary rules.

One of the most confusing rules involves the verb "to go" when it is being used as the wildly popular substitute for "to say."

For example, you might think the past tense of say (said) is "went." It's not. It's "goes," as the sentence: "I go 'whatcha doin' and she goes 'nothin.' "

You'd never say: "I went whatcha doin' " and "she went nothin.' "

It's especially important for people in my journalism profession to master the rules of this modern idiom because we want to make ourselves clear to the young who do not comprehend traditional English.

For example, say you're reporting on a presidential press conference and trying tell your readers that Mr. Clinton says he'll use the line-item veto on a welfare bill.

You don't write "The president went 'I'm gonna, like, veto that suckah.' " That would be incorrect. Instead you write: "The president goes 'I'm gonna, like, veto that suckah.' "

> *"You don't write 'The president went I'm gonna, like, veto that suckah.' That would be incorrect."*

We'll get to proper use of "like" in a minute. For now, just remember that when used as extraneous punctuation like the above, it's, like, set off by commas.

But back to the verb to go, again: We've covered the past tense. The present tense is easier. There isn't any. One never says "And then I'm going: 'that's cool.' " It's always "And then I go: 'that's cool.' "

I just finished reading a piece by a California language professor who was explaining how "like" has recently expanded into something more than just punctuation.

Now, he explained, it is used to describe a reaction to something, as in his example:

"He goes: 'You can't do that here' and I'm like (long significant pause) 'I can't believe this!' "

In our example of the press conference, we might report: "Clinton goes: 'I'm gonna veto that suckah' and Newt Gingrich is like 'yuck!' " (The "yuck" may be audible or it may be facially mimed.)

I was telling my wife about all this and she goes: "Why can't you express yourself like a grownup?" and I'm like, wow — I just stare at her and roll my eyes and go: "To, like, be or not to be, that is the question" and she's like "I can't stand it!" and I'm like would you believe speechless?

Did Ghengis Kahn have "bad hair days"?

W hat's all this about bad hair days?
Are there any other kind?
You want to see bad hair? On *any* day, just come with me to the back of my photo and I'll show you some positively evil hair.

Luckily, I never have to go there so it doesn't undermine my self-esteem, but I know it's there. My wife/barber told me.

Occasionally I'll catch a glimpse of it when I open the mirrored door of the medicine cabinet and see its reflection in the shower door mirror, but it's only fleeting.

Sometimes I'll be looking at an old photo album dating back 30 years or more and I'll ask my wife, "Who's the bald guy who looks a little like me?"

But I think it's silly to think of hair as bad or good. Hair is hair.

To scowl at it and say, "Bad hair, BAD hair!" is fruitless. It does about as much good as shouting "BAD DOG!" Hair and dogs just laugh and shrug off such intemperate outbursts.

But wait: As long as we've gone this far on this silly subject, let's at least try to be clinically accurate:

What we're talking about in my case is a round patch of pale skin about four inches in diameter surrounded by thinning white hair that is neither good hair nor bad hair but simply *there hair.*

As you might guess, this subject popped into my increasingly hairless head while reading another of those "new studies."

This one was by a professor of "psychology and gender studies" at Yale. She claimed that "bad hair" can trigger real psychological "trauma." It can make you pathologically self-critical and antisocial.

Women react with shame and embarrassment when their hair looks unattractive. Men withdraw and can become antisocial and even dangerous, she said.

I have to admit that I was inclined to scoff at this scientific study, but then I thought of all the historical figures, like Genghis Khan, whose unsociable behavior could easily have been caused by too many bad hair days.

If Hitler had not had serial bad hair days, combined with persistent "stupid moustache" days, even years, might he have turned into an amiable house painter instead of a genocidal murderer?

If the Boston Strangler had been befriended by a kindly hairstylist, would he have spared his victims? Did he ever say, "My hair made me do it"?

Think about it.

I know I do.

Script ideas for a last episode

J erry Seinfeld got me thinking: How would I want my final episode of this column to unfold, assuming I one day decide to take my millions and begin a new career while I'm still at the top of my game?

"How about revealing that deep underneath you're really a rabid right-wing Republican who hates dogs and secretly loves nothing better than working on his lawn and cleaning the basement?" my wife suggested.

"You mean give up my hard-won reputation as the last of the knee-jerk, bubble-headed liberals, international conspirators and infidels? I don't *think* so. Who would carry on my great work?" I wanted to know.

"Nobody," she said. "Liberalism is dead. In the final episode you reveal that for all these years you've been living a lie, pretending you're out of step with the times when in fact you think Rush Limbaugh is a left-wing wimp."

"Not bad," I had to admit. It sure would hype the ratings.

We toyed with the idea of having the last episode opening with me down in the basement gun room, lovingly polishing my AK-47 assault rifle.

"Give up my hard-won reputation as the last of the knee-jerk, bubble-headed liberals? I don't **think** *so."*

"Going hunting?" my wife asks.

"Nah. Stevie's third grade teacher wants to me to give a hands-on demonstration. I'm going show the kids how I converted this baby to full-automatic. I'll tell them how those kids in Arkansas would have doubled their body count if they'd had my know-how and one of these."

On the wall behind me are racks and racks of guns of all types. In the corner are some fishing rods alongside creels full of hand grenades.

Mounted heads of various animals, including one cow and a golden retriever puppy, line the walls.

Another scenario has us sitting in the den. I'm reading an item from the *Wall Street Journal*.

"Get this: `Investors hail announcement of vast layoffs,' it says. Now we'll see some action on Wall Street! There's been entirely too much emphasis on research and new product development in this country. I wondered when they were going to wake up and fire more people."

To let the readers enjoy the full impact of this final episode, I feel obliged to continue my mush-headed knee-jerking right up the end, at the same time hyping the "Big Surprise - Coming Soon!"

I want to leave 'em laughing.

What did Neanderthals talk about?

Anthropologists are excited about new research that suggests humans could talk as early as 400,000 years ago when our ancestors were known as Neanderthals.

Skeletal evidence shows that the position of the larynx, or voice box, of the Neanderthals was low in the neck, enabling them to make a wide variety of sounds.

Apes' larynxes, like those of newborn human infants, are high in the neck, so they can only grunt. (Only when an infant's larynx descends, can it begin to learn to talk.)

Naturally this discovery and other related evidence involving nerve pathways and tongue development, has scientists wondering what Neanderthals talked about.

It is only a question of time before tape recordings of cave-dwelling Neanderthals' conversations are discovered by sheepherders and eventually reprinted in the tabloids.

But why wait? The answers are right here in this column:

It is obvious to me from my reading of subsequent human history that the first conversation among early humans went something like this:

First Neanderthal: "Gimme that!"

Second Neanderthal: "Uh-uh."

First Neanderthal: "Take that!"

Third Neanderthal: "Oooh, look! Og squish Hank like bug!"

First Neanderthal: "Gimme!"

Third Neanderthal: "Sure thing, Og. No problem."

Eventually civilization developed subtle variations on this basic theme, such as exchanges of gunfire, germ warfare and terror bombing of the major population centers.

The report that inspired these thoughts appeared Sunday in the *New York Times* and was illustrated by two busts of Neanderthals. One Neanderthal is depicted as saying: "The rain in Spain . . ." His companion replies: "mainly in the plain."

Somehow, I find this clever but historically doubtful. Neither even remotely resembled Eliza Doolittle or Prof. Higgins of *My Fair Lady*.

However, I'll concede that not all conversation among these early ancestors were necessarily hostile.

It is not inconceivable that Neanderthals had their moments of genuine concern for each other. I can see them sitting around the fire, resting between aggressions:

First Neanderthal: "Ah Choo!"

Second Neanderthal: "Gesundheit."

FN: "Lot of it going around."

SN: "Here, have some prehistoric chicken soup."

Science explains springtime fancies

"Keep your hands to yourself, buster," the girls used to tell us guys when we were teenagers back in the 1930s and sex education hadn't yet been invented.

Now that we're older and smarter, and living an age of scientific research and discovery, we realize that if we'd been born 50 years later, we could have explained ourselves more adequately and soothed their apprehensions.

"It's just that this time of year my suprachiasmatic nuclei start acting up in response to the lengthening daylight," we might have said.

"It's all perfectly natural, biologically speaking."

They'd have been impressed by our erudition and apologize for misjudging our motives.

The luscious object of our purely scientific interest would have been reassured:

"Oh, well, in that case, proceed with your investigation," she'd say. "I thought you were just being fresh. Please continue, but remember, I'm ticklish."

The scientific purity of our motives having been established, we'd move right along:

"It's just that at this time of year my suprachiasmatic nuclei start acting up..."

"As I was about to say, paraphrasing the great poet, Alfred Lord Tennyson (1808-1892), 'In the spring a young man's fancy lightly turns to thoughts of love, inspired by the secretions of his pineal gland which serves as an internal biological clock.'"

"How fascinating!" she'd exclaim.

"Yes, isn't it! You see, the suprachiasmatic nuclei is located in the brain's hypothalamus and moderates the function of the pineal gland which produces melatonin, a hormone that slows down activity in the fall and increases it in the spring."

"You're so smart! But keep your voice down. You'll wake up my parents."

"In the spring, as daylight lasts longer melatonin secretions decline and all animals, including us, are energized. They go searching for romance, as you and I would be doing if we weren't so deeply engaged in this purely scientific study."

According to the latest biological studies I've been reading lately in preparation for this scientific paper, all this activity is timed to get under way in the spring so we animals can mate and give birth in the warm months when food is plentiful.

It's a holdover from the days when we used to hunt and gather for a living.

But there's no need to get into that mating part just yet.

Give it a little time. We mustn't spook our research partner this early in the study.

Motherhood at 60? What about dad?

A column on our op-ed page Monday said there was no medical reason why women over 60 couldn't have babies.

They'd have to get a fertilized egg from a younger woman, but recent studies have shown that age and menopause are no barrier to pregnancy.

Syndicated columnist Suzanne Fields was commenting on a study of 77 pregnant post menopausal women reported in the *Journal of the American Medical Association*.

"What do you say, kiddo," I asked my wife at the breakfast table; "Want to go for it?"

She said she'd have to think it over. A fraction of a second later she said: "I've thought it over."

"And your answer is...?"

"Been there, done that. I may be over 60 but I'm not losing my mind yet," she said.

I'm glad she feels that way because I can't see myself being a father and a grandfather simultaneously. Imagine being drafted again as a Little League umpire at age 96 and being called a blind bum by some kid's irate 30-year-old mother!

That happened to me once. I thumbed her out of the bleachers, but everyone thought I was kidding and just laughed at me. Never again!

It was just five years ago that we had a five-week-old golden retriever puppy. That just about did us in. Puppies and babies are for young folks.

We remember the heartbreak when he flunked out of obedience school and we thought he was headed for a life of delinquency and crime. A year or so later, he suddenly snapped out of it and began earning Boy Scout merit badges.

An awkward hurdle for us would be the problem of arranging to provide my spouse with an egg from a younger woman. I'd have to fertilize it without committing adultery.

I suppose a fertility clinic could arrange it somehow, but, still, there's that third party aspect that complicates things.

There are lawyers who claim that a clinic's refusal to help a woman in her 60s get pregnant would amount to age discrimination.

I don't buy that.

Do the arithmetic, I'd argue.

If you ask me, becoming a mother at that age is asking for severe geriatric fatigue at the very least.

Old age is not for sissies.

And at the very worst, pregnancy at that age risks creating a premature teenage orphan.